C000318898

# Grant Morrison

*the early years*

# Grant Morrison

*the early years*

Timothy Callahan

Sequart.com Books Edwardsville, Illinois

***Grant Morrison: The Early Years***
by Timothy Callahan

Copyright © 2007 Timothy Callahan. Zenith and related characters are trademarks of 2000 AD © 2007. Animal Man, Arkham Asylum, Batman, Doom Patrol, and related characters are trademarks of DC Comics © 2007.

First edition, March 2007. ISBN 978-0-6151-4087-2.

All rights reserved by the author. Except for brief excerpts used for review or scholarly purposes, no part of this book may be reproduced in any manner whatsoever, including electronic, without express written consent of the author.

Cover by Kevin Colden. Design by Julian Darius. The cover depicts Grant Morrison and refers to a classic scene from his *Animal Man*. Interior art from Zenth is © 2000 AD; please visit www.2000adonline.com. Interior art depicting Batman, Animal Man, Doom Patrol, and related characters is © DC Comics; please visit www.dccomics.com. Thanks to Grant Morrison, 2000 AD, and Paul Levitz.

Published by Sequart.com Books. Co-Edited by Julian Darius and Mike Phillips.

For more information about other titles from Sequart.com Books, visit www.Sequart.com/books/.

Material in this volume has previously appeared, in part and/or in previous editions, on Sequart.com.

# Contents

# Introduction

Comic books and graphic novels have received more critical attention in recent years than ever before, yet most studies of sequential narrative focus on the big picture – they tell about the history of the medium, or provide a biographical overview of a major creator, or provide a synopsis of various important storylines.

In this book, I'm doing something different.

I'm taking a look at a few works by comic book writer Grant Morrison, and through close textual analysis, I'm going to show what the stories are *really* about. I'm going to show you how to read his work by pointing out the recurring patterns and motifs. I'm going to show you how he explores a few dominant themes again and again. I'm going to show you what he's doing with words and images to challenge the very foundations of narrative. I'm going to show you what these comic books reveal about life.

My focus is the work from Grant Morrison's early career. He burst onto the comic book scene and produced a series of masterpieces within a few short years. Between 1987 and 1992, he published *Zenith*, *Arkham Asylum*, *Animal Man*, *Batman: Gothic*, and *Doom Patrol*, all of which deserve a close, analytical reading – the type of reading I'll provide in these pages. All of these works are, basically, super-hero comic books, and super-hero comic books get little respect. They dominate the shelves of the local comic book stores, but they aren't taken seriously in the critical community. I hope this book shows how much super-hero comic books have to offer, especially if they're written by a master.

# *Zenith*

*Zenith*, an epic story told in four distinct Phases over the course of five years, is not only Grant Morrison's first major comic book project, but lays the framework for his future work in the medium.[1] By the time the prologue for Phase One was published on August 15, 1987 in the 535th prog[2] of *2000 AD*, Morrison had already published dozens of stories in a variety of locations. He had been a comic book writer (and occasional artist) for nearly a decade, but much of his work until that point had focused on licensed characters like Zoids,[3] or short pieces published as one or two-page "Future Shocks."[4] With *Zenith*, he created something different. First of all, *Zenith* was a super-hero strip in a magazine which had avoided super-hero strips entirely for 534 issues. Second, it was a series which, because of its ultimate length, would allow him to tell a story of immense scope and grandeur. And third, it was a

---

[1] Every *Zenith* installment was drawn by Steve Yeowell, an artist whose appeal lies in his ability to ground extraordinary characters by placing them in a solid context. He tends not to use extreme angles or dynamic perspective to tell the stories, but rather, he uses clean pen lines and solid blacks to give bold form to the proceedings. This is a particularly effective technique when working with Grant Morrison, since Yeowell's artwork adds an understated context for Morrison's outrageous stories.

[2] *2000 AD* issues are called *progs*, short for *programmes*, in keeping with the science fiction nature of the series.

[3] Grant Morrison wrote several back-up stories for the UK comic book entitled *Spider-Man and Zoids*, which featured separate Spider-Man and Zoids tales in each issue. Zoids were robotic creatures created by TOMY, the Japanese toy company.

[4] "Future Shocks," a recurring section of *2000 AD*, were brief science fiction stories with clever twist endings.

chance for Morrison to play the revisionist super-hero game, while, at the same time, expressing his own unique perspective on the nature of fiction and the nature of reality.

The first episode of Phase One doesn't even show the title character, Zenith, at all, which should be a bit of a warning that things may be a little unorthodox in the chapters that follow. Throughout all four Phases, in fact, Zenith is not your typical protagonist. It could be argued that he isn't even the protagonist at all. He's merely the character around whom the story events revolve. As I'll illustrate later, Peter St. John, politician and former '60s radical superhuman, is actually the hero of the story at almost every step of the process. And Zenith himself is a selfish, sarcastic brat who, although likable, never develops or grows in any significant way, even after overcoming impossible challenges and helping to save the universe. One possible criticism of *Zenith*, as a story – a criticism that I wouldn't be willing to make – is that Morrison includes only superficial attempts at characterization (pop culture references, snappy comebacks, etc). This may be true, but to criticize *Zenith* on that ground is to miss the point. *Zenith* is about patterns. *Zenith* is about perspective. *Zenith* is about our paths as we journey through space and time. "There's a pattern here somewhere," says Zenith, "...all we have to do is put the pieces together." Or, as the evil Iok Sotot says, "I love to watch the mindless patterns they make in spacetime." *Zenith* is not about reality as we know it – it's a commentary on a larger sense of reality, a commentary on the big, multidimensional picture, a commentary which (luckily for us) has giant robots, super powers, secret agents, evil scientists, and dark gods bent on world domination.

## Phase One

Phase One begins with a flashback to WWII, where we find the British superhuman Maximan[5] fighting his Nazi counterpart, Masterman in Berlin. Over their heads, an allied plane drops and atomic bomb, destroying them both. We flash forward to the present day, identified as 1987 in a caption. A German woman, Fraulein Hass, stands in front of the preserved body of Masterman and describes her plan to awaken him.

---

[5] Maximan, a creation of Morrison's, is an archetypal national hero in the vein of a British Captain America, a super-soldier who wears the flag of his nation on his shirt.

From *2000 AD* prog 547 - An ineffective Zenith and a floating Peter St. John confront Masterman after the death of Siadwel Rhys. Art by Steve Yeowell. Copyright © 2000 AD.

This prologue misdirects the audience in several ways: (1) The tone of the series is far more ironic than the prologue indicates; (2) Masterman, established here as the antagonist, is revealed later to be a hollow vessel for a much larger evil; (3) The idea of the heroic legacy, and the concept of duty and honor embodied by Maximan's sacrifice in the prologue is antithetical to everything Zenith, as a character, represents. All of which, presumably, is the point. Morrison gives us a conventional super-hero story for all of one episode (if you consider nuking the hero conventional) before subverting our expectations in the very next installment.

The main narrative of Phase One goes something like this: Zenith, the world's only active superhuman, is a bored pop star who finds himself on the front line of a battle against extra-dimensional beings. Ruby Fox, a retired and supposedly depowered superhuman who used to be known as Voltage, is attacked by Masterman (who is merely the host body of an evil god, one of the "many-angled ones" – entities inspired by H.P. Lovecraft's Cthulhu tales)[6] and then runs to Zenith to warn him about the danger. Zenith is reluctant to get involved until Fox tells him that she'll reveal what really happened to his parents (who died mysteriously when he was a child) if he helps her. The pair tries to enlist politician Peter St. John, formerly the hippy hero known as Mandala, but he coldly rebuffs them. Their last hope is in the form of an overweight drunk of a former hero: Siadwel Rhys, known once-upon-a-time as Red Dragon. After a quick sobering-up and a bit of practice with his newly rediscovered powers, Rhys joins Zenith as they fly back toward London. Fox takes the train, and therefore misses the entire battle. In London, Rhys is quickly disintegrated by Masterman, and just when it looks like Zenith's soul is about to be devoured, St. John shows up to save the day. Zenith destroys the Masterman host body, but the duo is confronted with the multi-dimensional form of Iok Sotot, the eater of souls, who proceeds to devour both Zenith and St. John. Unbeknownst to the reader, St. John had imparted a post-hypnotic suggestion into the mind of Iok Sotot in an earlier

---

[6] Cthulhu, an otherworldly entity, first appeared in Lovecraft's 1928 short story entitled, "The Call of Cthulhu," published in *Weird Tales* magazine. Lovecraft filled his fiction with alien gods and extra-dimensional beings with multiple eyes and tentacles. His stories, and the expansion of Lovecraft's mythology by writer August Derleth, has inspired a popular role-playing game, the evil forces in the *Hellboy* movie, and a lot of bad teenage writing. *Zenith*, thankfully, rises above its influences.

episode, and when St. John shouts "Tyger! Tyger!," the many-angled one contorts in an epileptic fit and spews out the two heroes. In the epilogue, during Rhys's funeral, St. John confesses that he played the hero role for the sake of political gain, and soon afterwards Zenith finds that his role as a savior has made him #1 on the singles and album charts.

What Morrison subverts, throughout this narrative, are the conventions of the super-hero melodrama. On the surface, he has the struggle of good (Zenith, St. John, etc) vs. evil (Nazis and evil beings from another dimension), but Morrison doesn't give us the story that we would normally expect. Zenith is not heroic. He acts purely on self-interest. He only aids Ruby when she promises to provide him with something (information about his parents) in return. And although Ruby fails to deliver on that promise by the end of the story (she goes on holiday instead), Zenith is rewarded for his "heroic" actions by achieving pop stardom. Peter St. John is the actual cause of the victory against the evil force anyway, but he doesn't win through usual super heroic means. There are a lot of punches and power blasts during the battle scenes, yes, but all of the expended energy doesn't amount to much. The battle is won because of a strategic move made off-panel halfway through the story. This type of anti-climax is typical of Morrison's work, and typical of *Zenith* in particular. Such a structure illustrates that each component of the narrative bears relevance, and while readers have been trained to pay attention to the emphatic points of the story by all of the comic books they've read previously, and while they've been trained to seek satisfaction from an exciting ending in which the hero overcomes the villains through force and ingenuity, Morrison's anti-climax effectively challenges their assumptions about what was and what was not important in the story, priming them for what will come later (most explicitly in Phase Four).

In addition to reconditioning audience expectations, Phase One also lays the groundwork for several themes and motifs which Morrison will explore throughout the entire *Zenith* series (and in future series extending from *Animal Man* to *Doom Patrol* and beyond).

The most dominant theme established in Phase One is the theme of *age*. The conflict between the young and the old, between one generation and the next is emphasized again and again throughout the text. Zenith, age 19 in 1987, says, "All this '60's stuff... who cares?" – revealing his contempt for the cultural artifacts of the previous generation and setting him up for a conflict between himself and his fellow heroes (both Ruby Fox and Peter St.

John were members of Cloud 9 – a 1960s super-hero group which rebelled in their own way against the generation which preceded them). The generational pattern Morrison establishes here works out to look like this: the 1940s, embodied by Maximan, represent an emphasis on duty and self-sacrifice. The 1960s of Cloud 9 represent rebellion and idealism. The 1980s of *Zenith*, however, represent selfishness and celebrity. Morrison, as a cultural anthropologist of sorts, gives each generation the hero which best embodies its spirit. Contrast this with most comic book heroes, and you'll find that in the 1980s, Marvel and DC were pumping out comic books featuring characters who lifelessly embodied the spirit of a bygone age.[7] For Morrison, the ethics of the 40s and the 60s no longer represented the world, while Zenith himself garishly represents his time and its focus on celebrity, superficiality, and the self.

A strong *mind / body* theme also runs throughout Phase One. Morrison himself has acknowledged that he was "straightedge" (no smoking, no drugs, no alcohol) at the time he was writing the first part of *Zenith*, and it shows. The major component of the straightedge philosophy is that drugs have a negative impact on both the mind and the body, and throughout Phase One, characters who use drugs or alcohol are adversely affected. When we first meet Zenith, for example, he is drunkenly flying through the skylight of his apartment. Because of his impairment, he crashes into the sofa. The major example, however, comes in the form of ex-super-hero Siadwel Rhys. He's an overweight alcoholic when he's introduced, and the implication is that the alcohol has dampened his superhuman powers. As he sobers up and ultimately renounces alcohol before the final battle, his powers grow stronger. Morrison doesn't preach to the reader, but there is an overt connection between clarity of mind and effectiveness of body throughout the series. Zenith's powers actually fluctuate with his monthly biorhythms. This fact, established when he initially appears, plays a role in a later storyline, but it also shows Morrison's interest in the cyclical nature of life, and the way patterns can both reveal and predict. Zenith, for example, can project which days of the month will be his strongest and which days will leave him

---

[7] The trend of recycling characters from an earlier age is arguably even worse today than it was twenty years ago. While both Marvel and DC try to update their heroes for each new generation, their attempts at what they call "Ultimate" or "Year One" stories sometimes result in nothing more than re-telling the same old stories at a much slower pace.

totally powerless. The two other primary appearances of the *mind / body* theme are found in the use of Masterman as host for the Iok Sotot entity and Peter St. John's ultimate method of victory over him. In the first case, the mind of Iok Sotot lacks a corporeal body and exists as pure thought until it is contained by Masterman's superhuman husk. In the second case, St. John uses his own mind as a weapon against Iok Sotot, causing the being to convulse into a type of epileptic fit, which allows St. John (and Zenith) to escape from the "belly of the beast" (they had been devoured by the disembodied being).[8] Mind trumps body in the climactic scenes of Phase One.

A *metaphysical* theme appears prominently in Phase One as well. In the prologue, Masterman (with his actual mind intact) points to the heavens and tells Maximan, "There's no-one up there," while Zenith's pop single is identified as "Heaven Can't Wait." The true hero of the story, Peter St. John is named after two apostles of Christ,[9] and he says this about his powers: "I can control your perception... I can make you see anything... Anything at all." If our concept of reality is based on our perception of it, St. John can alter reality as we know it. The other religious / metaphysical references I've mentioned don't provide answers to any questions (Masterman tries to, but he's wrong – there is someone up there, and he's dropping an atomic bomb on Masterman's head), but they identify issues that Morrison explores over the span of the four Phases. The nature of God is something that Morrison deals with many, many times, and in the case of Phase One, the only gods we see are the many-angled ones, who are clearly evil. Morrison does give us a reference to something called the Omnihedron, but its ominous potency is not revealed until a later Phase.

Morrison also explores the nature of *power* in Phase One. Three characters seek power in the story, and each searches for it in a different way. Zenith seeks celebrity and popularity, which he equates with power. He has no interest in physical might. When Ruby Fox tries to engage him to fight against the threat of Masterman, Zenith scoffs and says he's "not a boxer." Zenith, who has an agent named Eddie (who acts as a revisionist version of

---

[8] How might a disembodied being devour someone? Iok Sotot lacks a corporeal form, but he does exist as a kind of indescribable energy, and within the story, he takes the shape of a giant mouth for just long enough to swallow the heroes. By the rules of comic book logic, it all makes sense.

[9] St. Peter and John the Revelator, respectively.

Bruce Wayne's butler, Alfred),[10] wants to make music videos and reach #1 on the charts. Peter St. John wants political power, and he appears willing to achieve it by any means necessary. He says, after the battle: "I didn't fight Masterman for you [Ruby]... I did it to pick up votes in the election." Heroism is a means to an end, just as it is for Zenith. The final approach to power is exemplified by Masterman / Iok Sotot. This creature kills anyone who opposes it (except St. John and Zenith, both of whom are allowed to live because the creature wants to use them to its advantage later – a choice which, not surprisingly, results in its own defeat), and what it wants is total domination. In essence, Zenith wants to sell records, St. John wants to govern, and Iok Sotot wants to destroy. The power they crave is essential only in so far as it helps them achieve those specific goals. Unlike traditional super-hero / super-villain scenarios, Morrison's *Zenith* doesn't show us characters interested in altruism, justice, or pulling a bank heist. Zenith, St. John, and Iok Sotot use their power for more globally selfish motives.

Besides exploring the themes above, Morrison also includes several motifs which provide a pattern throughout the narrative. The three major motifs include *fashion*, *flying*, and *doubling*. Fashion comes to the foreground in the character of Zenith, whose super-hero outfit is a fashion choice, not a crime-fighting costume. He also accessorizes his outfit with a jacket, providing a stylistic twist on the traditional uniform. Adding a jacket[11] to "update" a character is a particularly common motif throughout Morrison's work from *Zenith* onward. To emphasize the costume-as-fashion-choice idea, one of the characters refers to "Jean-Paul Gaultier's 'Superhuman Collection.'" Another example of the fashion motif occurs the moment Siadwel Rhys says, "I'm ready now." He doesn't say those words until he has the old costume back on. And to offer a counterpoint to that, Peter St. John never dons his old costume at any point in the story (or in any following story). His "costume" is a business suit throughout this Phase,

[10] If the support for a young, male hero from the 1940s like Batman was a butler, then what could be more appropriate for a young, male hero from the 1980s like Zenith than an agent? Morrison is always commenting upon these cultural shifts by playing with archetypes like this.

[11] *2000 AD* artist Brendan McCarthy designed the characters for the *Zenith* strip, even though Steve Yeowell drew every installment. McCarthy basically invented the contemporary tradition of super-hero-costume-under-a-cool-jacket in 1983 with the creation of the Paradax strip for Eclipse Comics' *Strange Days*, in collaboration with writer Peter Milligan.

even when he's using his powers.

The flying motif is linked to many of the themes in the story. In *Zenith*, power is linked with flight. For example, Zenith triggers Siadwel Rhys's powers by flying him into the air and dropping him. Before Rhys hits the ground, his powers kick in, allowing him to fly to safety. Ruby, earlier in the story, flies out of her window to escape Masterman, and then, later in the story, she is too drained to fly, so she takes the train (thereby sparing her life – she certainly would have died, just as Siadwel did). The most interesting use of the flying motif is a panel transition in Chapter 10 when St. John says, "There's not much we can do, except pray. And hope someone up there likes us." The very next panel shows the apparent saviors, Zenith and Rhys, flying overhead. The flying motif links most of the themes together and reinforces the concept of the superhuman as a god, a concept Morrison explores more deeply in later Phases.

The final and most obvious motif is that of doubling. Right away we have the mirror images of Maximan and Masterman. We later find out that the Masterman of 1987 is the twin of the one killed in Berlin. Heroes are constantly shown in pairs. First, it's Ruby Fox and Zenith trying to enlist help. Then, Zenith is paired with Siadwel Rhys as they train with their powers together. Then, in the final battle, Zenith and Peter St. John are paired against Iok Sotot. At no point in the story are all of the heroes fighting together as a big group. Morrison always uses pairs. The idea of doubling doesn't stop there. Spook, a member of '60s super-hero group Cloud 9, disappeared through a mirror, a symbol of the doubling effect. And Iok Sotot itself comes from a parallel dimension. Morrison expands upon all of these ideas in future Phases, but he lays the foundation here.

By the time Phase One comes to a close, the world has been saved, and the extra-dimensional threat of the many-angled ones has been halted, if not totally eradicated. Zenith, a self-centered character from the beginning, whines throughout the story and even cries to his agent, Eddie, for help when he's in the bowels of Iok Sotot. If he learns a lesson from his experiences, it's that he can profit from looking like a hero. St. John, meanwhile, gains immeasurable political clout from his actions, and Ruby Fox gets a vacation. Ultimately, though, all of these things are just patterns in spacetime, but they aren't (contrary to what Iok Sotot says) mindless patterns. They are patterns defined by Grant Morrison. He continues to weave these patterns, these themes, these motifs, and expand upon all of them, throughout the next three

Phases.

## Interlude

Two months after Phase One of *Zenith* ended, and several months before Phase Two launched in August of 1988, Grant Morrison provided a two-part interlude in *2000 AD*, progs 558-559. The interlude allowed Morrison to reveal some backstory without the exposition getting in the way of the upcoming storyline, and it also established the dominant theme of the second Phase: *hubris*.

As I mentioned in my analysis of Phase One, Peter St. John defeated dark god Iok Sotot with a post-hypnotic suggestion. The trigger he used was "Tyger! Tyger!" – a reference to the famous poem by William Blake:

"The Tyger"
by William Blake (1757-1827)

Tyger! Tyger! burning bright
In the forests of the night,
What immortal hand or eye
Could frame thy fearful symmetry?

In what distant deeps or skies
Burnt the fire of thine eyes?
On what wings dare he aspire?
What the hand dare seize the fire?

And what shoulder, & what art.
Could twist the sinews of thy heart?
And when thy heart began to beat,
What dread hand? & what dread feet?

What the hammer? what the chain?
In what furnace was thy brain?
What the anvil? what dread grasp
Dare its deadly terrors clasp?

When the stars threw down their spears,
And watered heaven with their tears,
Did he smile his work to see?
Did he who made the Lamb make thee?

Tyger! Tyger! burning bright
In the forests of the night,
What immortal hand or eye
Dare frame thy fearful symmetry?

Without getting into too much poetic analysis here, I'll just say that Blake's poem questions what sort of God could have constructed something as beautiful and terrifying as a tiger. A close reader should note of the speaker's tonal shift from the end of stanza one, when he asks "What immortal hand or eye / *Could* frame thy fearful symmetry?" to the end of the final stanza, where the intent of the sentence is changed by replacing one word: "What immortal hand or eye / *Dare* frame thy fearful symmetry?" The poem is about the act of creation, and the speaker, at first, is unable to comprehend *how* the tiger was made, but by the end of the poem he's more concerned with *why* the tiger was made.

The reference to this poem in Phase One of *Zenith* seemed like an irrelevant literary allusion, but Phase Two takes that single allusion and expands it into a structure. Simplistically put, the "Tyger[s]" of the poem equal the manufactured superhumans in the world of *Zenith.* And the role of God, in *Zenith,* is played by Dr. Michael Peyne, who, as we find out in the second part of the Interlude, created "the children of the quantum era," the generation of superhumans who ended up calling themselves Cloud 9. Just so we don't miss the connection, Peyne himself refers to his "children" as "Tygers" and has named his unpublished memoir, from which we get this backstory, "Seizing the Fire," in reference to the eighth line of Blake's poem.[12]

All of which relates to the idea of hubris. Hubris is god-like arrogance. In ancient myths from around the world (including the stories found in the *Bible*), whenever humans thought themselves to be equal to, or better than, the gods, they were punished severely. Peyne, a man of science, a Nobel Prize winner in the field of "Engenics,"[13] would have benefited by

---

[12] It's worth noting that Blake's "The Tyger" has an impressive pedigree in the revisionist super-hero genre. Alan Moore alludes to the Blake poem in *Watchmen,* which I'll discuss in the next chapter of this book, and in his his seminal *Marvelman* work originally published in the *Warrior* magazine in the early 1980s (and reprinted and expanded years later under the name *Miracleman,* published by Eclipse Comics). *Marvelman,* a dark re-imagining of the Captain Marvel / Shazam archetype, is a vicious, ironic, thrilling piece of work which influenced Grant Morrison's approach to super-heroes in the early part of his career. Morrison would later use *Animal Man* to break free from Moore's influence, as I'll demonstrate later.

[13] Engenics is not a Nobel Prize category, nor is it a recognized scientific field. Morrison uses the term to combine the idea of genetic engineering with the social science of "eugenics," which advocates selective breeding for optimal human performance. The Nazis, not surprisingly, were big fans of eugenics, and Morrison

remembering these old stories. But he's not the only one, as we'll find out when we actually get to Phase Two.

Before we do so, I'd like to point out a few more facts we learn during the Interlude. We learn that Dr. Peyne "dreamed of a purer world" and vowed "to build that world" through the creation of a race of superhumans. Using the serum which granted Maximan his powers a generation before, Peyne created ten children with superhuman abilities. Two of them died, or were killed, during the moment of birth, seven of them grew up to be the members of Cloud 9 (Ruby Fox, Peter St. John, Siadwel Rhys – all of whom we met in Phase One – plus Lux, Spook, Dr. Beat, and White Heat – all of whom disappeared in the late '60s), and one of them, a bizarre being described as a "storm of shapes" and called Chimera, was trapped by Peyne in an electromagnetic field snare and presumably forgotten. We also discover that the seven surviving children were trained to be part of a government super-group called Taskforce UK, but they rebelled from their masters and began calling themselves Cloud 9 on their own. Dr. Beat and White Heat were Zenith's parents, but they, like Lux and Spook, vanished mysteriously twenty years earlier. At the end of the interlude, we see that Peyne has created two new superhuman females in the present day. He calls the girls only by the super-hero names Shockwave and Blaze, and completes the interlude by implying that he wants them to begin breeding a new race of superhumans as he says, "I needed Zenith."

## Phase Two

Once Phase Two actually begins, in prog 589 of *2000 AD*, we are thrown into an alternate reality[14] where we find that Lux (David Cambridge) and

---

implies that negative connotation in the word he chooses for Peyne's scientific pursuits.

[14] Alternate realities and parallel universes are common in science fiction stories and even more common in comic books, especially since the Silver Age of the 1960s when inconsistent continuity was explained away by creating multiple earths. How could Batman fight crime in the 1940s and still be youthful a generation later? Because the Batman from the 1940s existed on a different Earth, along with the other WWII heroes. When the heroes began crossing over and meeting their counterparts, things became interesting. Just to be clear, though, in the alternate reality seen in the opening of Phase Two of *Zenith*, we are actually seeing the "real" Lux and Spook, not alternate versions of the characters. They crossed over to this other reality when they disappeared from Zenith's Earth all those years ago.

Spook (Penelope Moon) are alive and well and living in a futuristic version of Sydney, Australia. Ruby Fox, who was talking about taking a holiday at the end of Phase One, has arrived on this alternate reality to find that, while she has aged twenty years since the 1960s, David and Penelope look as young as the day upon which they disappeared. As they update Ruby, we learn that the victory over Iok Sotot in Phase One was just a small battle in a much larger war. We learn that the many-angled ones who were threatening to take over the world in Phase One are actually called the Lloigor (based directly on beings from the Cthulhu mythos), and we hear a bit about the Omnihedron and something called The Alignment. All of this is just a taste of what's to come, however, for once the prologue of Phase Two ends, we don't see any of these characters again until the epilogue.

All in all, the prologue and epilogue provide a cosmic framing sequence for what is basically a straightforward, earth-bound narrative. The main conflict in Phase Two exists in the form of a newly-introduced character, Scott Wallace, a former computer whiz-kid with twisted utopian ideals. Wallace teams up with Dr. Michael Peyne (who clearly has his own utopian ideals, which may or may not mesh with those of Wallace), and the two of them initiate a nuclear attack on London using some hijacked missiles. Wallace wants to remake civilization into something more peaceful, more civilized, and he's not afraid to use brutal tactics to rid the world of its corruption. Peyne, on the other hand, uses Wallace to set the stage for what he imagines will be a superhuman paradise, for who else will repopulate the world and take control once the world is inhabitable again?

The two villains are opposed by two heroes, Zenith and another new character, Phaedra Cale, an American intelligence agent who, like Ruby Fox in Phase One, promises information about Zenith's parents in exchange for his help.

In this story, however, Zenith actually does learn the fate of his parents (they were assassinated by CIA "shadowmen"), although he soon realizes that there is more to the story than that. But before he learns the whole truth, he confronts Dr. Peyne and meets Shockwave and Blaze. Their interaction before and after this scene indicate that Zenith apparently copulated with one, or both, of the young ladies off panel. Awkwardness and disgust arise when he finds out that the two girls are clones of Ruby Fox and Zenith's own mother. Later still, as he battles a giant robot by the name of Warhead, Zenith discovers that Warhead is actually a cybernetic organism built around

From *2000 AD* prog 599 – Dr. Michael Peyne reveals the truth about Blaze and Shockwave to a stunned Zenith. Art by Steve Yeowell. Copyright © 2000 AD.

his father's body. At one point during their battle, Warhead's helmet comes off, revealing the disfigured face of Zenith's father in a moment echoing the famous climactic scene in *Return of the Jedi*. Unlike Luke Skywalker, though, Zenith punches his father's head off.[15]

As these events transpire, Scott Wallace, locked in a bunker, readies himself to launch two nuclear missiles toward London. Peter St. John, the real hero of Phase One, hovers over London, preparing to stop the missiles with the force of his mind. Phase Two, just like the previous Phase, ends with an anti-climax. Zenith infiltrates Wallace's bunker with some telepathic help from St. John, talks to Wallace and convinces him not to bomb London. No fighting. No explosions. Just Zenith rationally explaining the consequences and Wallace agreeing not to go through with the plan.

We learn, however, in a series of epilogues, that although the London problem has been solved, three larger issues remain: (1) Peter St. John's political machinations are becoming more blatant as he is directly encouraged by Prime Minister Margaret Thatcher to engage in political assassination; (2) Chimera, the creature created by Peyne as mentioned in the Interlude, was accidentally freed by Zenith during his battle with Warhead, and, at the end of Phase Two, Chimera expands to fill the entire universe, then mysteriously contracts into a hand-held pyramid; (3) The Lloigor are taking control of alternate realities and a multi-dimensional war is already underway.

Phase Two answers some of the unresolved questions from Phase One, but the implication inherent in the framing sequence illustrates that the story is far from over. In a way, the entirety of Phase Two feels like a prologue to Phase Three, but there is still plenty of thematic unity in Phase Two, and to understand *Zenith* as a whole, it's necessary to look at the themes and motifs emphasized in Phase One to see what new perspective is illuminated by the events of Phase Two.

*Age*, a dominant theme in Phase One, is superseded in Phase Two by the theme of *fatherhood*. Age is still an important concern in the world of *Zenith*, and it is brought to the fore almost immediately in the prologue when Ruby Fox realizes that David and Penelope have not aged in the alternate

[15] Morrison often evokes nostalgic connections to popular culture in his work, and, just as often, he adds a subversive twist. He's no sentimentalist like George Lucas, that's for sure.

dimension. In the main narrative of Phase Two, however, fatherhood is such an overwhelming issue that age is not mentioned to any significant extent. Regarding fatherhood, we have the following two plot points: Dr. Michael Peyne is the father of the superhumans. When Peyne reaches out to Zenith, to help lift him off the ground, their reaching hands mimic the hands of God and Adam from Michelangelo's famous fresco.

This is the moment at which Peyne refers to Zenith as "evolution's perfect child," and he hopes that Zenith will breed with his two new creations. Most prominently in Phase Two, Zenith must battle, and eventually kill, his own father, an event which actually causes him to get serious for the first time in either Phase One or Phase Two. Only after he kills his own father (or the mockery that was once his father) does Zenith show any sign of anger and aggression. At this point, as he confronts Peyne, Zenith has changed. The change doesn't last long, but there remains a loss of innocence after the death of his father, and it's doubtful that the frivolous, self-centered Zenith of Phase One would have been able to talk Scott Wallace out of blowing up London.

Another important theme from Phase One was the concept of the *mind / body* connection. Phase Two isn't explicitly straightedge in its philosophy like Phase One, but it does emphasize that theme on several occasions. The idea of inducing seizures through an attack on the senses appears in this Phase, and Zenith uses a stroboscopic[16] effect to paralyze Warhead. Later in the story, Peyne teaches Zenith more about his potential power, revealing that his abilities are only limited by his mental control. To further this point, Zenith actually develops telepathic abilities in Phase Two, abilities which he uses to link with St. John and figure out how to bypass Scott Wallace's security system. The biorhythm cycle which determines the ebb and flow of Zenith's powers proves to be a plot point in this Phase, as Wallace and Peyne plan to kill Zenith (because he has presumably already impregnated one of the girls – although this is never explicitly stated) when he is at his low point. Their calculations are wrong, however, since they were based on the publicity material about his birthday.[17]

The *metaphysical* theme emphasized in Phase One is certainly prominent

---

[16] One of Zenith's newfound powers is the creation of strobe-light flashes. He is a pop star after all.

[17] Eddie, Zenith's agent, had told the public that Zenith shared a birthday with Elvis Presley. This promotional falsehood ended up saving his client's life.

here as well. Immediately, we are told of the existence of alternate universes, and Ruby Fox says, of the alternate Sydney, "It's like the cities in my dreams." Peter St. John, on the other hand, awakens from a horrible nightmare in which he envisions a desolate London beneath a black sun – an image which will reappear years later in a future Phase. Dreams, Morrison implies, act as a portal between different realities (or potentialities). We also learn, through Peyne, that Zenith has the power to consciously manipulate "the quantum process." In other words, Zenith can alter reality once he learns to fully control his powers. The creator has imbued his creation with the actual powers of a god.

Speaking of *power*, that theme is important in Phase Two also. In Phase One, Zenith measured his power by how many albums he sold and how popular he was. Phase Two, however, shows him slipping in popularity as even the local cab driver criticizes his new record. Perhaps because of the decline in that aspect of his life, Zenith is more willing to seek other forms of power – in this case, power over others, using his superhuman abilities to change things. Peter St. John, shown in Phase One using his powers for political gain, is now accused of doing exactly that by the media in Phase Two. St. John keeps a relatively low profile during this Phase, probably to avoid overt use of his power, although without his telepathic help, Zenith would not have penetrated Scott Wallace's bunker. Wallace himself is another type of power-seeker. He reached the pinnacle of his profession. He was the most successful computer programmer of his day, but he wants to impart order into the world. He wants to world to make sense, and he thinks that he can, through force and through fear, will such a world into being. That sort of power, using force to bring order to chaos, will reappear as a dominant theme in Phase Three.

As far as motifs are concerned, the *doubling / pairing* pattern abounds once again. Peyne, for example creates two new superhumans, and they are clones. We learn about the Einstein-Rosen Bridge which connects two alternate realities. When we first meet Warhead, we see Zenith reflected in his helmet, providing a visual doubling, in addition to emphasizing the connection between the two characters. And finally, Mantra, one of the alternate universe heroes, says in the epilogue, "You will come to the secret of your being both dark and light in contradictory union and you may join with this source or remain separate from it." Mantra's words give us the union of two contradictory forces, and her words give us two options on how to deal with those forces.

As I said at the beginning of this section, though, *hubris* is the dominant idea of Phase Two: the hubris of Phaedra Cale, who is easily killed when she tangles with superhumans because she overestimates her own abilities; the hubris of Scott Wallace, who thinks he can control the world and make it better because he wants to, and who fails because he lacks conviction; the hubris of Dr. Michael Peyne, who thinks he can manufacture gods on Earth. These three humans are playing with forces they cannot fully understand. And they are all punished for it – if not now, then soon.

As Phaedra, prophetically, says, "You superhumans... it's like we've been invaded by aliens, you know?"

## Phase Three

Only a few months after Phase Two ended, Grant Morrison resumed the story of *Zenith* with the launch of Phase Three in prog 626 of *2000 AD*, cover-dated May 13, 1989. The longest *Zenith* story arc by far, Phase Three features the climactic battle for the fate of the multiverse, heroic sacrifice, and an ultimate evil that wishes to destroy life. It's Morrison's take on Marv Wolfman and George Perez's *Crisis on Infinite Earths*,[18] using his own pastiches of superhumanity coupled with actual characters from British comic book history. In fact, because of Morrison's problematic use of copyrighted characters in this Phase, *Zenith* trade paperbacks are nearly impossible to find in America.

The multitude of characters (over 50 different characters in a 27-part story, in fact) overwhelms the narrative at times, and Zenith find himself on the sidelines more often than not, but Morrison keeps everything balanced around a traditional good vs. evil plot line. This time, the many-angled ones, the Lovecraftian creatures known as the Lloigor, are in the process of taking over the bodies of the mightiest superhumans on every version of earth throughout the infinite alternate universes. Their plan is to initiate "The Alignment," which would bring about the ascension of the Lloigor, granting

[18] *Crisis on Infinite Earths*, published as a 12-issue series by DC Comics from 1985 to 1986, was a wildly-popular "maxi-series" which attempted to include every character from the DC Universe in a cosmic story involving the death of multiple worlds. It was an ultimately failed attempt to simplify the continuity at DC, but it was a seminal moment in super-hero comics, not just because of its grand scale, but because it spawned so many other company-wide crossover events.

them ultimate power. This is clearly a direct reference to the plot of *Crisis on Infinite Earths*, which featured a destructive being, the Anti-Monitor, whose annihilation of the multiple realities resulted in only one version of earth surviving. In the *Crisis*, popular heroes like the Flash and Supergirl sacrificed themselves for the good of humanity. In *Zenith*, Morrison uses reader familiarity with that prior story to set up the reader expectation, but of course Morrison subverts those expectations to delirious effect.

The basic plot takes place over a five-day span. As the story begins, Zenith is struggling with diminishing popularity and potential humiliation in his career as a pop star. He's soon saved from the inglorious position of appearing on a children's television program by the arrival of Robot Archie, a British character from the '50s, '60s, and '70s, and the first heroic member of the *Zenith* cast whom Morrison took directly from another source (in Robot Archie's case, a publication called *Lion* magazine). Archie tells Zenith that he is needed; as Archie puts it, "Big trouble coming. End of Universe." Zenith willingly joins him, probably just to get out of his embarrassing television gig. Meanwhile, Peter St. John's former colleagues, David Cambridge, Penelope Moon, and Ruby Fox, arrive to enlist St. John's aid. Shortly thereafter, Zenith and St. John arrive together at Axis Mundi, on Alternative World 23, where a parallel universe Maximan, a blind, cloaked version of the WWII hero, commands an interdimensional force of heroes against the Lloigor.

Under Maximan's leadership, two factions of heroes venture out into two alternative universes intending to destroy the worlds overtaken by the Lloigor.[19] In both cases, the corrupted worlds are destroyed by bombs which unleash chaos energy, but the heroes learn, to their horror, that Maximan himself is a Lloigor being, and his plans were sinister from the start. St. John confronts the Maximan creature, and after a futile battle, the Lloigor appear poised for victory. It is only the last-minute sacrifice by Zenith, who stays behind to detonate an unused chaos bomb, which prevents the Lloigor from achieving ascension, thereby saving the multiverse.

As the heroes celebrate victory and mourn those they've lost, Zenith appears alive. We soon discover that the heroic sacrifice was made by a

---

[19] This, of course, massively subverts super-hero norms. Morrison gives us heroes willing to sacrifice entire worlds (and the human populations therein) to serve the greater good. Contrast this with *Crisis on Infinite Earths*, which is predicated on the desire of the heroes to save worlds, not destroy them.

parallel version of Zenith, a hero named Vertex from Alternative 300.[20] Zenith scoffs at the idea that he would have actually sacrificed himself in such a manner. As the story ends, Zenith turns to Peter St. John and says, "So, we saved the universe then? How do we follow that?"

Unlike Phase Two, Phase Three ends with a decisive finale. The Lloigor seem destroyed, and the parallel realities that weren't infected seem saved. At the end of Phase Three, the *Zenith* saga feels like it has come to an end.

Thematically, Phase Three continues where Phase Two left off, and although it is much more cosmic in scope, the same concerns are still evident.

*Age* is again emphasized in this Phase, as Zenith himself indicates at the beginning of the story, "I'm 21," he says, "I'm over the hill." This comment is not just hyperbole on Zenith's part. Zenith, 19 years old when he reached the pinnacle of his music career at the end of Phase One, is now past his prime. One of Morrison's conceits in the *Zenith* series is that the characters grow older in each successive storyline (unless they alter their age through some other means, as I'll discuss a bit later). In the pop music industry, youth is essential, and the same goes for the world of super-heroes. Think of eternally youthful heroes like Superman or Wonder Woman, who have not aged noticeably in over 60 years of publication.

To make matters worse for Zenith, not only is he replaced on the charts by a boy band, but he is scheduled to appear on a television program for children. His career is obviously in decline because he is no longer considered "cool." Throughout the series, Eddie has been giving Zenith advice on the upcoming trends in pop music, but now at age 21, Zenith is behind the curve and has lost his relevance. This attitude matches Morrison's thoughts on the cyclical nature of super-hero popularity. As a creator, he recognizes that super-heroes become stagnant, and he continually reinvents characters for each generation. He has done it throughout his

---

[20] Vertex, who appears several times before his demise, looks exactly like Zenith, except he has a lighting bolt "V" on his shirt, while Zenith has a "Z." Vertex is the anti-Zenith: he's polite, friendly, and selfless. This, of course, is a subversion as well. In traditional "mirror universe" tales, like we might see in *Star Trek*, the alternate reality characters are evil reflections of the protagonists. You can tell this by their sour demeanor and threatening facial hair. Because Zenith is such a selfish ass, though, his "evil doppelganger" is actually an altruistic hero.

Alternative 23 was created "purely by thought," a literal manifestation of Descartes' *cogito*.[22] Maximan himself tries to define the plans of the Lloigor: "[The Omnihedron will be] a vast, that is to say incomprehensible, crystal structure. A superdimensional geometry composed not of lines and angles but of continuums." The Lloigor, according to the corrupted hero, Streamline, "plan to ascend along [the Omnihedron's] ge-geometry... its unique geometry... towards something called Point-Zenith... th-the godhead... once they do they can change the universe with a thought." By rising beyond mortal comprehension, the Lloigor will be able to shape reality with their collective mind. It's the ultimate *mind / body* connection and within *Zenith* it provides the foundation for the *metaphysical* realm. Morrison defines God as the ultimate mind, with the universe (or multiverse) as its physical manifestation.

Within such a universe, the power of the old gods has faded. One classic British comic book character who makes an appearance is Thunderbolt Jaxon. His superhuman abilities derive from a magical belt which links him to the Norse god Thor. In Phase Three, Jaxon's belt is powerless. His link with the realm of the gods has been severed. Such a literal example of *loss of faith* is not without context in the story. Another hero, Prince Mamba, describes the end of his world with horrifyingly poetic imagery: "The vicar's body has been impaled on the weathercock and it creaks as it turns." Even Maximan, who understands the true nature of reality, says, "Words sometimes lose their significance." In the face of this crisis, there is no higher power, no greater meaning, just the Lloigor, who wish only to infect and destroy.

One character provides an antithesis to this godless reality: Hotspur,[23] a refuge from a corrupted world. He survives possession by the Lloigor through sheer force of will. Once his humanity, and his health, is restored, he inspires the collected heroes by standing on high and speaking of the

---

[22] "Cogito, ergo sum," translated as "I think, therefore I am," is the famous philosophical statement made by Rene Descartes. Descartes later reworded it to the less inferential phrase, "I am, I exist," but Morrison seems to equate thought with a higher form of existence throughout *Zenith.*

[23] Hotspur is, of course, a hot-headed character from William Shakespeare's *Henry IV, Part I.* In the play, he's killed by young Hal, the character who will later become Henry V. Morrison's Hotspur seems to take his name and temperament from Shakespeare's Hotspur, but he takes his look (militaristic) and deeds (rousing speeches) from Shakespeare's Henry V. Such a character is, no doubt, doomed.

Lloigor as "devils" and refers to the superhumans as an "army of God" fighting on behalf of the "Almighty," before concluding by shouting, "Hallelujah!"

The rousing speech motivates the troops, but Hotspur doesn't survive the final battle. If God does exist in Morrison's story, he is an absent deity. The Lloigor are the only gods present, and they are defeated by *chaos* and by *sacrifice*. These two themes bring about the conclusion of the story, and therefore deserve close attention.

In Morrison's cosmology, chaos trumps order. This is not an unusual perspective in scientific circles, but traditionally, in comic books, order is the goal and chaos the corrupting force. In *Zenith*, order is corrupt, as foreshadowed in Phase Two with the cruel utopianism of Scott Wallace, and as exemplified in Phase Three with the Lloigor's intention to impose a rigid geometry on the multiverse. As Mantra says, "We owe our existence to chance and chaos. You can't turn the universe into a piece of clockwork." The Lloigor's intentions are paralleled by the Order of the Black Sun, who are shown working with two infected superhumans, archetypal characters based classic British comic book characters, Ace Heart and Captain Miracle. The corrupted heroes see a swastika hanging on a wall and identify it as the "sigil of the Black Sun." Morrison has linked the "plan" developed by David Cambridge to the Nazi "final solution" in an earlier chapter, and now he directly links the fascism of an artificially-imposed human order to the Lloigor's geometric reconstruction of reality. In Morrison's stories, life is sloppy and random, and imposing order on such chaos is a destructive act. As a creator, however, Morrison is forced to impose such an order on his fictional characters. *Zenith* is an early attempt to reconcile Morrison's internal struggle between the desire for chaos and the need for order, a thematic concern he returns to frequently in his work.

The resolution of the plot of Phase Three, the order imposed by Morrison, hinges on the apparent sacrifice of Zenith. The archetype of the sacrificial hero is an ancient one, and although we might not have expected Zenith to be selfless enough to give his own life to save others, we have been conditioned to believe that a hero would do such a thing, especially a hero in need of redemption like Zenith. Morrison foreshadows such a sacrifice near the beginning of Phase Three when a character named Tammy willingly gives her life to detonate the first chaos bomb. When Zenith agrees to act the same way during the climax of the story, we believe he might die to save humanity. But we are also aware that super-heroes rarely die (especially title characters), and the attempt at self-sacrifice is enough to redeem his continually selfish behavior. When it comes to sacrifice, it's the thought that counts.

Morrison, though, subverts even this expectation. Instead of giving us the archetype of the self-sacrificing hero who is reborn (as seen in the stories of Osiris, Jesus, Jean Grey, and Superman, to name just a few),[24] he gives us the sacrifice of an irrelevant character. The Zenith doppelganger, Vertex, plays no significant role on the plot until the finale. Zenith himself doesn't even attempt to take credit for Vertex's heroic act. "You must be joking," Zenith says when he realizes that the other heroes thought he sacrificed himself. Even after an epic life-and-death struggle to save reality as we know it, Zenith is as selfish and sarcastic as always. Morrison mocks the tradition of the heroic sacrifice, but he also points out the static nature of comic book heroes. After all, characters like Superman never really change, either. Superman's altruistic on page one of a story, and (whatever happens between) he ends up being altruistic by the end of the story as well. We expect Zenith, however, to develop a sense of morality if he doesn't have one, since he wears a costume and his name is the title of the series. That's what we've been conditioned to expect anyway, but not by Morrison, and not in this story.

Structurally, Morrison organizes the story around the same motifs he's been using since Phase One. *Doubling* appears repeatedly, with the doppelganger Vertex, the parallel universes, and the head-to-head confrontation between Peter St. John and Maximan. The *apocalypse* motif is obviously the center of this Phase, since the heroes are defending the multiverse from destruction. Throughout Phase Three, we see end-of-the world imagery: London destroyed, super-heroes literally crucified, and the white-light explosions of the chaos bombs. Morrison also introduces a sophisticated *vision* motif with the blindfolded Maximan, the blinding of the

---

[24] Osiris, from Egyptian mythology, was torn into 14 pieces and thrown into the Nile, but the devotion of his wife Isis restored Osiris to life. Jesus, from Christian mythology, was raised from the dead on the third day after his crucifixion. Jean Grey, from Marvel mythology, died in a crash but was reborn as the nearly omnipotent Phoenix. Superman, from DC mythology, "died" in a battle with a creature named Doomsday, but was "reborn" after his Kryptonian cells regenerated themselves.

possessed Mr. Why, and the warning given by the dying Hotspur who uses his eyelids to blink a message in Morse code indicating that Maximan is a Lloigor.

In this Phase, Morrison equates sight with power and goodness. Corrupted characters are blind or blinded, and when their sight is taken from them, they become ineffectual. The exception to this is Maximan, who says, "[I] ripped out my own eyes. And for the first time, I saw." He still has immense power, even in blindness, but his lack of sight directly corresponds to his evil nature. Vision, in Phase Three, ties many of the major themes together. It's a direct link between the *metaphysical* theme and *mind / body* theme I've analyzed earlier. The eyes are the connection between the brain and reality, and by tearing out his own eyes, Maximan rejects conventional reality to gain a higher understanding. Because the connection with visual reality has been severed, he becomes corrupted.

In Phase Three, *Zenith* reaches its overall climax and apparent conclusion. As I stated in my discussion of Phase One, Zenith really isn't the hero of his own story, and this Phase helps to emphasize that fact. He's not even present during the climax. We think he is. We think he makes a heroic sacrifice, but he's actually completely outside the action. While Morrison provides us with an actual climax this time, as opposed to the anticlimaxes of Phase One and Phase Two, it's a misleading climax at best. Once again, Morrison teaches us to look at the patterns in his work, and he teaches us to distrust the traditional comic book structure. Phase Three is not about a hero learning his lesson and making a heroic sacrifice. It's a pastiche of *Crisis on Infinite Earths*, and it's an exploration into the nature of corruption. It seems to offer a final verdict on the battle between order and chaos, with chaos achieving victory. Yet even when it seems to bring the *Zenith* story to an end, Morrison hasn't given the final word on the themes he's been exploring. He saves that for the strange epilogue known as Phase Four.

## Phase Four

Although Grant Morrison began Phase One of *Zenith* in 1987, Phase Four wasn't published until 1992, beginning in prog 791 of *2000 AD*. My commentary on *Zenith* thus far might lead you to believe that he composed it within a relatively short time period, as if Morrison wrote one *Zenith* script after another until he was finished telling the entire story. That's clearly not the case. Between 1987 and 1992, in addition to writing *Zenith*, Morrison produced some of his most famous American work: his run on *Animal Man*, his *Arkham Asylum* graphic novel, his *Batman: Legends of the Dark Knight* story (entitled "Gothic"), and his early issues of *Doom Patrol*. *Zenith* is part of a much larger creative output, and if we look at the big picture, we can see that many of the dominant themes and ideas weave throughout those other series as well. Throughout this book, I'll explore those connections, but what is amazing about this period of Morrison's career is that even though he was producing a variety of work on both sides of the Atlantic, he was able to maintain the unity of the *Zenith* narrative until the very end. Phases One through Four provide a single thematically-unified whole. If my descriptions of *Zenith* until now have led you to believe that *Zenith* was written page-by-page until the whole thing was completed, that's because it reads that way. It feels like a single, uninterrupted text.

So what does Morrison do in Phase Four to top the cosmic nature of the previous Phase and yet bring about a satisfying conclusion to the saga? He kills the heroes and destroys the world. In Phase Four, we realize that things weren't what they seemed.

Phase Four of *Zenith* occupies an odd place within the larger story. On one hand, it feels like an epilogue to the events of Phase Three; it feels like yet another anticlimax. On the other hand, it seems that Morrison has been building toward this Phase the entire time, and it is the logical conclusion to the scheme he established from the very beginning. It's an epilogue if you think the overall story was about building an inter-dimensional defense against the dark gods known as the Lloigor. If that's your take on the story, you might feel as though Phase Three wrapped everything up already. The good guys won. The multiverse was saved. In that case, Phase Four might seem like an afterthought. I propose, however, that Phase Four is the very essence of *Zenith*. It's Morrison's ultimate word on the themes he's been exploring since the first page of Phase One. It cannot be dismissed as merely an epilogue.

Phase Four[25] is about the remaining members of Cloud 9 (excluding

---

[25] In this Phase, Steve Yeowell, for the first time in the series, works in full color. The previous three Phases had been presented in stark blacks and whites, while Phase Four is filled will murky blues and grays, contrasted with moments of brightness. Even in color, Yeowell maintains the simple geometry of his earlier compositions and tells the story with clarity and grace, but the characters seem to

Peter St. John) and the resistance group known as Black Flag (plus one or two others) now calling themselves Horus,[26] attempting to bring about a superhuman utopia. This recalls "the plan" mentioned as early as Phase One, the misguided utopian dreams of Scott Wallace in Phase Two, and the fascist order the Lloigor attempted to impose in Phase Three. What makes this Phase different, however, is that the members of Horus (David Cambridge, Penelope Moon, and Ruby Fox, especially) succeed where the others failed. They construct their version of a perfect world.

Phase Four is narrated by Dr. Michael Peyne, the geneticist who created the members of Cloud 9 decades before. In this Phase, however, Peyne is the last surviving human in a world that's been twisted beyond recognition.

The superhumans have granted him one final gift as a token of thanks for his part in their creation: his aging process is reversed. Throughout Phase Four, Peyne ages backwards, beginning the narrative as an old man, before transforming, ultimately, into a fetus and then a disembodied voice. Peyne tells the tale of the end of humanity. He describes the battle between the superhumans, with Peter St. John, Archie, and Zenith as the heroes, and the members of Horus as the villains. He describes how the members of Horus have become like gods, and he describes how easily they dispatch the three heroes. Archie is decapitated, Zenith is incinerated, and St. John is impaled upon the raised fist of the Maximan statue.

Peyne tells how the members of Horus ultimately destroy the Earth before flying out into space. They fly farther and farther through the galaxy, out into the unknown reaches of the universe, before receiving a shock. They hit the end of the universe, and then they look up. They see the face of Peter St. John. This world they have dominated, this whole universe, exists within the Chimera pyramid, and St. John holds it in his hand.

As established all the way back in Phase Two, Chimera became an exact copy of our universe, but in miniature. That seemed like a throwaway moment then, a way for Morrison to dispose of a powerful character that was

---

have more weight with the added color. This added physicality provides a counterpoint to the goal of the unburdened consciousness as idealized by David Cambridge and his compatriots. The art reminds us that their plan was flawed from the beginning. They can never escape the bonds of their existence.

[26] Horus, from Egyptian mythology, is the god of the sky. His symbol was a large glowing eye, and image which reoccurs throughout *Zenith* and appears in other work by Morrison.

irrelevant to the story, but in Phase Four we find out how essential that moment was. If you remember, Morrison used a similar technique in Phase One as St. John's defeat of Iok Sotot hinged on an apparently minor scene from an early chapter. Looking at *Zenith* as a whole, an identical pattern emerges. A minor scene, one quarter of the way through the entire story, provides the moment of victory at the end. It's a narrative version of fractal geometry;[27] the patterns repeat on both scales, large and small.

This type of fractal pattern, where events and images reoccur at various levels, is the overarching structure of *Zenith*, as a matter of fact. The repeated themes, the motifs, the endless doubling – all of these devices have provided a fractal narrative framework for the entire story. This isn't surprising. Fractal geometry is an aspect of chaos theory.[28] If Zenith is about anything, it's about chaos. In Phase Four, the patterns established from the beginning continue as reality within the story shifts and changes. The world is literally coming to an end, but the themes from earlier Phases still resonate.

The concept of *age*, of the young vs. the old, dominated Phases One through Three, and in Phase Four it becomes ironically inverted in the persona of Dr. Michael Peyne. Even before he begins to age backwards, he recognizes his inferiority to the superhuman gods. "I feel like a child," he says.

A few chapters later, he actually regresses to childhood, symbolically becoming the embodiment of vulnerability as he transforms into a helpless infant. He, like almost all of the characters in *Zenith* (with the notable exception of Peter St. John, who is embarrassed by his younger days), has coveted youth, and now that desire will lead to his own demise. Peyne's physical regression isn't the only device Morrison uses to explore the theme of age. He also emphasizes Zenith's advancing years, as Ruby (who was 20 years older than Zenith in Phase One, remember) says to him, "why don't

---

[27] The concept of the *fractal*, the recursive pattern that appears the same at all levels of magnification, is integral to the work of Grant Morrison. Nearly every series or story I'll analyze in this book contains fractal patterns or a reference to fractal geometry.

[28] Chaos theory, much like Morrison's comic book work, deals with the relationship between chaos and order. In chaos theory, a tiny, seemingly insignificant event can be shown to have wide repercussions. In other words, even the seeming randomness of some events can be seen to have a root cause, and therefore, a predictable pattern. Chaos theory shows that order and chaos are inextricably linked.

you shut up, you old bore." Zenith, the former symbol of irreverent youth, is seen as an irrelevant fossil, and he's only 24 years old. He's a relic of the 1980s, and as David Cambridge says, "a new age is dawning."

In previous Phases, the *mind / body* connection was thematically significant, and that theme arises again as the events of Phase Four unfold. In this Phase, though, the minds actually become disconnected from the bodies. Peyne describes that the superhumans communicate telepathically "at all times, speech being far too slow and clumsy to accommodate their thought processes." Later, David Cambridge explains the power of their expanded awareness as they ascend like divine beings in halos of light: "We've been reborn from the egg of the sun," he says, "We've given up flesh and become pure consciousness extending across a multitude of dimensions." They are now transcendent beings who float above humanity.

This ties into Morrison's *metaphysical* explorations within Phase Four. Reality and dream weave together in the narrative. Peyne, "imprisoned," as he says, "in a dream come true," describes how "the contours of the city are altered and amended" by the "superhumans with complete psychokinetic control over the structure of matter." He declares, "here were the gods walking the earth." Ruby Fox later amplifies that thought by saying, "We are God and this is our heaven."

As *Zenith* has progressed, the characters have grown more and more powerful, and reality has become more and more elastic. In earlier Phases, we saw Ruby Fox become younger, we saw Peyne teaching Zenith how to manipulate the quantum process, and now we see the end result of such power: humanity is twisted beyond recognition and the sun has turned black. The physical reality is transformed by the minds of the superhumans who have ascended to godhood. Zenith and Peter St. John cannot hope to match that level of power because they are still attached to their physical desires. They have not achieved pure consciousness because they are too attached to humanity: Zenith wants to be popular – he wants adoration; St. John wants to effect change within the political machine built by humans. Both heroes are incapable of achieving their dreams without humanity, therefore they are as vulnerable as all flesh-and-blood creatures. They are both killed quickly when they try to resist the ascendant ones.

The ultimate evolutionary end in *Zenith* is mind without body. To emphasize this further, Peyne describes that "the people outside have got hands instead of heads." This is not a metaphor. Within their utopia, the

From *2000 AD* prog 803 – Zenith is apparently destroyed by his own offspring. Art by Steve Yeowell. Copyright © 2000 AD.

superhumans have transformed the humans and replaced their heads with giant hands. Physicality thereby becomes a symbol of humanity, of stupidity, while consciousness belongs only to the gods. Once they are free from the bonds of the flesh, the superhumans have no more need of the material goods on planet Earth, so they destroy the planet as well. Yet, when they think they have achieved a state of perfect consciousness, they find themselves trapped within the body of Chimera. The mind can never be free from the body, Morrison seems to be saying. There is no escape. The mind and body are inextricably linked.

Because Phase Four provides the capstone on the *Zenith* story, it also concludes the patterns that began in Phase One. The motif of *flying*, a symbol of freedom and power in the early parts of the *Zenith* story, becomes fully realized. The superhumans who have declared themselves gods no longer walk on the ground. They fly or hover exclusively every time they appear. In contrast, when Peter St. John is defeated, he plummets from the sky before being impaled. Then, of course, the superhumans fly out into space, thinking they have attained ultimate freedom and the ultimate power.

Phase Four also wraps up the *fatherhood* motif that arose in Phase Two. We discover that Zenith's off-panel liaison with Shockwave and Blaze back then has resulted in the birth of a baby boy. In Phase Four, Zenith's son transforms into Iok Sotot, the Lloigor who Zenith fought in Phase One. Iok Sotot kills Zenith; the son murders the father.[29] Youth dispatches age. The new eradicates the old. This action is paralleled by Dr. Michael Peyne's metaphorical children, his "Tygers" (the superhumans he helped create), destroying the old world and reducing him to nothingness. Phase Two, which seemed much less cosmically significant than the other Phases, is now seen, in retrospect, as the linchpin of *Zenith*'s thematic unity. It's all about the act of creation and the consequences of that act.

The other dominant motif in Phase Four is that of *vision*. In the early chapters, when the CIA attempts to dispose of the superhuman threat before they turn on humanity, the shadow agents use their limited psychic powers to cause blindness, thereby rendering their victims powerless. Sight, an essentially mental process in which the brain transforms physical stimuli into

---

[29] Such an act has Oedipal resonance, in the Freudian sense, and in the classical-tragedy sense. *Zenith*, and all super-hero narratives are, after all, based on ancient heroic structures – a point which I'll elucidate more fully in my analysis of *Arkham Asylum*.

a notion of "reality," is linked with Morrison's exploration of the *mind / body* theme. Related to this, the Eye of Horus symbolically represents ascendant superhumans who say they hatched from the sun.[30] He who controls sight controls the world, and that idea becomes concrete in Phase Four as Peyne describes how "[everyone] saw his or her own vision of the end of the world." Reality in *Zenith* is not only subjective, but its subjectivity is manipulated by a higher power. The superhumans revise those below them, but they find that they are manipulated, ultimately, by an even higher power, Peter St. John, who, like a true god, holds their universe in his hand.

At the beginning of our discussion of this Phase, I referred to the fact that some things weren't what they seemed. Morrison provides, in Phase Four, a shocking twist as we learn that the serum Peyne used to create the superhumans derived from the dark gods, the many angled ones, the Lloigor. David Cambridge reveals, "We are, we were, we will be, the Lloigor." If we assume Cambridge's statement to be true, this throws the entire narrative of *Zenith* into disarray, because it means that Peter St. John and Zenith are Lloigor as well. Therefore, the victory at the end of Phase Four, with St. John holding the corrupted miniature universe in his hand, is a hollow victory. Yet, Morrison has established that sons rebel against their parents in this story, so we can believe that St. John and Zenith are not necessarily destined to follow the paths of their Lloigor "parents." Then again, Morrison has also established that chaos is the natural, dominant mode of the universe, so St. John's imposed order (he has not only controlled the Lloigor threat, but he has become Prime Minister of England) is not likely to sustain itself for long.

By the time Morrison concluded the story of *Zenith,* he had begun to explore many of the themes that would drive his work for years to come. His close look into the relationship between mental and physical processes, his sense of cosmology and creation, and his investigation into the nature of reality all dominate the work that I'll be analyzing throughout this book. *Zenith* is Morrison's ur-text: it provides a template for everything that follows. He expands, revises, and deconstructs the template over the years, but his thematic concerns remain essentially the same. Morrison's work, at its core, deals with the link between creator and creation and all the

---

[30] For what is the Sun if not a giant, glowing eye? The Egyptians believed that the Sun was one eye of Horus, and the moon was the other.

complexities inherent in that relationship. *Zenith* exemplifies this approach, and, as a comic book story, it's super-heroics on a grand scale.

# *Arkham Asylum*

After the initial success of *Zenith*, Grant Morrison was invited to meet with editors from DC Comics while they visited London looking for new talent. Morrison pitched an *Animal Man* mini-series and a 48-page *Arkham Asylum* story. Both were accepted, and both were expanded. My analysis of the *Animal Man* story (which DC expanded into an ongoing series) will appear in the next chapter, but for now I'd like to focus my attention on the 120-page controversial masterpiece that was published in 1989 as a hardcover graphic novel called *Arkham Asylum: A Serious House on Serious Earth.*

The subtitle comes from the final stanza of Philip Larkin's poem "Church Going," which describes the emptiness of a church no longer in use:

> A serious house on serious earth it is,
> In whose blent air all our compulsions meet,
> Are recognised, and robed as destinies.
> And that much never can be obsolete,
> Since someone will forever be surprising
> A hunger in himself to be more serious,
> And gravitating with it to this ground,
> Which, he once heard, was proper to grow wise in,
> If only that so many dead lie round.

Larkin's words: "compulsions," "destinies," "hunger," "serious," "wise," and "dead," indicate some of the ideas Morrison had in mind for the *Arkham Asylum* graphic novel. He's not writing about a church, though – he's writing about a fictional house for the criminally insane that first appeared in a 1974 issue of the *Batman* comic book. Such is the method employed by Grant Morrison throughout the graphic novel; he takes conventions from the world of the *Batman* comic books and he treats them with the seriousness of literature and the vicious playfulness of experimental art. As Morrison explains in the 15th Anniversary edition of *Arkham Asylum*,

> The story's themes were inspired by Lewis Carroll, quantum physics, Jung and Crowley, its visual style by surrealism, Eastern European creepiness, Cocteau, Artaud, Svankmajer, the Brothers Quay, etc. The intention was to create something that was more like a piece of music or an experimental film than a typical adventure comic book.

He certainly succeeded at not creating anything typical.

*Arkham Asylum* begins with an epigraph and an image. The epigraph is from Lewis Carroll's *Alice's Adventures in Wonderland*:

> "But I don't want to go among mad people," Alice remarked.
>
> "Oh, you can't help that," said the Cat: "We're all mad here. I'm mad, you're mad."
>
> "How do you know I'm mad?" said Alice.
>
> "You must be," said the Cat, "or you wouldn't have come here."

Morrison not only establishes the theme of *madness* with such an epigraph, but he also indicates that what follows will, like Alice's journey, resemble the illogical world of a dream.

The image which accompanies the epigraph (albeit on the opposite page) depicts artist Dave McKean's[31] stylized adaptation of "The Moon" tarot card. "The Moon," with its two foreboding black towers bracketing the glowing lunar form, represents, according to Morrison, "trial and initiation – the supreme testing of the soul, where we must face our deepest fears, confront them and survive or be broken. In this single image are encoded all the themes of our entire story." Morrison will repeat this image, and the ideas embodied by it, throughout the narrative, just as he will repeat the *Alice in Wonderland* motif and the theme of madness. Certainly not the stuff of a "typical adventure comic."

If anything, the techniques Morrison uses in *Arkham Asylum* bear a closer resemblance to the high Modernist poetry of T. S. Eliot, as best exemplified in "The Waste Land," than to anything in the comic book

---

[31] Dave McKean, the artist of *Arkham Asylum*, gives the graphic novel a unique look. He's anything but a traditional super-hero artist. His work mixes painting and collage to create a dream-like realism which perfectly complements the Grant Morrison script. McKean takes the mythic, symbolic story and turns it into a mad hallucination which alternates between beauty and savagery.

tradition. Morrison may not have been thinking about Eliot's "The Waste Land," when he wrote this graphic novel, but the parallels are numerous. Both rely on fragmented narrative and disembodied voices, both use the iconography of the Tarot to provide symbolic unity, both allude to the story of the grail-knight Parsifal, both contain references to the Vesica Pisces (the Jesus fish), and even some of the images from the poem are echoed directly in the graphic novel. If Morrison wasn't influenced by "The Waste Land," then both he and Eliot were tapping into the same mythic structures, filtered through some of the same antecedent sources such as Sir James George Frazer's *The Golden Bough* and Jessie L. Weston's *From Ritual to Romance*. Weston and Frazer identify ritualistic patterns that connect various cultures together, and they show how early pagan rituals became adapted by the dominant religions of the world. Eliot's "The Waste Land" uses such material to illustrate the emotional and spiritual void which followed the first World War, while in *Arkham Asylum*, Morrison uses it to illustrate the disorienting depravity and madness of the late 20th century.

I'll return to the connection between "The Waste Land" and *Arkham Asylum* throughout my analysis, but I'd just like to take a moment to point out that both works seem to share something else in common: critical disdain, at least by the general public. Many readers of poetry (a small subculture of humanity, no doubt) think "The Waste Land" is a pretentious mish-mash of nonsense, the embodiment of style at the expense of substance. Likewise, many readers of comic books (another small subculture of humanity, for sure) think of *Arkham Asylum* in much the same way. Peruse a sampling of reader "reviews" at Amazon.com and you'll find negative comments like "I couldn't tell who he was fighting, who was talking or what i [sic] was looking at. And then the book ended. I kept turning back the pages to see if I missed something. Frankly the book wasn't worth the money," and "Top this lack of any decent plot off with some really strained attempts at deep symbolism (just throw in lots of religion and philosophy for no good reason), and you have yourself a shocking bore."[32] Such reaction is

[32] Ironically, *Arkham Asylum* is the best-selling graphic novel ever, with over 500,000 copies in circulation. Even Grant Morrison admits that the timing of the release had more than a little to do with its success: It came out during the "Batmania" that followed Tim Burton's *Batman* feature film. The mass audience who bought *Arkham Asylum* looking for a traditional Batman story surely responded

obviously heartfelt, but it clearly misses the point of *Arkham Asylum*.

As Morrison has indicated with the image of "The Moon" card, the graphic novel is about "trial and initiation." In many ways, it does contain a very conventional plot. Batman is the hero of a monomythic adventure, an epic quest of the variety found in the work of Joseph Campbell,[33] in which a character descends into the unknown world (Arkham Asylum itself), confronts challenges (bad guys), overcomes obstacles (more bad guys), and returns to bring about a rebirth to the world through some kind of self-sacrifice. (Batman wins at the end, but not without paying a price.) Expressed in those simplistic terms, the core narrative of *Arkham Asylum* is really no different than most super-hero adventure stories, but it's the manner of the telling that's so different: the elliptical dialogue, the fractured transitions between scenes, the fluidity of time, and the symbolic weight of the images. All of these aspects make *Arkham Asylum* a more fully realized combination of words and images than almost any comic book story ever published.

According to Grant Morrison, the idea for the graphic novel came from the "Arkham Asylum" entry in Volume 1 of DC Comics' *Who's Who: The Definitive Directory of the DC Universe*.[34] The relevant portion of the entry, written by Len Wein in early 1985, describes how the asylum was first established:

> Founded in 1921 by Dr. Amadeus Arkham, on a parcel of land deeded to him by his mother, who had herself been a victim of mental illness, the asylum was the first such facility of its kind in Gotham County. Dr. Arkham, a vigorous social reformer, had been appalled by conditions in the Gotham penal system, where those who were not mentally responsible for their actions were incarcerated side-by-side with hardened career criminals, and he was determined to improve this situation. To that end, he transformed his ancestral home into a high-security mental facility,

---

with a collective "huh?!?"

[33] Joseph Campbell, the scholar of comparative mythology, wrote *The Hero with a Thousand Faces* (1949), which outlines the path followed by every questing hero. For examples of this journey, see *Star Wars*, *The Lord of the Rings*, *SpongeBob SquarePants: The Movie* and basically everything else Hollywood has produced in the past thirty years.

[34] *Who's Who* was a 26-issue series which provided images and information on nearly every character in the DC Universe. Arkham Asylum was one of the few locations deemed important enough to warrant its own entry.

> and staffed it with some of the most prominent psychologists and physicians of the time.
>
> Ironically, one of Arkham's first inmates was one "Mad Dog" Martin Hawkins, who had been arrested and tried for the brutal murders of Amadeus Arkham's own wife and infant daughter, then found not guilty by reason of insanity. It is to Dr. Arkham's everlasting credit that he treated Hawkins with great concern and compassion, right up to Hawkins' accidental electrocution two months after his incarceration.
>
> In 1929, six days after the now-legendary stock market crash, Dr. Arkham, who had lost his entire fortune in the crash, apparently went berserk, and was subdued and arrested while attempting to electrocute his former stockbroker. Found not guilty by reason of insanity, Amadeus Arkham was committed to his own Asylum, where he spent the remainder of his days carving indecipherable inscriptions on the floor of his cell with his fingernails while softly singing "The Battle Hymn of the Republic."

"It occurred to me," says Morrison, "that having one's wife and daughter slaughtered by a man named 'Mad Dog' might have been sufficient cause for a nervous breakdown, so I decided to explore and expand upon the life of this throwaway character, and from this seed the story that became 'A Serious House on Serious Earth.'" The narrative of Amadeus Arkham's descent into madness opens the graphic novel and runs parallel to the Batman storyline for the rest of the book.

After the Carroll epigraph and the image of "The Moon" card, the sequential narrative of *Arkham Asylum* begins with an excerpt from Amadeus Arkham's journal and accompanying images which establishes Arkham's connection to the house and expresses the motif of the shadow world where chaos reigns. "During the long period of mother's illness," reads Arkham's journal entry, "the house often seemed so vast, so confidently real, that by comparison, I felt little more than a ghost haunting its corridors. Scarcely aware that anything could exist beyond those most melancholy walls. Until the night in 1901, when I first caught glimpse of that other world. The world on the dark side." Dave McKean's painted panels on the following page depict Arkham's bed-ridden mother. Beetles crawl from her mouth as she repeats, "I've eaten. I've eaten." Insects often reoccur in Morrison's work, usually as a symbol for something foreign or otherworldly – he seems to use them to represent the antithesis of humanity. In this instance, Arkham's journal entry explains that the beetles represent something very different from what Morrison normally intends: "Many years later, when I became aware of the significance of the beetle as a symbol of rebirth, I realized that she was simply trying to protect herself from something, in the only way that made sense to her." *Rebirth* is a theme that will appear in the form of various motifs and symbols throughout *Arkham Asylum*, and it's yet another connection to Eliot's "The Waste Land," which centers around an implied question: *how can life emerge from desolation?* The same question might be asked about Arkham Asylum.

The rebirth in the case of Arkham's mother is quite different, though, as Arkham himself explains: "Mother had been born again, into that other world. A world of fathomless signs and portents. Of magic and terror. And mysterious symbols." The world he alludes to is, of course, the world of madness. Notice how Morrison defines that world as the world of "signs" and "magic" and "symbols." Throughout the graphic novel, Morrison attempts to convey a different type of reality. A non-literal realm, "from the point of view," Morrison himself explains in the 15th Anniversary edition, "of the dreamlike, emotional and irrational hemisphere, as a response to the very literal, 'realistic' 'left-brain' treatment of super-heroes which was in vogue at the time."[35]

After introducing young Amadeus Arkham and his unstable mother, Morrison shifts the narrative to the Batman storyline. While the early Arkham flashback sequences are illustrated in panels which are embedded in imagery from the house itself (i.e. as young Arkham ascends the stairs to his mother's room, his panels are inset among a full-page illustration of the facade of the house, symbolically demonstrating his imprisonment within its walls), the early Batman sequences are illustrated as alternating sequences, with one vertical image showing a Batman silhouette against a color background followed by a sketchy black and white vertical stripe of panels showing Batman and Commissioner Gordon. That pattern continues, three slices of vertical narrative at a time, creating a triptych on each page. The color sequence shows Batman in the narrative present, slowly approaching Arkham Asylum. The sketchy black and white sequence shows the recent

---

[35] Morrison here refers to the late 1980s preponderance of "grim-and-gritty" comic books which had none of the charm or sense of wonder that super-hero stories had in the past. By the late 1980s, American comic books were filled with storylines with names like "Mutant Massacre" and "Gang War."

past and reveals why he must undertake this journey into the madhouse. The three distinct time periods (the distant past of Amadeus Arkham, the recent past with Commissioner Gordon, and the present with Batman alone) alternate throughout the first 16 pages of the graphic novel until Batman finally arrives at the front door of the asylum. From then on, the narrative only alternates from Batman's present to the distant past of Amadeus Arkham. By providing so much temporal fragmentation, Morrison not only employs yet another technique which parallels Eliot's "The Waste Land," he also disorients the reader, replicating the very state of delirium and madness which the characters experience throughout the story.

The central Batman plotline, occurring in the recent narrative past, starts with a hostage situation at Arkham Asylum. As Commissioner Gordon explains, "The inmates seized control of the building early this morning... They're holding the asylum staff hostage, making all kinds of crazy demands." The last demand is to speak with Batman, who talks to the Joker[36] via speaker phone. The Joker immediately adopts a perverse familiarity with Batman, asking, "How's it hanging?" Morrison presents Joker as a sexual creature throughout the graphic novel, and he had originally intended to take the depiction even further. As he explains in the 15th Anniversary edition, he originally imagined the Joker dressed as Madonna from the "Open Your Heart" video, complete with "a black basque, seamed tights and lace-up stiletto boots." His original draft of the script explains, "[the Joker] projects an absolute confidence that confers upon him a bizarre kind of attractiveness and sexuality. It is the attraction of the perverse and the forbidden. The Joker personifies the irrational dark side of us all." Editor Karen Berger and the powers-that-be at DC Comics ultimately required Morrison to tone down his hyper-sexualized Joker, but Morrison still managed to include a few innuendos and a panel later in the story where the Joker actually grabs Batman's buttocks. Contextually, though, the Joker's actions are not really about sexuality or perversion; they are about *chaos* and *subversion*, providing a funhouse mirror image of the uptight and orderly Batman.

---

[36] The Joker is Batman's classic enemy, but he's almost a cipher. His identity and behavior shifts depending on who's writing the story. Morrison plays upon this fact in *Arkham Asylum* and actually provides a reason for his inconsistent characterization.

During the telephone conversation, two other motifs emerge, and the Joker's violence compels Batman to visit Arkham Asylum personally. The first motif appears in the form of a woman's name: *Pearl.* She is one of the hostages in the asylum. The second motif, *vision,* follows immediately, as the Joker implies that he is going to stab her in the eye. "Pearl wants to be an artist, don't you, Pearl darling?" the Joker says, "She just drew me a beautiful house. She drew it with this pencil. The one I've just sharpened. Open your eyes wide, Pearl! Beautiful. Blue. Oh." Batman shouts "Jesus, No!" as he hears a harsh scream from the other end of the telephone line.

The character of Pearl, and the word "pearl" will reappear in the graphic novel several times, each time taking on more symbolic weight, most specifically regarding Batman's murdered mother, who was wearing a string of pearls the night she was gunned down.[37] The vision motif, less explicit here than in Morrison's *Zenith,* seems to appear mostly by its inverse: blindness and not-seeing. The world of madness, after all, is described by Amadeus Arkham as the "world on the dark side." Once again, both motifs recall Eliot's "The Waste Land," which alludes to Shakespeare's *Tempest* by stealing the line, "Those are pearls that were his eyes."

In addition to the introduction of the two new motifs, the sequence also repeats the house imagery (Pearl drew a picture of a house, according to the Joker), and in Batman's profane exclamation, "Jesus," he invokes the Christian symbol of rebirth. His shout may seem like a throwaway reaction to a horrific event, but by referencing Christ, he's continuing to establish the motif of *ritual and initiation* that began with "The Moon" card on the opening pages. All of this ties into the same anthropological sources Eliot used to inspire "The Waste Land": Frazer's *The Golden Bough* and Weston's *From Ritual to Romance.* Both of those books describe the connection between the pagan fertility gods and the adoption of those fertility

---

[37] Batman's origin can be summarized like this: Young Bruce Wayne and his parents, on their way home from a movie theater, take a shortcut though an alley where they are robbed. The robber shoots and kills Bruce's parents, and the boy grows to adulthood with a passion for vengeance which he will wreak on the world of crime. After a bat flies through his window, inspiring him, Bruce Wayne adopts the identity of Batman because criminals are a "superstitious, cowardly lot." Every major Batman story deals with his origin in some way, and *Arkham Asylum* is no exception.

From *Arkham Asylum* – In the narrative present, Batman discovers salt around the asylum, while in the recent narrative past he discusses madness with Commissioner Jim Gordon. Art by Dave McKean. Copyright © DC Comics.

rituals by the early Christians. Christ is the embodiment of a fertility god. He has sacrificed himself to bring about a rebirth. The cycle of death in rebirth is apparent in the natural world each year, as the agrarian world moves from planting to growing to harvesting from season to season. The fertility god, and therefore Christ, represents this cycle, and the monomythic hero parallels the cycle as well, as the hero descends into the bowels of the underworld before emerging to bring about a rebirth in the world above. Morrison draws on all of these mythic structures in *Arkham Asylum*.

One of the archetypal moments of the heroic quest is the refusal of the call. This occurs early in the story when the hero doesn't quite think he has what it takes to succeed. In *Arkham Asylum*, Batman doesn't outwardly refuse to confront Joker and the other inmates, but he hesitates a moment and talks to Commissioner Gordon before rushing into action. "This is something I have to do," Batman says. "Listen, I can understand if even you're afraid," says Gordon. "Afraid? Batman's not afraid of anything," says Batman, referring to the character he plays while in costume before continuing his thought:

> It's me. I'm afraid. I'm afraid the Joker might be right about me. Sometimes I... question the rationality of my actions. And I'm afraid that when I walk through those asylum gates... when I walk into Arkham and the doors close behind me... It'll be just like coming home.

Batman's indication of his split psyche shows a self-awareness not usually seen in his regular comic book adventures, and it also takes the theme of madness to the next level, directly stating the questions that his quest into Arkham Asylum will seek to answer: *Is Batman as mad as the inmates? Can he rise above the wasteland of insanity?*

Throughout this flashback to the recent past, we've seen a shadowy Batman approaching the asylum in the narrative present, so we know he's going to undertake the mission (as if there were ever any doubt), but he only gets as far as the exterior grounds before Morrison cuts away (on Batman's use of the word *home* in the excerpt above) to an extended flashback of Amadeus Arkham's return to what was then the family home after his mother's funeral.

"She opened her own throat with a pearl-handed razor," writes Arkham in his journal, continuing the pearl motif and connecting it to another dead mother. Speaking of mothers, Morrison also indicates that the intention of his Joker-as-Madonna image wasn't just to show the Joker's perverse sexuality, but it was also to reinforce the motif of the "madonna," the holy mother, which would symbolically connect Arkham to Batman to Christ.

Arkham continues his 1920 journal entries by alluding to his plans, thoughts of which are interrupted by "dreams... haunted by beating wings," a poetic evocation of Batman's future impact on the asylum which Arkham begins to plan. The Arkham flashback continues for several pages, revealing some of the back story as expressed in the *Who's Who* entry but enlarged by Morrison. In the flashback, Arkham meets a new patient in Metropolis: "Mad Dog" Hawkins, a prisoner from the state penitentiary who destroyed the faces and sexual organs of his victims. When Arkham asks Hawkins why he cuts his arms with a razor, Hawkins replies, "Just to feel. Just to feel something." Arkham vows to create a place for people like Hawkins, "Men whose only real crime is mental illness."

After he announces his plans to his wife and daughter, Arkham describes his dream that night in another journal entry:

> That night I dream I am a child again. Lost in a funhouse, I find myself in the Hall of Mirrors. There are strangers in the mirrors and I freeze, not daring to go any further... That night, I dream that the mirror people haveescaped from the glass and come looking for me. I wake, sweating and adult, and for a moment. Just a moment. I feel as though I'm back. Where I belong. Back in the old house.

Dreams and unreality run rampant through *Arkham Asylum*, but the key motif in Arkham's nightmare is the *mirror*. The mirror which reflects and distorts provides a symbol for the relationship between Batman and the Joker, Batman and every other insane villain he confronts, and most emphatically, Batman and himself. It is in the mirror that Batman must confront his own psychosis. The mirror reference also reminds us of the *Alice in Wonderland* epigraph, and the description of the dream shows that the mirror, as Alice discovered, is a portal between worlds, between order and chaos, between sanity and madness.

On the word *house*, Morrison returns us to the narrative present, where Batman stands outside the walls of Arkham Asylum, a small black figure against a looming stone facade. His fingertips are white from examining the mysterious salt on the ground. When the Joker emerges from the house, he asks Batman, "Why don't you sprinkle some on me, honey? Aren't I just good enough to eat?" Besides the implied sexuality in the questions, the

Joker's words connect the moment back to pagan fertility rituals which occasionally contained literal or metaphorical cannibalism. Such a ritual can be still witnessed in the Christian sacrament of the Eucharist, in which the body of Christ is symbolically eaten. These implications connect the story of *Arkham Asylum* to its mythic roots.

Because Batman fulfilled the inmates' final request by showing up in person, the Joker allows the hostages to go free, including Pearl who is clearly shown to possess two good eyes. Batman asks, "But what about her eyes? You said..." To which the Joker replies maniacally, "April Fool!"[38] In the dark world of Arkham Asylum, it's all just a twisted game.

As the Joker leads Batman into the asylum, they pass by a statue of Anubis. Anubis was the Egyptian god of the underworld; thus Morrison literally signifies Batman's descent into the realm of ritual and initiation. In Aleister Crowley's Tarot design, called the Thoth Tarot deck, a mirrored Anubis is depicted on both the left and right of "The Moon" card. Anubis, by the way, is depicted with the face of a dog, which connects the symbolism back to Amadeus Arkham, whose family was killed by "Mad Dog" Hawkins (as we'll find out later).

The panels throughout the story so far have been rigidly rectangular, but once the doors to Arkham Asylum open, Dave McKean paints a double-page splash with jagged inset panels and collage effects. Juxtaposed with the chaotic images, the disembodied word balloons say things like, "Some say God is an insect," "Who killed Bambi," and "Oranges?" The Joker shouts, "Let the Feast of Fools begin!"

These two pages are packed with images, and Morrison's script indicates that he wanted the scene to allude to "the Mad Hatter's Tea Party in 'Alice' and also to the Last Supper." "What we want," he writes, "are a few nice, disturbing images and a sense of the world gone mad. Something to give Francis Bacon nightmares." A table is featured at the center of the image, but McKean has not painted anything resembling a tea party or the Last Supper. Instead, he gives us winged characters, skeletons, beheadings, and brutality. In the midst of it all, in place of a chandelier, a featureless human hangs with one leg suspended from the ceiling. The figure, with its arms

---

[38] The date, April 1st, is another important pattern in the story. It's the day of the year which not only inverts social norms, but within *Arkham Asylum*, it connects the past with the present.

outstretched and one leg bent to form a "figure four" across the other leg, perfectly replicates another Tarot card from Crowley's Thoth deck: "The Hanged Man." "The Hanged Man" card represents the fertility god, and if you flip the card upside down, the figure of the man suspended by one leg with his arms outstretched exactly duplicates Christ in the crucifixion pose. Morrison is packing it all in here, all the symbols of ritual and initiation, with the moon lurking through the giant windows of the dining hall.

The multitude of disembodied voices in the scene offers sense of the swirling chaos, but some of the words have more significant meaning within the story. The word balloon which reads, "Oh, daddy, make him stop! He's hurting me! The dog's hurting me!" is, according to Morrison, "Arkham's daughter's ghostly voice coming in through time from earlier in the book," and the line which reads, "well... a... a boy's best friend is his mother," comes from Hitchcock's *Psycho*. The line, as spoken by Anthony Perkins's Norman Bates, resonates deeply throughout *Arkham Asylum*, connecting the theme of madness with the motifs of the *mother* and *transvestism* (a thread that was partially lost when Morrison was forced to remove the Joker from Madonna drag). Anthony Perkins actually appears in the graphic novel as an image on a television screen on a later page.

After the overwhelming imagery of the two-page splash, the panels return to their normal geometric rigidity as the Joker introduces Batman to some of the "normal" citizens who've stayed behind like Ruth Adams, a psychotherapist, and Doc Cavendish, the hospital administrator, who, according to the Joker, "just loves to administer current to ECT patients." ECT, or electroconvulsive therapy, involves inducing a seizure in a patient by passing an electric current through the brain.[39] By the time of *Arkham Asylum*'s publication in 1989, such treatment was reserved for extreme cases, but it was used much more widely in the early 20th century. The motif of *electricity* gains greater prominence in the last stages of the graphic novel.

In this sequence, Batman also discovers his old villain, Two-Face,[40]

---

[39] Morrison, here and in his later work like *Doom Patrol*, doesn't reveal much fondness for psychiatry or psychotherapy. Perhaps it's because Morrison draws a different line between sanity and insanity (if he draws a line at all) than the one commonly accepted by medical professionals.

[40] Two-Face was once Harvey Dent, prosecutor, before one side of his face was burned with acid and he went insane. Two-Face's gimmick is that everything is doubled. He wears a suit with two distinct designs, he always commits crimes

relieving himself as he sits on the floor because he's unable to make a decision. As Dr. Ruth Adams explains to Batman,

> we've successfully tackled Harvey's obsession with duality... He used to make all his decisions with [his coin], as though it somehow represented the contradictory halves of his personality. What we did was wean him off the coin and on to a die... He did so well with the die that we've been able to move him onto a pack of tarot cards. That's seventy-eight options open to him now, Batman.

Yet, as Batman points out, "he can't even make a simple decision, like going to the bathroom, without consulting the cards? Seems to me you've effectively destroyed the man's personality, Doctor." Meanwhile, Two-Face, building a house of cards with the Tarot deck, holds up "The Tower" card as Batman talks to Dr. Adams. "The Tower" symbolizes destruction, and it usually indicates that false institutions are going to tumble to the ground. McKean gives us two consecutive panels of "The Tower" card, emphasizing its importance in Morrison's narrative, as Batman expresses doubt about the effectiveness of the asylum (the literal embodiment of a false institution).

Regarding the Joker's mental state, Dr. Adams says,

> It;s quite possible we may actually be looking at some kind of super-sanity here. A brilliant new modification of human perception. More suited to urban life at the end of the Twentieth century... the Joker seems to have no control over the sensory information he's receiving from the outside world. He can only cope with that chaotic barrage of input by going with the flow. That's why some days he's a mischievous clown, others a psychopathic killer. He has no real personality. He creates himself each day.

Like T. S. Eliot, who presented the fragmentation of early Twentieth century society as a multitude of voices, Morrison gives us a shattered sense of identity – an identity in tune with a postmodern culture in which personality shifts occur as quickly as flipping through the channels.

The Joker, meanwhile, attempts to delve into Batman's psyche, first with a Rorschach test.[41] The inkblot clearly resembles a bat, and Dave McKean

---

relating to the number two, and he has a two-sided coin with one side scratched out. He typically uses that coin to make all his decisions. If the clean side comes up, he does something good, but if the scarred side comes up, he does something evil.

[41] The Rorschach test is a dubious psychological tool involving a series of ten cards with inkblots. The subject describes what he sees in each image and the psychologist evaluates the subjects responses.

follows the ink blot panel with a full-page splash of a bat (presumably the very bat which flew through Bruce Wayne's window and inspired his super-hero origin), but Batman says he sees "nothing." He doesn't want to play the Joker's game, but yet he goes along with a word association test conducted by Dr. Adams. He says, "I'm not afraid. It's just words." Although he declined to define the images in his mind with the Rorschach test, he willingly participates in word association. He understands the symbolic power of images, giving the reader a clue about how to read *Arkham Asylum*.

In the word association test, Morrison repeats some of the same words and images that he has patterned throughout the graphic novel. When Dr. Adams says, "Mother," we see a picture of a well-dressed female, a photograph of a praying holy Madonna figure, and a string of white pearls. Batman says, "Pearl." In response to "Father," Batman says, "Death." Batman quickly abandons the game, perhaps because he's afraid to continue, or perhaps because his psychic depths have already been plumbed. That's as deep as it goes: resentment and anger over the death of his parents.

Morrison provides more image patterns in another Amadeus Arkham flashback which frames the word association test. In the flashback narrative, Arkham writes in his journal about the erection of a St. Michael statue. The statue, as rendered in the graphic novel by Dave McKean, shows a looming winged figure, with a spear, atop a defeated serpent. As Arkham explains, it is "an image of the triumph of reason over the irrational." A spear and a reptile will appear later in the Batman narrative, and the wings, of course, remind us that Batman is the saintly hero (of the rational) who is questing for a dragon (madness). Except Morrison has complicated things by implying that even Batman knows that madness is a part of him as well. But that's what the ritual and initiation is about in this story: confronting madness to defeat it from within.

The symbolism continues in the flashback narrative, as Amadeus Arkham returns home to sit beside his dreaming daughter. Strewn about the floor are red crayon drawings of savage dogs (foreshadowing of her brutal death by "Mad Dog" Hawkins) and a single playing card: a joker. The joker card is more than a mere reference to Batman's enemy, though, it's another Tarot allusion. The joker, also known as "The Fool" is the only surviving card from the major arcana[42] of the Tarot to make its way into a deck of playing cards. Not only are jokers wild, but there are games played with Tarot cards in which playing "The Fool" exempts the player from the rules of the game. Also, "The Fool" traditionally represents the inexperienced, questing human in search of meaning. It symbolizes the protagonist of a story. Therefore, Batman, not the Joker, is "The Fool" in this graphic novel.

Arkham's flashback continues by describing his meeting with two controversial figures: Aleister Crowley and Carl Jung. By referencing these two names, Morrison is giving us the keys to understanding *Arkham Asylum*. Crowley is significant because he created the Thoth Tarot which Morrison references continually in this graphic novel, while Jung's psychological theory of archetypes relies heavily on the relationship between what he calls the *Self* (unified consciousness) and the *Shadow* (the instinctive and irrational side of human nature). Batman and the Joker physically represent these archetypes, although Batman is not a fully realized *Self* until the end of the graphic novel. At first, and until he achieves victory over the various *Shadows* (as embodied not only by the Joker, but by other rogues as well), he is a mere *persona*, as the Joker so readily points out when one of the inmates asks to see Batman's real face: "[The mask] is his real face," says the Joker, "and I want to go much deeper than that."

One more significant symbolic image in the flashback sequence is Arkham's wife's purchase of a Japanese clown fish. As Morrison explains in the 15th Anniversary edition,

> Clown Fish are represented for the purpose of illustrating the circus clown / Joker imagery. Their ability to change sex being another reference to the shamanistic transvestism theme which appears throughout. The Fish is also representative of Christ (think of the classic Christian Fish symbol which appears on bumper stickers across America, also known as the *Vesica Pisces*).

Morrison loads each symbol with meaning, because in *Arkham Asylum*, as in a dream or a nightmare, the symbols are the meaning.

---

[42] The Tarot deck comprises 78 cards, 56 of which are the minor arcana which later evolved into common playing cards (the Tarot's page and knight combined to become the "jack," and the four suits changed their names – swords became spades, etc. – but otherwise, the minor arcana are familiar to anyone who has played a game of poker). The major arcana, the much-more-powerful 22 cards with names like "The Lovers," "Justice," "The Tower," and "Death," no longer show up in decks of playing cards. "The Fool," or joker, is the only one that remains.

In the narrative present, the "plot" of the graphic novel kicks into gear with the Joker threatening the kill the remaining civilians one by one unless Batman plays a game of hide and seek. Joker demands that Batman hide in the asylum, with a one hour head start, before the deranged inmates begin looking for him. To prove his intentions, Joker shoots a security guard in the head. As Batman walks away, Joker yells, "The game ends at midnight! Run! Run!" This is all a narrative contrivance to get Batman through the various rooms of Arkham Asylum, and in this sequence Morrison shows us an unusually inactive Batman. Surely the traditional Batman wouldn't simply walk away from Joker threatening to murder innocent civilians. Surely he'd heave a batarang the Joker's way or give him a flying kick to the head. Not in Morrison's world. Not in the dream logic of *Arkham Asylum.*

As Batman stalks through the hallways of the asylum, he flashes back and forth between his boyhood and the present. Images of his parents' brutal murder (accompanied by images of a torn pearl necklace) juxtapose with his descent into the darkness of Arkham. He lashes out in the present and, as Morrison writes in his script, "as though it will somehow stop the memory from reaching its awful and inevitable conclusion, Batman snaps his fist up to smash the convex mirror." We have mirrors and mothers and pearls in almost the same instant, but what Batman does after smashing the glass has even deeper symbolic weight. Over the course of fourteen panels, he takes a shard of the mirror and thrusts it through his left hand. Morrison explains,

> This act deepens some of the ritual symbolism of the story. The recurring Fish motif – which relates to Pisces, the astrological attribution of the Moon card – also relates to Christ, who in turn can be linked to the Egyptian God Osiris, whose life and descent into the underworld parallels with the story of Amadeus Arkham.

He further elucidates the sequence by describing his initial conception of the architecture of Arkham Asylum as taking the shape of Vesica Pisces (two overlapping circles, which was developed from the Greek symbol for Christ):

> The Vescica Piscis [sic] symbol is a very basic representation of the holographic process in which intersecting circular wave patterns produce three dimensional images. Physicist David Bohm believes the hologram to be an analogy for his vision of a vast interconnected universe, in which every part is in some sense a reflection of every other part... In the same way, everything in this story reflects and comments upon everything else.

Morrison's metaphysical concept of reality, via David Bohm's theory in which everything is recursive, is visually mirrored in *Arkham Asylum* in every sequence. The patterns that emerge occur again and again, and if it seems like I'm repeating myself by pointing them out to you, well I am. But so is Morrison. On purpose. The world of *Arkham Asylum* is a grand, unified work of symbolism.

After gazing at the moon, Joker and the inmates decide to "pretend" that it's been a hour, so they can chase down Batman, but Morrison cuts away from that promised action to show a highly significant Amadeus Arkham sequence, from April 1st, 1921. Arkham returns home to find his wife and child dead – their mutilated bodies on the floor, and the words "Mad Dog" scrawled in blood on the wall. Arkham can't find his wife's head, but when he looks at his daughter's doll house, he sees the eyes of his wife looking back at him through the tiny windows. As painted by McKean, it's a horrifying scene, and as Morrison says, "this single image [of the head inside the house] is the pivot around which the entire story revolves." The entire story, basically, takes place within Batman's own mind, and Arkham Asylum represents his head as he journeys deeper and deeper into his subconscious. The Mad Hatter, one of Batman's old, deranged villains, states this idea literally in a later scene in the graphic novel: "Sometimes I think the asylum is a head. We're inside a huge head that dreams us all into being. Perhaps it's your head Batman. Arkham is a looking glass. And we are you." Morrison admits that here, "The Mad Hatter obligingly explains the book for anyone who hasn't figured it out yet."

In the Amadeus Arkham flashback, Arkham loses his mind after finding his wife and child in such a condition and he dons his mother's old wedding dress. Morrison claims in the 15th Anniversary edition that his original draft of the script featured Arkham turning to ritualistic cannibalism at this point, which would have bound everything more tightly together: the mother imagery, the transvestitism, the fertility rituals. Not surprisingly, the act of eating his own wife and child was deemed too offensive by DC Comics, so we're left with an image of a weeping and vomiting Arkham instead.

In the narrative present, inside the asylum itself – or inside Batman's head, depending on your point of view – Batman faces one nemesis after another. The first villain he encounters is Clayface, portrayed here as a green, withered, naked humanoid.[43] According to Morrison, this version of

[43] Batman has met several villains going by the name of Clayface. The most famous

Clayface represents "Batman's fear of sexuality as something intrinsically unclean." "AIDS on two legs," Morrison calls him. Batman quickly dispatches Clayface (and presumably his fear) with a swift kick to the knee.

Next is Dr. Destiny,[44] whom Morrison does not clearly define for us. This particular villain has the power to control dreams, though, and would fit nicely into the narrative without any additional symbolism. Yet here he's portrayed as a sickly, wheelchair bound man with a skull for a face, while he's usually shown in other super-hero comic books as having the physique of a steroidal weightlifter. Also, he's looking around for Clayface, so perhaps Dr. Destiny represents another aspect of Batman's sexual fear: impotency. In any case, Batman kicks him and his wheelchair down the stairs.

Scarecrow[45] shambles past, but Batman does not confront him. The act of letting the Scarecrow, the master of terror, walk by seems to show that Batman is not ready to confront his deepest fears. Instead, Batman focuses his attention on the floor of a cell. Millions of words have been carved into the stone, a sight to which Batman can only respond, "My God." The words represent Amadeus Arkham's final project. He carved them while a prisoner in his own asylum, and the climax of the graphic novel will reveal why.

Batman's journey leads him through a hall of infinite mirrors, and the mirrors lead to (who else?) the Mad Hatter.[46] It's here that the Hatter tells Batman that everything is happening inside his head, but he also discusses David Bohm's theory, saying, "The apparent disorder of the universe is simply a higher order, an implicate order beyond our comprehension." This

---

is the one with the ability to change shape, but the one in this graphic novel bears little resemblance to any of the Clayfaces Batman has encountered before. He has been re-imagined here, by Morrison, as something more sordid.

[44] Dr. Destiny is not one of Batman's regular nemeses. He's traditionally more of a Justice League villain, and Morrison doesn't do much with him to justify his particular presence in this story.

[45] Scarecrow is a classic Batman villain. He uses fear gas to cause dementia in his victims. Morrison doesn't do much with Scarecrow either, but Batman's lack of confrontation with him seems to have symbolic value.

[46] The Mad Hatter is not portrayed in his usual fashion here. Morrison wanted McKean to present the Hatter as he was illustrated in the Alice books, and that's how McKean does it. Even the Hatter's words seem uncharacteristic. In the Batman comic books, he's a giggling inventor of mind-controlling hats, but here he's a loony sage. Morrison is clearly trying to allude to the dream logic of the Alice books rather than the literal Batman continuity.

conflict of (and relationship between) order and chaos appears repeatedly in Morrison's work, from *Zenith* to *Doom Patrol* and beyond. In *Arkham Asylum*, order doesn't stand a chance. Batman doesn't "win" until he confronts his own madness within the midst of the chaos.

The Hatter sequence leads into another Amadeus Arkham flashback, culminating in the deeds of April 1, 1922, one year after the death of his family. Arkham has begun treating "Mad Dog" Hawkins (as explained in the *Who's Who* entry), but in Morrison's interpretation of events, Arkham's "treatment" of Hawkins is a ruse. And on the one-year anniversary of his family's murder, Arkham straps Hawkins into the electric chair (that electricity motif appearing again, only this time with substance), and as he writes in his journal, "[he burned] the filthy bastard... There is ozone and the smell of burned skin in my nostrils. But I feel nothing." His mental state now mirrors Hawkins when the two first met – the time when Hawkins said he cut himself "just to feel." As Arkham wanders the hallways of his asylum, he knows how deeply he's sunk. He says, "The house is an organism, hungry for madness. It is the maze that dreams. And I am lost."[47]

Batman, in the narrative present, has his encounter with electricity in the form of obscure villain Maxie Zeus.[48] The wall in the electroconvulsive therapy room bears a Greek marking, words which translate as "Discover Thyself." It is a message for Batman, since he is the questing hero, the grail-knight, the fool on his errand. Essentially, *Arkham Asylum* is simply about Batman's self-discovery. Maxie Zeus is connected to wires, a halo of blue electricity hovers around him. He is a madman who thinks he's Zeus, god of the sky, and as the attendant jolts him with electricity, he likes it, and he says, "For I am Zeus. Lord of ECT. God of electric retribution. I give, so that thou shouldst give. Here. My gift to you. Do you want power? I can give power." As he says these last two lines, his body surges with voltage and his skull glows beneath his skin. He represents *hubris*, the arrogance of a god, and the trap which Batman could easily fall into. How can Batman not think of himself as superior to the mass of humanity? How can Batman not think

---

[47] All of the significant events in the graphic novel, past and present, occur on April 1st. As the Joker would no doubt point out, it's all just a tragic joke.

[48] Maxie Zeus, a mob boss with delusions of grandeur in the Batman comic books, is portrayed here as a spirit of electricity. He's a visual link between the present and the past, between Batman's quest and Amadeus Arkham's journey into madness.

of himself as a god? Batman offers no reply as he walks out of the room.

In the next Amadeus Arkham flashback, Arkham describes the attempted treatment for his "ill health," as some friends take him to see Wagner's *Parsifal*. Parsifal, or Sir Percival, was a grail-knight, and as alluded to in Eliot's "The Waste Land," he represents fertility because he seeks the end of the desolation. The grail will provide rebirth. In Wagner's *Parsifal*, though, he also finds the spear used to pierce Christ's body on the crucifix. In many ways, this imagery connects him to the statue of St. Michael, as described earlier, and to Batman, as seen later. Batman, after all, is undergoing a trial of initiation, much like the one faced by Sir Percival on his quest. To connect the symbolism even further, Arkham himself, in his journal, describes the movement of his two clown fish in their tank: "[they] glide toward one another. And make the sign of Pisces. Pisces! The astrological attribution of the moon card of the Tarot pack! Thy symbol of trial and initiation. Death and rebirth." It's yet another instance of Morrison directly stating the connections in the graphic novel through the words of a character.

Batman reaches his final physical challenge when he confronts his dragon: Killer Croc, the reptilian beast[49] – one of Batman's most malicious villains. As Morrison explains in the 15th Anniversary edition, "Killer Croc stands in for the Old Dragon of Revelations. The Dragon can be seen to represent primal chaos, the R complex lizard brain." Batman, recognizing his own role within the monomyth, within the rite of initiation, says, "Like Parsifal, I must confront the unreason that threatens me. I must go alone into the dark tower. Without a backwards glance. And face the dragon within." The word *within* alludes to what lies inside the tower and what lies within his mind. Batman's strength is no match for the gigantic monster, and Batman, thrown out of the window, finds the statue of St. Michael and the serpent as he falls. After landing, Batman grasps the spear and (re-enacting that Biblical moment) slays his dragon, sending a bloody Croc into the depths of the asylum with a cry of "Mother!"

Morrison explains:

> The spear, the weapon of rational intellect, is used to conquer the brute appetites of nature and man... In Qabalistic numerology, Christ = Satan = Messiah, which is why Croc appears here in a

---

[49] Killer Croc is as self-explanatory as you can imagine. He's a giant crocodile man with a temper.

> crucifixion pose [as he is impaled upon the spear], taking the place of Christ in this blasphemous cross. In this scene, Batman reunites Christ and the Serpent, then confronts and overcomes his own attachment to his Mother in a perverse nightmare of lizards, lace and bridal embroidery.

He has slain the dragon and seems to regain his *Self* (in Jungian terms) by confronting his fears and destroying his subconscious maternal obsession. "Where then is my grail?" asks Batman, "My treasure horde?"

He soon finds his reward in the form of knowledge. The only true reward that will benefit "The Fool." He returns to where he began, just like every monomythic hero. (After descending into the depths and defeating the monster, remember, the hero returns to the living world to provide some type of rebirth.) But like all heroes, he must defeat the ultimate evil on the final threshold to prove himself once and for all. He finds Dr. Cavendish and Dr. Adams, the two volunteers who stayed behind when the hostages were set free. Because of the understanding and confidence gained through his trials, Batman recognizes that Cavendish is the one who let the inmates loose, the one who caused all the chaos. When asked why, Cavendish directs Batman to Amadeus Arkham's journal, and Morrison transitions us into another flashback where we learn the dark secret of Dr. Arkham.

Arkham, in his delusion, writes about how he finally saw what had driven his mother mad: "I see it. And it is a bat. A bat." Then we discover that he killed his mother to protect her. She did not commit suicide – he sliced her open with a straight razor. Then, wearing his mother's wedding dress, Arkham says, "I shall contain the presences that roam these rooms and narrow stairways. I shall surround them with bars and walls and electrified fences and pray they never break free. I am the dragon's bride, the son of the widow." As Cavendish explains, Batman is responsible for Arkham Asylum because Batman "is the bat." The words Batman found carved into the floor were a binding spell, scratched into the stone by Arkham with his own fingernails. Cavendish says about Amadeus Arkham, "He's read the 'Golden Bough,' he'd studied shamanistic practices and he knew that only ritual, only magic, could contain the bat."

Cavendish, after recently finding Arkham's journals, realized that the bat had escaped, and so he realized that he had to complete the spell himself. The salt around Arkham Asylum was part of Cavendish's binding spell to trap Batman in the asylum forever. During this expository scene, Cavendish

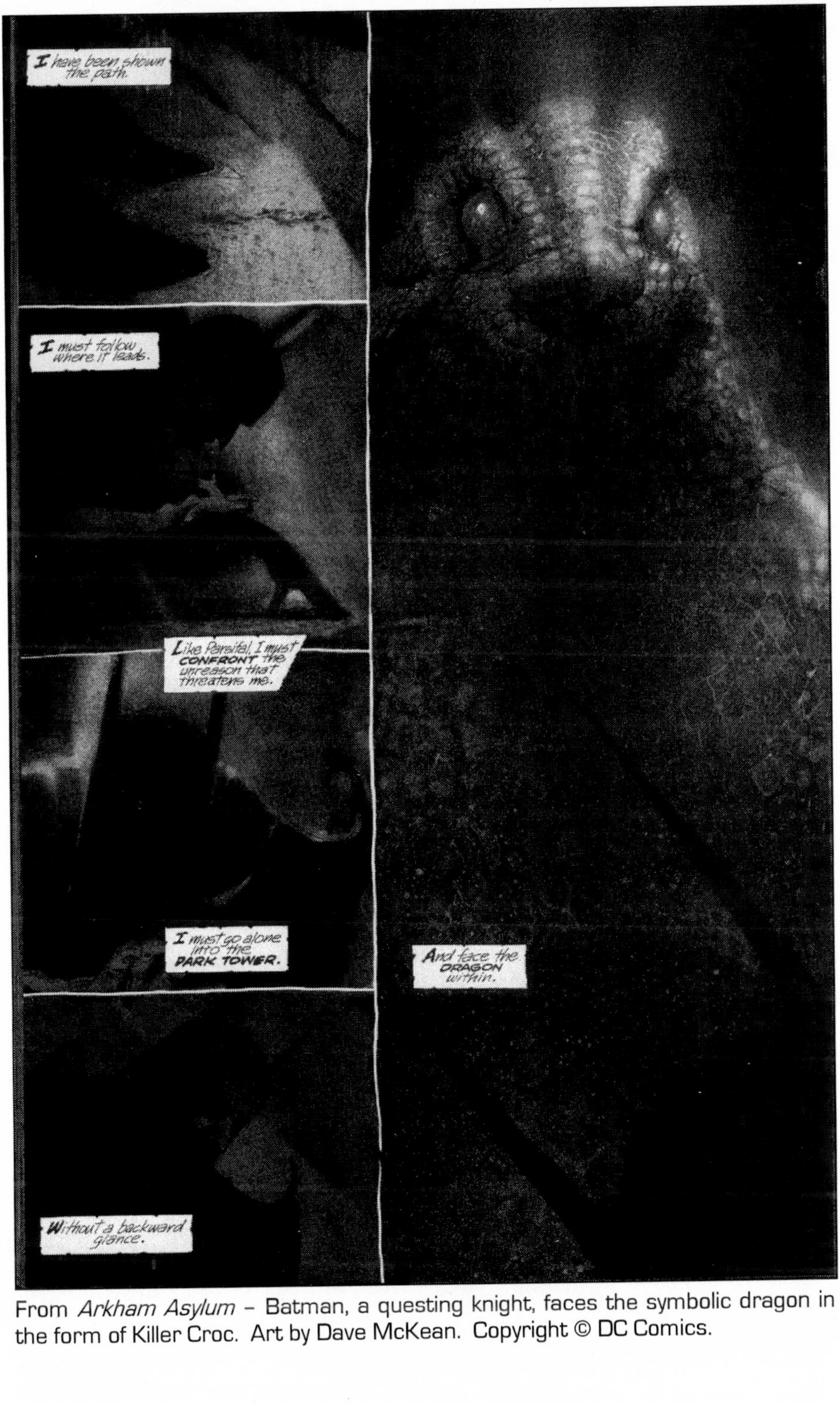


From *Arkham Asylum* – Batman, a questing knight, faces the symbolic dragon in the form of Killer Croc. Art by Dave McKean. Copyright © DC Comics.

is dressed in Arkham's mother's wedding dress, continuing the *transvestite / mother* pattern that Morrison has shown again and again. And because Batman is not fully unified (psychologically) – he's defeated the dragon, but not the final challenge – Cavendish is able to hold Batman down and strangle him. As Morrison explains,

> Batman, at his most ineffectual, is here wrestling the very embodied heart of his own insanity. Under normal circumstances, of course, a superb martial arts master such as Batman would have no trouble defending himself against a skinny, lunatic doctor, but here we are watching the very essence of Batman crumble in the face of his own potential abnormality.

Dr. Adams, an innocent bystander, finally gets involved after the fallen Batman cries out for help.

If this all inside Batman's head, then Cavendish represents Batman's ultimate fear: that he, Bruce Wayne, is responsible for his parent's death. That he is the "bat," the evil force that has caused all the problems in the world. Batman is unable to defeat that deep-rooted fear without calling for help, but if it's all in his head, then the help he calls for, represented by Dr. Adams, is just another aspect of his psyche. Nevertheless, Dr. Adams does come to Batman's aid, slicing Dr. Cavendish's throat with a razor in a reverse image of Arkham's matricide.

Dr. Adams, shaken by the murder she's been compelled to commit, realizes that Batman is different now, stronger, complete. His *Shadow* has been defeated, and his *Self* is whole. She senses that he's going back into the bowels of the asylum. "Who are you?" she asks. "Stronger than them. Stronger than this place. I have to show them," is his only reply. "That's insane," says Adams. "Exactly," replies Batman, "Arkham was right; sometimes it's only the madness that makes us what we are. Or destiny perhaps." At that moment he verifies his new psychological state. If it's madness, or destiny, that makes us what we are, then he cannot be responsible. He cannot be responsible for the villains who inhabit the asylum, and most importantly, he cannot be responsible for his mother's death. His acceptance of the madness has healed him.

With that self-recognition, he grabs an axe and begins to demolish Arkham Asylum from within. He smashes through the electrical lines, he cleaves a door off its hinges, he destroys everything in his path. As Morrison explains in the original script,

> Batman is physically demonstrating his new-found dominance over the spirit of Arkham House... The images here are designed to recall Christ's clearing the temple and even more importantly, the Harrowing of Hell... In the story of Hell's Harrowing, Christ descends into Hell, has a confrontation with the Devil and his minions and then, at the climactic moment, tears the Gates of Hell and sets free the tormented souls within.

Batman, literally at this moment, tells the inmates of the asylum that they are all free.

The Joker, however, says, "We know that already." They have always felt free, he implies, but then he asks if Batman is free. If Batman should be *allowed* to go free. Batman decides to leave the choice to Two-Face, who had just been given his old coin back by Batman. Two-Face flips the coin, a crack of lightning flashes in the background, and Two-Face looks at the result. "He goes free," says Two-Face. The Joker escorts Batman out of the ruined asylum, a moment which Morrison comments upon in the 15th Anniversary edition:

> The Joker's role as a Trickster / Guide through the underworld is no more apparent than here, where he seems happy to let Batman go. The Joker's work is done, he has broken and remade his old enemy. In the reversal reality of the Feast of Fools, it's the arch-villain who does the most good, while the hero is ineffective and lost until the conclusion. This seemed a much richer, more satisfying and more adult way to consider the Batman / Joker dynamic.

As the Joker guides Batman out into the world, the Joker says, "Enjoy yourself out there. In the asylum. Just don't forget – If it ever gets too tough...There's always a place for you here."

Two-Face returns to his house of cards (made from the Tarot deck he'd been using), and he looks down at the coin in his hand. It shows the scarred side, the evil side, revealing that Two-Face let Batman go out of his own free will. He quotes the end of *Alice's Adventures in Wonderland*: "Who cares for you? You're nothing but a pack of cards," before sweeping his arm through the fragile levels of cards, sending them flying across the room, destroying the "house" he'd made, in symbolic parallel with the destruction of the asylum. "The Moon" card, from the Crowley Thoth deck, spins across the panels, growing larger each time, until the story ends. The ritual of initiation is over.

"Batman has faced his own personal Abyss," says Morrison, "integrated his psychological demons and emerged stronger and more sane from the other side of the looking glass. The dream ends here."

It almost ends, but not quite, because Grant Morrison's most ambitious graphic novel ends with a reflection of the opening two pages. "The Moon" card, less stylized at the end, a stretched version of the Thoth design, occupies one page, while a different Lewis Carroll quotation concludes *Arkham Asylum*:

> And is not that a mother's gentle hand that withdraws your curtains,
> And a mother's sweet voice that summons you to rise?
> To rise and forget, in the bright sunlight,
> The ugly dreams that frightened you so when all was dark –
> — *Alice's Adventures in Wonderland*

Batman's nightmare voyage has ended with the promise of a bright future. His healed self will allow him to move past his nightmares of guilt. Morrison concludes Batman's symbolic journey with hope, just as T. S. Eliot ends "The Waste Land" with the holy words, "shantih shantih shantih," which translate as, "the peace which passeth understanding." Batman, with his unified psyche, has overcome the fragmented, postmodern wasteland, and he has achieved, at least temporarily, peace.

*Arkham Asylum* is Morrison at his most symbolic. His dream-like narrative explores the nature of Batman's relationship with both himself and the world. It's dense storytelling that packs thousands of years of allusions into a single super-hero tale. Morrison pushes the artistic boundaries of the genre with this graphic novel, and whether he has succeeded in creating a masterpiece or not, *Arkham Asylum* exists as a distillation of many of his major concerns. Even a casual reader who finds it obscure, pretentious, or impenetrable will have to acknowledge the loftiness of its aim and the beauty of its execution. And if he or she looks closely enough, an attentive reader may see a distinct order beneath the apparent chaos.

# *Animal Man*

Grant Morrison's first American work, *Animal Man*, was launched in the summer of 1988. He'd completed *Zenith* Phases One and Two by that time, and had already begun work on the *Arkham Asylum* graphic novel (though it wouldn't be published for over a year). He had proposed *Animal Man* as a four-issue mini-series, but before publication, he was given the green light to turn it into an ongoing. Morrison claims to have rushed to generate the initial idea for the series on the train to London where he was to meet with the editors from DC Comics. He had the *Arkham Asylum* pitch already prepared, but he wanted to have something else to show them. *Animal-Man*, an obscure, underutilized character from the 1960s, seemed to offer some revisionist possibilities, but once the series expanded from its original four issues, Morrison took the series in a more personal direction.

## Being Alan Moore: The First Four Issues

Regarding the series, Morrison said (in an interview with sequentialtart.com), "I hated the post-*Dark Knight*[50] school of pain-and-guilt comics and I'd lost interest in the claustrophobic 'realism' of the *Watchmen*[51] camp, so by the

---

[50] *The Dark Knight Returns*, by Frank Miller and Klaus Janson, presented a dystopian future in which an elderly Batman had to come out of retirement to fight against the corruption of society. After its success, many comic book heroes, especially Batman, were revamped as darker versions of themselves.

[51] *Watchmen*, by Alan Moore and Dave Gibbons, was a milestone for super-hero comic books in its depiction of a "real world" affected by a small cadre of

time I got hold of *Animal Man* in 1987 I was ready to bring all my favorite four-color John Broomist crap back in a tidal wave of self-referential madness." He wanted to bring "The Flash of Two Worlds" sensibility[52], the delirious Silver Age mentality of John Broome and Garner Fox,[53] back to comics. He didn't do it right away, though. The first four issues of *Animal Man* are clearly inspired by Alan Moore, and although the content is quite different than *Watchmen*, the technique is similar.

*Animal Man* #1 begins with a pretentious narration by a mysterious, shadowy creature: "The smell of people squeezed together like grapes in a press... the sour bouquet of sweat... of all the tiny lives that go unnoticed in the belly of the monster... Why did we come down out of the trees?" This is immediately followed by the first panel on page two showing Buddy Baker, the protagonist of *Animal Man*, climbing in a tree to rescue a cat. The opening narration is ridiculously prolix, almost in a mockery of Alan Moore's style. Morrison clearly believed, or was encouraged to believe, that Americans wanted another *Watchmen* and *Swamp Thing*,[54] and poetic caption boxes and fancy transitions were the way to satisfy the audience. Luckily, Morrison became bored with such hollow imitation rather quickly, and although he continued to use clever scene-to-scene transitions, he abandoned the Moore-like captions and high-seriousness in favor of a metafictional,

---

superhumans. *Watchmen*, along with *The Dark Knight Returns*, spawned many superficial imitations as creators latched on to the idea of presenting "realistic" super-heroes but lacked the style of Alan Moore or Frank Miller.

[52] "The Flash of Two Worlds," published in *The Flash* #123, by DC Comics in 1962, was the first crossover between a Golden Age DC hero from the 1940s and a Silver Age DC hero of the 1960s. This story initiated in the multiple universe (or "multiverse") concept which culminated in *Crisis on Infinite Earths*.

[53] John Broome and Gardner Fox were two of the best writers from DC's Silver Age. Between them, they created many of the most memorable stories from that era of DC Comics. They were best known for their work on *The Justice League, Green Lantern,* and *The Flash.* Fox, in fact, wrote "The Flash of Two Worlds."

[54] Alan Moore's other major American work in the 1980s was his revamped version of *Swamp Thing*, which re-imagined the series as a poetic, Gothic horror comic. Moore's narrative captions could tend toward purple prose, as in the opening of *Swamp Thing* #21: "Plump, warm summer rain that covers the sidewalks with leopard spots. Downtown, elderly ladies carry their houseplants out to set them on fire-escapes, as if they were infirm relatives or boy kings." In context, Moore often uses such language ironically, but when other writers attempt to copy his style, they mimic only the superficial elements. Even Grant Morrison falls into that trap with his early *Animal Man* scripts.

playful, style by issue #5.

Although issues #1-4 are superficially written like an Alan Moore pastiche, they do contain some interesting ideas and some new perspectives on classic heroic archetypes. First of all, the initial issues establish Buddy Baker and his family. Until Morrison's series, Animal Man was an insignificant player in the DC Universe. He had appeared in a few Silver Age back-up stories, had joined the uninspiring Forgotten Heroes for a couple of Bronze Age[55] adventures, and had made a cameo or two in *Crisis on Infinite Earths*. If anything, he was a joke of a character with his bright orange and blue costume (covered with scales), his goggles, and his silly power to duplicate animal abilities. Unlike Beast Boy from the Teen Titans,[56] Animal Man couldn't even change shape. He could simply swim like a fish, or jump like a grasshopper, or, presumably, hibernate like a bear (assuming that any of those animals were near him when he wanted to use their power). Buddy Baker, his alter ego, was a cipher. He was just a guy who put on a costume until Grant Morrison came along.

Even burdened with the unnecessary task of aping Alan Moore, Morrison was able to create some depth of characterization and provide Buddy Baker with a personality, a family, a life. Morrison does this by keeping Baker out of his Animal Man costume for the first 17 pages of issue #1.[57] We don't see him in his super-hero garb until page 18, and, even then, it's an image on a television as Animal Man is mocked by a local TV personality. Both of these ideas (keeping the title character out of costume for so long, and

---

[55] The Bronze Age has gained acceptance as the appropriate term for comic books published in the 1970s and 1980s. (As contrasted with the Golden Age of the 1930s and 1940s or the Silver Age of the 1950s and 1960s.)

[56] Beast Boy, also known as Changeling, has the ability to transform into any animal at will. The only drawback is that everything he turns into is colored green. He is most closely associated with The Teen Titans, a super-group made up of former kid sidekicks and other teenage heroes. They are known as the "Junior Justice League." The point is that Animal Man has traditionally been more pathetic than almost every hero in the DC Universe.

[57] Chas Truog drew almost every issue of Morrison's *Animal Man*. While not as accomplished as an artist at Steve Yeowell or Dave McKean, Truog brings an organic quality to the comic book with his soft lines and cartoony faces. His work emphasizes the humanity of Buddy Baker and his family, and his tendency to draw overly large eyes makes the characters look extremely vulnerable. His compositions are open and accessible, and his storytelling is clear. Truog complemented Morrison well on this series.

ridiculing his heroic persona) were not brand new in 1988, but they were unconventional enough to keep things interesting. Morrison didn't waste those out-of-costume moments in the first issue, either. He establishes the suburban setting of the series, another unconventional choice in a market dominated by urban vigilantes. As he introduces Baker's neighbors like Mr. and Mrs. Weidemeir (a grumpy middle-aged man and his frumpy, middle-aged wife who owned the rescued cat) and Roger (who is clearly older than Baker and offers to act as his "manager" in a nod to Zenith's relationship with Eddie), and Roger's selfish trophy wife, Tricia, we see that *Animal Man* will not be filled with an elegant supporting cast. There will be no Alfred or Jarvis;[58] instead, Animal Man is surrounded by normal, average Americans. Morrison further emphasizes this milieu by not only giving Baker a strong, unglamorous wife in the form of Ellen Baker, but also by giving the Bakers two children, the mullet-sporting Cliff and the innocent, young Maxine. This is yet another unconventional decision by Morrison. Super-heroes don't have children, especially in the DC Universe (or if they do, they spring up years later, fully grown). By placing Buddy Baker in this type of setting, surrounded by such characters, Morrison is able to provide a new perspective on the super-hero genre, and he takes full advantage of that.

The motif of the *strong female* supporting character is as old as the super-hero genre. Lois Lane was a career woman (even if she was a helpless victim more often than not) before such a thing was the norm, and The Flash and The Atom had love interests who were often more confident and aggressive than the men were.[59] In *Animal Man*, Morrison continues and expands upon that tradition. I've already referred to Ellen Baker as "strong" and "unglamorous," because she is depicted as a typical suburban mom. She wears short, permed hair, jeans, and t-shirts. She is the pragmatic one in the relationship. When Buddy says he wants to "go full time into the super-hero business," she curtly undercuts him by saying, "feet off the table!" She

---

[58] Alfred, Batman's butler, and Jarvis, the butler who works in Avengers Mansion, are similar supporting characters. They often provide a practical perspective on events, but they comport themselves with grace and dignity befitting European aristocracy. Nobody in *Animal Man* can be accused of anything like that.

[59] Lois Lane dressed like Rosalind Russell, from *His Girl Friday,* in the *Superman* comics, while Iris West, the fiancée of Barry Allen, the Flash, often mocked Allen's absent-minded nature. Jean Loring, who dated Ray Palmer, the Atom, was an attorney who worked with the crimefighter on several cases.

continues to point out the unrealistic nature of his dreams by saying, "you paid 800 dollars for those Animal Man costumes and they've only been out of the closet a half-dozen times in eight years." The relationship between Buddy Baker and his nuclear family, so clearly established in the early issues, serves both to mark him as a different kind of hero and to provide a greater and more serious sense of jeopardy in future issues. While we know Lois Lane isn't really going to die in Luthor's death trap, we aren't so sure about Ellen, Cliff, and Maxine.

The first storyline also brings the issue of *animal rights* to the foreground. Since Animal Man's powers derive from a close connection with the animal kingdom, it seems natural that Buddy Baker might oppose cruel treatment towards animals. Logically, he might be a vegetarian. Prior to Morrison, nobody wrote the Animal Man character with these concerns in mind. Even Buddy Baker himself seems not to have considered the ethical issues surrounding the treatment of animals because Morrison uses the first four issues to open Buddy's eyes to the cruelty inflicted upon animals and to make him rethink his own connection with nature.

The storyline that raises Baker's awareness of animal rights, the same storyline that's thick with Alan Moore-style techniques, comprises two narrative threads. The main plot features an obscure DC character known as B'wana Beast, a.k.a. The White God of Kilimanjaro, who is even more ridiculous than Animal Man.[60] B'wana Beast is on a quest for vengeance, but Animal Man has been called upon by S.T.A.R. Labs[61] to help discover what sort of creature has somehow fused a group of lab monkeys together into a grotesque monstrosity. (And to undercut Buddy Baker's pretense at being a super-hero, Dr. Myers, of S.T.A.R. Labs, makes a point of saying, "we were hoping for Superman's help. However, apparently this is one of his busy days.") The core of this main narrative is that B'wana Beast wants revenge on S.T.A.R. Labs for its inhumane anthrax tests, which caused the

---

[60] B'wana Beast, with his leopard-print loincloth, looks as silly as he sounds. He first appeared in *Showcase* #66, published by DC Comics in 1967.

[61] S.T.A.R. Labs, which stands for Scientific and Technology Advanced Research Laboratories, first appeared in DC Comics in 1971, and since then it has become the generic scientific organization of the DC Universe. Whenever a writer needs to include a science-related subplot, S.T.A.R. Labs makes an appearance in the story.

suffering, and later, death, of his beloved ape companion, Djuba.[62] Animal Man, although shocked by the revelation of such tests, is forced to stop B'wana Beast from causing further property damage and fatally injuring the humans in his path. It's a good guy vs. bad guy plot structure, but Animal Man is on the defensive most of the time, and the supposed bad guy, B'wana Beast, is justified in his intentions, if not in the harmful consequences of his actions. B'wana Beast is dying because of these experiments, and he's lashing out before he goes.

The subplot running throughout the first four issues provides a parallel to the main events, showing another side to the animal rights issue. In the subplot, which takes place in the woods near the Baker house, a small cat pounces upon a rat. Shortly after, in the very same area, hunters kill a deer. At this point, Morrison seems to be indicating that predators and prey are simply part of the natural cycle of life. Soon, however, Morrison explodes this notion as Ellen Baker, along with daughter Maxine, strolls through the woods and comes across the carcass of that newly slain deer. By lingering on the consequences of such brutality, Morrison creates a sense of unease in the reader. He amplifies this shortly thereafter as the hunters return and see the apparently vulnerable Ellen as their new prey. To intimidate her, one of the hunters grabs the cat that had earlier pounced upon the rat and throws it to the hunting dogs. While Maxine runs for help, Ellen is held at gunpoint and nearly raped before Mr. Weidemeir shows up to defend her. As the tension mounts, one of the hunters turns on his hunting companion and blasts a hole in him. By the end of the sequence, several animals (including one man) are dead, and we discover that the cat was protecting a nest of kittens. Morrison seems to provide a glimmer of hope as Ellen and Maxine rush the kittens back to their house in an effort to reclaim some goodness out of the day's events.

Both the main storyline and the subplot deal with cruelty toward animals, but it's also interesting that Ellen's life was in peril and her own husband, a super-hero, played absolutely no role in saving her. It was the apparently unconcerned neighbor, Mr. Weidemeir, who came to her rescue. While

[62] Djuba, B'wana Beast's best friend, is a gorilla. Morrison clearly wanted to show that he could make the most ridiculous characters in the universe seem sympathetic with the right story.

Animal Man was out defending a corrupt organization (S.T.A.R. Labs)[63] from a threat of their own manufacture, his family was in genuine danger. Morrison doesn't belabor the point, but the scenario is enough to remind us, and Buddy Baker, about the importance of *family* and the cost of playing *the role of hero*.

As dark as the first four issues are, they do end with a sense of hope. Animal Man saves B'wana Beast from certain death by using B'wana Beast's own animal fusion powers to reproduce more white blood cells to destroy the anthrax virus. The cure is the type of pseudo-scientific explanation that Silver Age comic books became famous for, and Morrison uses it to great effect here. He makes it believable within the context of the story. As the first narrative comes to a close, Buddy Baker can't simply go back to his old, naive mindset. He says, "I can't stop thinking about what B'wana Beast said... About the mess we're leaving for our kids... There must be some hope. Just some." Immediately after that reflection, Baker, and the reader, discovers that one of the rescued kittens survives.

Morrison doesn't wrap it all up with rainbows and flowers, though. In an epilogue at the end of issue #4, the rejuvenated B'wana Beast sneaks into S.T.A.R. Labs and, using his animal fusion powers, combines the head scientist, Dr. Myers, with the dead body of the ape, Djuba. The new creature he leaves behind is a distorted ape-man, who is unable to speak as he is carted off toward some new, inhumane experiments the next morning. The reader is left with the feeling that justice has been served, even if it is justice of the cruelest kind.

## The Gospel of the Coyote: Moore no More

Once Morrison got the first story arc out of his system, he was able to take the *Animal Man* series in a different, more creative direction, beginning with issue #5, "The Coyote Gospel." This story, a bizarre homage to the Road

[63] Up until this time, S.T.A.R. Labs was generally portrayed as a benevolent scientific organization. It was a harmless conglomerate in most stories, used whenever a writer needed to explain where some stolen high-tech equipment originated. Morrison, however, portrays it negatively, in keeping with an anti-corporate mentality that is consistent throughout his work. His writing reveals an abhorrence of faceless order and conformity.

Runner cartoons of Chuck Jones,[64] expands *Animal Man* to a whole new level. The serious-minded captions and internal monologues of issues #1-4 are replaced by an omniscient narrator, and although the narration is presented in a serious, high-minded tone, the absurdity of the visuals provides an ironic counterpoint. I think that's the real essence of the difference between Alan Moore and Grant Morrison. Moore is an ironist, while Morrison is an absurdist. When Morrison was pretending to be Alan Moore for the first four issues of the series, he seemed to feel constrained. He tried to focus the irony too tightly, and his targets were perhaps too narrow for his liking. The first four issues present some fresh ideas, but the story does feel a bit constipated. Starting with issue #5, he opens himself up to the cosmic irony of existence and the absurdity of life in all its forms, and he's able to explore his favorite themes with complete freedom. "The Coyote Gospel" is when Grant Morrison really arrived in American comic books.

Unlike issues #1-4, there are no heroes or villains in "The Coyote Gospel." Animal Man doesn't fight any criminals or save any lives. Nobody has any evil plans for mass destruction. The only part of the story resembling a traditional comic book narrative is the revenge subplot. The revenge is misguided, of course, but it does provide the small bit of action that occurs in the story. Basically, "The Coyote Gospel" is the tale of a cartoon character, modeled on Wile E. Coyote, who has come to life in "the real world." Like the character from the Looney Tunes episodes, this Coyote can regenerate himself from even the most terrible injury. As he falls from a great height, exactly mimicking the typical Wile E. Coyote plummet that we've seen a hundred times, the narrator describes the process in gruesome detail: "An outcrop breaks its spine. A second impact crushes its skull. Unhinges its jaw. Snaps both legs." Yet the cartoonish image as he falls from panel to panel even includes the puff of smoke as he hits the ground. What Morrison does in "The Coyote Gospel" is to add pathos to the pathetic Coyote character. For the first time, we feel his pain. If Morrison stopped there, it would still be an interesting story, and it would certainly tie in with the animal rights theme that was so vigorously considered in the first storyline. After all, Buddy Baker does decide to turn the family vegetarian at

---

[64] Chuck Jones, the famed director of many Warner Bothers shorts, created the Road Runner and Wile E. Coyote in 1948.

the beginning of issue #5, much to the dismay of Ellen and the kids, showing that he has taken the events of the previous issues to heart.

By the time the reader gets two-thirds of the way through "The Coyote Gospel," everything seems to indicate that this issue will be an interesting, albeit odd, variation on the themes of issues 1-4. The reader is led to assume that we'll all learn an important lesson about the way animals are improperly treated in our society, and we'll be shown how children's cartoons contribute to that treatment by using animal cruelty as forms of entertainment. That's where Morrison seems to be heading. Until page 17.

On page 17, Animal Man swoops down into the story and the Coyote hands him a rolled up piece of parchment that he's had tied around his neck. It turns out to be the "The Gospel According to Crafty," and it tells the tale of the brutal world from which Crafty, the Coyote, originated. In the tale, Crafty confronts the "God" of his universe, who we see only parts of: gingham pants, short-sleeved shirt, wrist watch, and paintbrush. Crafty challenges "God" to end the suffering and violence in his world and offers his own life in trade for the peace he desired. The bargain causes Crafty to be reborn in Buddy Baker's world as a flesh-and-blood creature, and the Gospel ends by saying, "While he lived, there still remained hope that one day, he might return. And on that day overthrow the tyrant God. And build a better world." As tragic as that story is, Morrison throws in yet another twist: Buddy Baker cannot read "The Gospel According to Crafty." We can, but he can't. To him, it appears to be just scribbles on paper. His profound message is lost. Crafty's words remain unread when he is suddenly killed by a silver bullet, a bullet made by a deranged trucker intent on getting revenge against what he believes to be the devil. The bullet, the trucker reveals, was made by melting down his most precious possession, a silver cross. From the trucker's perspective, he was slaying the devil.

Clearly, the story, by the end, has veered into a whole new direction.

Then, Morrison gives us the final page.

The last page of the story starts with a close-up on the crying Crafty as Animal Man leans over his dying body. The camera pulls back until we see Crafty lying in a crucifixion pose, the pool of blood beneath him a stark white. The penultimate panel shows a giant hand with a paintbrush coming in from the sky, painting Crafty's blood red. As the camera pulls back farther, so does the giant hand, leaving a drop of red paint on the crossroads.

From *Animal Man* #5 – The hand of God paints the blood red as Animal Man helplessly watches Crafty die. Art by Chas Truog and Doug Hazlewood. Copyright © DC Comics.

Animal Man, with his head down in sorrow, never acknowledges the presence of the divine force. That paintbrush is the very same one that Crafty's God was carrying, according to his Gospel.

It's a bold final few panels. It suggests that the "real world" of *Animal Man* is itself a construct of a manipulative God, with Crafty's sacrifice as the salvation of the fictional world. It's a metafictional comment that changes the whole meaning of the series. It's not unheard of in the medium, though. It's an allusion to "Duck Amuck," the Daffy Duck short directed by Chuck Jones in which a playful animator puts Daffy through one visual gag after another based purely on capricious whim, and it's also an allusion to "The Flash of Two Worlds" story by Gardner Fox in which the writer of the story, Gardner Fox himself, is mentioned as the conduit between what would eventually be known in the DC Universe as Earth 1 and Earth 2. Nevertheless, it is a profound ending, and although the implications of the "hand of God" are not directly felt in the issues that immediately follow, "The Coyote Gospel" is the turning point in the series.

## Crossing Over and the Passive Hero

If "The Coyote Gospel" in issue #5 was the turning point of *Animal Man* as a series, then it naturally follows that issues #6 and #7 would continue with that new, metaphysical direction. That is, of course, supposing that Grant Morrison had total control over the content of the storyline. Since he was at the whim of DC Comics, however, he had to succumb, perhaps willingly, to an editorial mandate: a crossover with a massive DC Universe crossover – *Invasion.*

In the company-wide crossover event, centralized on a three-issue *Invasion* mini-series, the alien race known as the Dominators join forces with various races from throughout the universe (like Hawkman's Thanagarians and Chameleon Boy's Durlans)[65] to invade Earth and eliminate the superhuman population of the planet. As you can imagine, the plan is

[65] Although Thanagarians, humanoids from Hawkman's home planet of Thanagar, had been appearing in the contemporary DC Universe since the Silver Age, many of the alien races in *Invasion* had not appeared in any stories set in the present day. The Dominators and the Durlans, for example, were seen in the 30th century as part of *The Legion of Super-Heroes* comic book series but were never used in 20th century stories. Until *Invasion.*

ultimately unsuccessful, and Earth's heroes prove victorious.

The primary stage of the *Invasion* crossover, planned to coincide with the first issue of the three-issue mini-series, was called "Invasion: First Strike." Every major DC super-hero title participated in this crossover, and *Animal Man* was no exception. In issue #6, a Thanagarian invader by the name of Rokara Soh plans to detonate a bomb which would destroy the planet, and it's up to Animal Man to stop him.

An average writer would churn out a mediocre story under such imposed conditions, but Grant Morrison takes the opportunity to put his unique slant on the event. The story begins with Rokara Soh narrating: "The geometry of nature, like the geometry of life itself, contains infinities." If this sounds at all familiar to you, it might be because it's very similar to Morrison's use of pattern and motif in *Zenith* and *Arkham Asylum*. When I analyzed *Zenith* and *Arkham Asylum* in my previous chapters, I established that the overarching storyline and each smaller story followed, essentially, a fractal pattern. Rokara Soh alludes to such fractal patterns on the very first page of *Animal Man* #6, and Soh's entire approach to life (and art) is based on the recurrence of geometric patterns, as he later explains. By using the fractal motif in *Animal Man*, *Arkham Asylum*, and *Zenith*, Morrison is able to reinforce the very ideas of fractal geometry: no matter where you look in his work – no matter how closely you look, no matter how broadly you look – similar, but complex, patterns emerge.

In issue #6, Soh is referred to not as an assassin or saboteur, but as an "art martyr." Soh states, "In the end, only one thing matters. The performance." He is using his art (via what's called a life fractal / memory bomb) to destroy himself and an entire planet. It's a process he describes as a "seismic poem" which, he says to Animal Man, has a "kind of beauty [that] is beyond the ability of your species to comprehend." This character combined with this type of destructive potential is interesting for two reasons: first, it's unusual, and second, it's revelatory. It's unusual because Morrison actually creates a complex and unique character to act as a villain for this one-shot crossover (Rokara Soh practically reveals more depth of character in this one appearance than Zenith or Peter St. John revealed in the entire run of the *Zenith* series). It's revelatory because it expresses something about Morrison's perspective on *art*. If art can destroy a world, then art must be a powerful weapon. Morrison plays with this concept – the notion that art can create, transform, and destroy – again and again throughout his career, culminating in later work like *The Invisibles*, which not only transformed him physically[66] as he composed it but was meant to act as a sort of art-virus, infecting the world with ideas. Rokara Soh is Grant Morrison, if Grant Morrison were raised in outer space under an oppressive Thanagarian regime.

Perhaps that's why Morrison couldn't bring himself to have Animal Man defeat Soh. In the climax of the story, Buddy Baker helplessly watches as the bomb reaches detonation, saying a pathetic, "I'm sorry," as he waits for the end of the world. Only the *deus ex machina* intervention of Katar Hol (Hawkman) in the final two panels of the story prevents Soh from achieving artistic devastation. "All you had to do was switch it off," says Hol, thereby undermining any sense of the severity of the crisis. It's a typical Morrisonian anti-climax. Just as we saw repeatedly in *Zenith*, the title character is ineffectual against the opposition and all the sturm and drang of battle ultimately amounts to nothing.

Interestingly, *Animal Man* #6 is also the second issue in a row where Buddy Baker is a passive witness to someone else's story. In the previous issue, it was Crafty's gospel, and this time it's the tale of the rise and fall of Rokara Soh. It's a rarity for a title character to take the back seat to a newly introduced minor character for even one story, never mind two in a row.[67] Yet, Morrison pulls it off, and he doesn't stop there, because in the very next issue, *Animal Man* #7, Buddy Baker passively listens to the story of yet another newly introduced minor character.

First, a bit of context: the second stage of the *Invasion* crossover, called "Invasion: Aftermath," featured less participation than the first month. Titles that did feature this part of the crossover showed heroes dealing with various stages of devastation and reconstruction. Once again, *Animal Man*

---

[66] Morrison nearly died from a sudden illness while writing *The Invisibles* in the 1990s. He said that the illness, and the act writing the comic book, transformed his life.

[67] Although, in the 1940s, Will Eisner used the technique occasionally in *The Spirit* and Gardner Fox wrote a few *All-Star Comics* stories in which a minor character takes center stage, it was quite uncommon to see any mainstream comic books' super-heroes (even one as insignificant as Animal Man) sitting on the sidelines in their own titles in the 1980s. After all, potential merchandising rights and brand recognition were involved.

played a role, as issue #7's subplot included Buddy Baker destroying some robots which had been set loose during the catastrophic alien attacks. Unlike other titles that crossed over that month, *Animal Man* issue #7 didn't feature the "Invasion: Aftermath" logo on the cover, indicating either that Morrison was not required to tie his story into the company-wide stunt that month or that the editor didn't feel that the issue was significant enough to label as part of the larger storyline. It doesn't really tie in to *Invasion*, but it does use the resulting chaos of that event as a backdrop for a small, character-driven story: "The Death of the Red Mask."

In this issue, Morrison's Alan Moore-style imitations linger, for one last time. Issue #7 gets it out of his system, though, because after this, we don't see the Alan Moore impression again. Even in issue #7, the mimicry is not as pronounced as it was during issues #1-4. The narration in this issue is not nearly as ponderous or faux-poetic. Morrison does, however, use some *Watchmen*-like transitions[68] from panel to panel and page to page, but he uses it appropriately and effectively (i.e. the repetition of the color red, in abstract patterns which turn out to be splattered blood, and in the way the panels show camera-like movement, moving from aerial long shots to closeups, step by step).

"The Death of the Red Mask," like the two issues immediately preceding it, tells the tale of a misunderstood, suicidal, minor character. In this case, it's an insignificant, aged "super-villain," who is neither super nor particularly villainous. Animal Man encounters the Red Mask as he is poised to jump off the top of a building, presumably to his death. Although, as the Red Mask points out to Buddy Baker, "What makes you think I can't fly?" Before Baker can really respond, the Red Mask admits, "Nah. You're right, I can't." The moment adds a bit of humor to the scene and undercuts Baker's role as self-appointed savior. The Red Mask, a bloated, balding old man, tells his tale of woe: he tells about the meteorite that gave him, "the worst super-power in history... Death Touch." Such a power made him choose the

[68] Besides the "realistic" approach to super-heroes, *Watchmen* also features more sophisticated visual transitions than most comic book stories. Alan Moore often employed match cuts to visually connect two separate scenes, and he also asked Dave Gibbons to repeat similar compositions from different distances, to provide the illusion of a camera moving toward or away from an image. Morrison copies some of those techniques here.

side of evil by necessity: a hero could hardly have a power like that.[69] He describes how, as a young man, he teamed up with another villain, "The Veil," and they "had a pretty good fight with Captain Triumph[70] once, but that was about it." The Red Mask goes on to explain how the Veil "ended up crazy... it got so bad he dug out his own eyes with a spoon." He admits, "All I ever wanted to do was fly. That would have been enough. I could have joined the Justice Society[71] and made something of my life." Instead, he was burdened with the power to kill, and he has accomplished nothing in all his years. Now, he's dying, and he tells Animal Man that he wants to "go out with some fireworks," hence he released some old robots onto the streets and is planning to leap to his death.

Unlike issues #5 and #6, this issue doesn't contain any profound metafictional subtext or overt link to the cosmic ideas that dominate other works by Morrison. It's a simple story about one character that just didn't amount to much in the grand scheme of things, and while that may not be a mind-blowing idea, *insignificance* is a recurring theme in much of Morrison's work. It's also another instance of Animal Man being an *ineffectual hero*, because after Buddy Baker convinces the Red Mask that he could at least stay alive and tell his story to the world, Baker flies off to dismantle the last of the Red Mask's robots before they cause any more damage. The Red Mask waits patiently for about two seconds before saying to himself, "ah, screw this!" He jumps off the rooftop and is given a splash page where he's surrounded by white as he shouts, "I can fly!" The next page reveals his shattered body on the ground below.[72] Animal Man never even finds out about the suicide, because by the time he knocks out the final

---

[69] Morrison seems to demonstrate how ill-conceived our notions of heroes and villains really are. While we tend to think that internal factors (like altruism, decency, compassion, etc.) lead characters toward the path of goodness, Morrison points out how much of it is all random. Would Superman choose to be a hero if his only power was a "Death Touch"?

[70] Captain Triumph is a Golden Age hero originally published by Quality Comics in the 1940s. DC Comics now owns the rights to him along with most other Quality characters. The Red Mask and the Veil, however, are pure Morrison creations.

[71] The Justice Society, the first super-hero team, initially appeared in *All-Star Comics* #3 (1940), written by none other than Gardner Fox.

[72] Not that the reader expected him to be able to fly, nor was the reader fooled into believing that this momentary jump into the white sky was true flight. Morrison established the character as doomed from the start.

robot, a black light freezes him in mid air and the caption tells us to read *Invasion* #2 (which explains that a "gene bomb" has been detonated by the invaders in an attempt to remove all superhuman powers from the Earth – the effect is reversed in *Invasion* #3, but Buddy Baker's powers don't recover properly for several more issues).

Ultimately, by the time issue #7 has ended, we are left with two of the strangest installments of a company-wide crossover event ever. In both issues the title character accomplished nothing and played a passive role while two new villains (who were never seen or referenced before and haven't been seen or referenced since, as far as I know) told their life stories. By using that strategy, Morrison avoids the typical crossover malaise, and he turns what could have been two throw-away issues into two thematically resonant stories.

## Revising Continuity: At Play in the Layers

While issues #5-7 largely focused on Buddy Baker's "adventures" away from home, issue #8 brings the suburban, domestic setting back to the forefront. In "Mirror Moves," Morrison revives a familiar supervillian name, Mirror Master.[73] This new Mirror Master is not the original. He's more lethal (and more Scottish) than his predecessor, and *Animal Man* #8 deals with this new threat invading the Baker home. The character is a tribute to Morrison's favorite Silver Age comic books, and the issue is "dedicated to John Broome, Gardner Fox, Carmine Infantino, and the late, great Barry Allen."[74] The main storyline contains nothing fancy or metafictional, as Buddy Baker tries, and fails, to defeat Mirror Master (once again, Animal Man is a completely ineffectual hero). It's Ellen Baker who, ultimately, sends the villain on his way with a bold statement: "You're an asshole," she says, before giving him a kick to the crotch.

Buddy Baker recovers by the end of this sequence to regain a shred of his

[73] The original Mirror Master, a creation of John Broome and artist Carmine Infantino, first appeared in *The Flash* #105, published in 1959. He died during the *Crisis on Infinite Earths*.

[74] Barry Allen, the Silver Age Flash who died in *Crisis on Infinite Earths*, is here referred to as if he were a real person, his name placed, as it is, along with the flesh-and-blood creators of his comic book universe. Morrison continually blurs the boundaries between reality and fiction.

dignity by punching Mirror Master hard enough to launch him out of the house, but it was Ellen who stood up to the threat and protected her family. Morrison just doesn't seem that interested in traditional super-heroics. Here we are, eight issues into the series, and Animal Man's heroic actions have basically amounted to nothing. He has good intentions, but he has accomplished little (although he did rescue that cat in the tree in issue #1).

The Mirror Master storyline is clearly intended to (a) remind us that *Animal Man* is about the Baker family, and (b) set up future story lines. Mirror Master himself reveals his motivation to Buddy Baker: "The people I work for want to teach you a wee lesson. They want you to know they can get to you. Disny matter what you're doing or where you are. Your family as well – distance no object."[75] We don't learn exactly who the mysterious employers are, but we see a shadowy triumvirate talking with Mirror Master in the first of three epilogues – a shadowy triumvirate with a U.S. government seal visible above their heads.

There's another shadowy character who makes an appearance in issue #8 as well. It's someone (or something) that looks like Animal Man himself, but he's hiding in the bushes outside the house, and he whispers Ellen's name. We see more and more of this mysterious character as the series unfolds, but this issue features his ominous first appearance. Also making his first appearance in the series, in the second epilogue of issue 8, is an unnamed American Indian character (called J. Highwater in the following issue) who, alone atop a mesa, considers is own *metaphysical* (and meta*fictional*) dilemma: "Is it only some existential terror that makes me feel as though I have been newly brought into the world with a full set of memories and a purpose already prepared for me?" That question is followed by the third, and final, epilogue, which shows a personal computer in what appears to be an apartment or living room. The computer screen features the following text: "'I cannot believe that God plays dice with the cosmos.' —Albert Einstein." The cursor moves, and beneath that quote, a response emerges: "He doesn't. I do." The character responsible for that reply will not reveal himself until almost the end of the series, but even without knowing his identity, it's clear that Morrison is dealing with both the

[75] Morrison indicates Mirror Master's Scottish dialect in his speech balloons. It's not a technique Morrison uses very often, but it works here to differentiate this new Mirror Master from the old one.

*chaos / order* conflict and the *nature of reality*, two of the primary themes of the *Zenith* series as well. He's alluded to such themes before in this series, most prominently in "The Coyote Gospel," but from issue #8 onward, it becomes increasingly central to the narrative of *Animal Man*.

Issue #9 is structured similarly to issue #8 and focuses on many of the same themes. Once again, the metafictional subtext and shadowy mystery character make brief cameos, but the main plot deals with the Baker family and the ineffectiveness of Animal Man himself. This time, it's not a threat to the house, it's a smaller-scale threat: a bully who causes young Cliff some trouble. This time, it's J'onn J'onzz, the Martian Manhunter[76] (visiting the Bakers to welcome Buddy into Justice League Europe),[77] who saves the day. The bully has stolen Cliff's bicycle, and J'onzz helps Cliff get it back (and terrify the bully for life) by transforming into a monstrous beast. Cliff emphasizes his father's uselessness as a hero at the end of the issue when he angrily says: "Why don't you get yourself some real powers, Dad?" Buddy Baker, of course, has no reply.

J. Hightower, the unnamed existential explorer of the previous issue, spends a few panels of issue 9 returning to his home (a home he does not remember) where he finds a copy of Lewis Carroll's *Through the Looking Glass* on the floor. As he flips through the book, he finds some words underlined: "You're only one of the things in his dream." He unfolds a piece of paper which says: "ASK THE PSYCHO PIRATE." Hightower and Buddy Baker will inevitably cross paths in the future, but for now, Hightower is following his own mysterious trail of clues.

While issues #5-9 were all self-contained, single-issue stories (with subplots or epilogues that foreshadowed events yet to come), the next three issues of *Animal Man*, #10-12, contain a much longer storyline. Perhaps because Morrison has 72 pages to tell the story, or perhaps because he's free from editorial mandates by this point, these three issues feel much more open

---

[76] The Martian Manhunter, basically a Martian version of Superman, but with shape-shifting powers and invisiblility, is widely regarded as the first super-hero of the Silver Age. He made his first appearance in 1955. He often plays the role of the calm, wise mentor whenever he appears.

[77] At this time in the DC Universe, the Justice League had gone international, and Justice League Europe was the first attempt at expanding the "franchise." The *Justice League Europe* series was mostly played for laughs, and Animal Man's adventures in that title had no bearing on the Morrison-scripted *Animal Man* series.

than the previous nine. They feel somehow less constrained, less dense; they move quickly, yet they contain plenty of ideas.

Throughout issues #10-12 a similar page reappears again and again. It's labeled, when it first appears at the beginning of issue 10, as "Ten Years Ago," and the panels depict part of the origin of Animal Man.[78] We see, for example, the exploding space capsule, the giant orange alien monster, Buddy and Ellen in their younger days (except they're wearing fashions from the late 1950's), and Buddy's friend Roger telling of how he spotted a space ship in the woods. That same sequence of panels appears several times over the three issues, always with slight variations. For example, it reappears on page 13 of issue #10, only this time it's partially torn up because it's actually the back side of a piece of paper held by J. Hightower. It again reappears on page 2 of issue #11 looking the same as it did at the beginning of issue #10, except the words are nonsensical this time around. Then, finally, it reappears in issue #12, on page 21, showing the same sequence of events but with more contemporary clothing on the characters and the dialogue has been shortened and clarified. Buddy Baker's origin has been revised, updated.

There's nothing unusual about updating a character's origin story. It's a typical trope of American comic books – every generation a character's origin is retold and altered to make it fresh and current. Except Grant Morrison doesn't just revise Animal Man's origin, he actually shows the process of revision within the context of the story. In fact, the revision is the point of the story, and Buddy Baker is an active participant of his own remaking. This is metafiction of the purest level, except Buddy Baker isn't yet aware of his own qualities as a fictional character. To him, it's a metaphysical story – he believes in the reality of his own fictional universe, but there's at least one character who can see the larger picture, the character known as the Psycho Pirate, who J. Hightower visits at Arkham Asylum.

What seems to be insane babble to the characters within the comic book makes sense to the reader. The Psycho Pirate refers to the tag line of *Crisis on Infinite Earths* – "Worlds will live. Worlds will die." – and he references the various alternate realities affected by the Crisis, like Earth S (which featured the Fawcett characters like Captain Marvel and his family) and

[78] In *Secret Origins* #39, published by DC Comics in 1989 (the same year in which *Animal Man* #10 was published), Grant Morrison contributed a story entitled "The Myth of Creation," which detailed Animal Man's "new" origin.

From *Animal Man* #10 – The Psycho-Pirate's awareness of pre-Crisis continuity has driven him mad. Art by Chas Truog and Mark McKenna. Copyright © DC Comics.

Earth X (where the Nazis won WWII). He asks if "The Wolfman" (Marv Wolfman, writer of *Crisis on Infinite Earths*) gave his name, and reveals his fear of being removed "from the continuity." Within the context of the DC Universe, characters were left with no memory of the alternate realities or of the specific events of the Crisis. Nobody else knows what Psycho Pirate is referring to, except the reader. It's more complicated than that though, because the Psycho Pirate is clearly aware of the metatextual level of his own existence, since he knows about "The Wolfman" and he knows about the concept of continuity. He is aware that he is part of a comic book universe, and that has driven him mad.

It all stems back to Morrison's fascination with the Silver Age *Flash* stories. As I explained in my analysis of "The Coyote Gospel," Gardner Fox, the comic book writer, played a role in "The Flash of Two Worlds" storyline. Yet, at the end of that storyline, the Golden Age Flash didn't think of himself as a fictional character, he just thought of Gardner Fox as the chronicler of his true adventures. Here, Morrison updates that notion by changing the cause and effect relationship between writer and subject. The characters are manipulated by the writers in his comic book universe, which, of course, is the way it really is. The consequences of this are that his stories have multiple layers of reality. There's the *foundation layer*, where the comic book characters interact with each other on their own level. Animal Man fights B'wana Beast, for example. Then there's the *secondary layer* where the "hand of God" comes from in "The Coyote Gospel" to paint the blood of Crafty into the panel. Then there's the *tertiary layer* where Grant Morrison is writing the script to the comic book. The reader normally pretends that the foundation layer is the only true layer, hence the endless debates over who's stronger – the Hulk or the Thing – or the anger that some fans experience when a favorite character is changed or killed off.[79] By pointing out the existence of the other layers of reality within and around a comic book story, Morrison subverts the normal expectations and frame of reference of the audience. In other words, the question of who's stronger becomes moot,

---

[79] The debates over which character is the strongest, or the complaints when a character has been altered in some significant way, have always occurred in comic book circles. With the advent of the internet, the debates and complaints have exploded, though. Many a message board is filled with conversations that treat the *foundation layer* as reality.

because the characters have no actual strength except what the writer creates, and the characters have no reality or life other than on the page. While this seems obvious, the suspension-of-belief contract between the writer and the reader implies that both will pretend that the fiction is really happening. Morrison, alternatively, not only points out that the characters are puppets, but he shows you the strings.

The Psycho Pirate scene is the single most powerful and profound moment in the story, but it's actually only a subplot. The main plot deals with Animal Man and the ex-Justice Leaguer, Vixen,[80] as they face unseen attackers who are finally revealed to be the very aliens that originally gave Buddy Baker his powers. By the end of issue #10, the aliens literally unmake Buddy Baker – he turns to nothingness. He's reborn in issue #11, remade with a slightly altered costume (the edges a bit more angular, the goggles sharper). "I feel terrific," he says, when he bursts forth into the world, fully formed. The remaking has caused inconsistencies in the comic book universe, though. That's when the words on the origin page begin to become incoherent, and on page 18 of issue #11, Ellen is puzzled because she doesn't remember having any children (the pre-*Crisis*, pre-Morrison Animal Man had no kids and she seems to have those older memories instead of the memories since issue 1). Issue #11 ends with the capture of Animal Man and Vixen by a crazed, Middle-Eastern, white ape character called Hamed Ali and his lethal assistant, Tabu.[81]

Hamed Ali and Tabu are basically insignificant characters in the larger scheme of things. They provide a superficial conflict for Animal and Vixen to overcome. After all, they exist only on the foundation layer, and the true threat to Buddy Baker's existence is on a much higher level. Baker actually helps move his awareness to the secondary layer (the layer of the cartoonist God and the layer manipulated by the aliens who granted him his power,

---

[80] Vixen first appeared in a 1981 issue of *Action Comics*, and although she does have powers that are very similar to Animal Man's – like him, she can mimic the power of any animal – Morrison may have included her for other reasons. She has been revised as well. Vixen was intended to star in her own comic book in the late 1970s, but her title was canceled before it was ever released. When she finally appeared a few years later, she looked a bit different and her name had been changed from "Marilyn" to the shorter "Mari."

[81] Hamed Ali originally appeared in the first B'wana Beast story from 1967, but Tabu is a Morrison creation.

apparently) when he escapes Hamed Ali and leaps into a pit which spews a kind of blank energy. In the bowels of the pit, Animal Man finds strange orbs that show various permutations of comic book reality, including the Silver Age version of himself. He confronts the alien manipulators, which leads to his participation in fixing his own continuity.

Buddy Baker aids the aliens and successfully "heal[s] the continuum." He therefore helps to manipulate the foundation layer. His awareness of the other layers, however, is still severely limited. He, unlike the Psycho Pirate, does not yet see the absurdity of his own situation, even when the aliens deconstruct Hamed Ali, making Ali regress backwards from comic book character, to pencil drawing, to rough shapes, to nothingness. Baker still doesn't get it.

After the mind-altering events of issues #10-12, Morrison gives us what feels like a fill-in issue with #13. It's still Morrison, but it feels like a step backwards in the overall storyline. He might be giving the audience a chance to catch it's breath, but issue #13 feels more in tune with what he was doing in the first four issues and less like what he'd been pulling off in the last few. It's actually a direct sequel to the B'wana Beast story, so maybe that's why it feels more closely linked to those early issues. Issue #13 demonstrates no awareness on Buddy Baker's part of the events he's just been through, and it has no J. Hightower subplot investigation or mysterious, shadowy figures, or anything that would link it to the more recent issues. It looks and feels like a story that could have taken place as early as issue #6 or 7. It's not a bad story, but it feels like a regression.

The story takes place in South Africa and it's basically a political story about civil rights abuses and the injustice inflicted by the white oppressors. It's about B'wana Beast finding a replacement for himself, through a spiritual method, much like, as he says, "the Dalai Lama in Tibet." Ultimately, a black activist, Dominic Mndawe, is given the mantle, but he has some new ideas about the role. That "white imperialist title [B'wana Beast] has got to go," he says. The former B'wana Beast, Mike Maxwell, is offended at that suggestion, and says that the name is about mythology, not politics. Mndawe's reply is, "today's politics is tomorrow's mythology."

The villain of the piece, a white police officer, had taunted Mndawe about the possibility of freedom and equality for the black people of South Africa, comparing their dream to the story of the unicorn, saying that both are just fantasy. In the climax of the story, Mndawe uses his animal transformation powers to create a unicorn which gores his former oppressor, and in the aftermath, Mndawe has an exchange with Buddy Baker and Mike Maxwell in which Mndawe says his name is now "Freedom Beast."

The story ends with Animal Man dropping off a roll of film to Perry White in Metropolis – photographs which Dominic Mndawe had taken to show the world of the cruelty inflicted upon his people.

Overall, issue #13 is a surprisingly straightforward "Apartheid-is-evil" story with nothing else to recommend it. It was certainly an attempt by Morrison to tackle a contemporary social problem, and to expand Animal Man's awareness of civil rights abuses, but it does nothing to further the multi-layered scheme of reality Morrison had been building over previous issues. If issues #1-4 are his Alan Moore impression, and issue #5 is his Chuck Jones riff, and issues #8 and #10-12 are his John Broome / Garner Fox imitation, maybe issue #13 is his take on Denny O'Neil.[82] It certainly feels *Green Lantern / Green Arrow*-esque in its didactic approach to a social issue.

## Things Fall Apart

By the time Grant Morrison passed the halfway point in his *Animal Man* series, he had shaken free from his comic book influences and began to run with all the ideas he had broadcast in issues #1-13. In essence, the next six issues focus on the four major aspects of Buddy Baker's life: (1) *the family*, (2) *animal rights*, (3) *the role of the hero*, and (4) *the nature of reality*. These four themes have permeated the previous storylines, and I've explored them all to some extent, but by this point in the series, Morrison allows Buddy Baker (and the reader) to come to a deeper understanding of each one of these pivotal ideas, culminating in one of the most surprising issues of any comic book ever.

*Animal Man* #14, "Spooks," shifts the focus away from Buddy Baker and reminds us about the importance of the entire Baker clan. While Buddy is en route home from his epic adventures in Africa, his family is confronted by a

[82] Denny O'Neil, with his *Green Lantern / Green Arrow* series in the early 1970s, in collaboration with artist Neal Adams, added a level of social realism that had never been seen in comics. In each issue, as Green Lantern (the conservative) and Green Arrow (the liberal) traveled to a new destination, they encountered a new social problem like drugs, or poverty, or racism.

mysterious apparition in an Animal Man costume. It's the same shadowy figure that's been appearing around the Baker house for the past several issues, but in "Spooks," the ghost actually interacts with members of the family. Issue #14 is also notable for the introduction of two pivotal characters: Grant Morrison and Lennox. Grant Morrison, the writer himself, becomes a character (albeit unnamed) in "Spooks," as he walks through the rain and ponders the mysteries of the universe and the act of creation. If Morrison is the God of the comic book universe which he inhabits, the character of Lennox is a demon, if not the Devil himself. Lennox is pure evil. He is an assassin without mercy, and in his introductory sequence, he is shown murdering a mother and daughter in their own home. It's clear that this character will soon pose a lethal threat to the Baker family.

Thematically, the focus of issue #14 is balanced between a consideration of the importance of the *family* and the *nature of reality*. When the shadowy Animal Man character appears in the Baker's backyard, he tearfully confronts a silent Maxine with the following speech: "I had a dream the other night, Maxine. I dreamed you grew up and everything was okay... You can't even hear me, can you? I can't even warn you... Oh, Maxine... I miss you. I miss you all so much." This is clearly some version of Buddy Baker speaking these lines. He's recognizable to us, and to Maxine, even if he is wearing a slightly different costume. It's a horrifying moment because we now understand that something terrible is going to happen, not only to Maxine, but to the entire family. We see that Animal Man's general ineffectiveness as a hero has cost him the thing that matters most in his life. We don't know what will happen to Ellen Baker and the children, but we know it will be bad. We can imagine how bad by the end of the issue when we see Lennox at work. By juxtaposing the eerie warning from the apparition with the sequence of the lethal Lennox, Morrison clearly foreshadows events that will soon occur. Like the ghost-like form of Buddy Baker, we are powerless to intervene.

Meanwhile, in an interlude on pages 6 and 7, a man painted in muted colors strolls through the rain, narrating about "the symbol of David Bohm's Implicate Order Theory.[83] A vision of a vast interconnected universe where every part contains the whole. Where the universe is a mirror reflecting

[83] As referred to by the Mad Hatter in *Arkham Asylum*. Everything connects.

itself. Everything is everything." The man, clearly a comic book version of Grant Morrison, continues his soliloquy: "What'll it be next? Choice extracts from the Oxford Dictionary of Quotations? Trotting out the Nietzsche and the Shelley and the Shakespeare to dignify some old costumed claptrap? Probably. Sometimes you wonder, in an interconnected universe, who's dreaming who?" At that moment he reaches down and, touching him on the shoulder, awakens J. Highwater, before disappearing as the page concludes. Besides the conceit of actually appearing in the very comic book he's writing (which was inevitable anyway, considering his nod to writer Gardner Fox's mention in "The Flash of Two Worlds," as I've explained previously), this interlude is interesting because (a) it reinforces the notion I've been advocating from my first analysis of *Zenith*, that everything in Morrison's universe is connected, and every aspect of it contains the whole; and (b) it shows his conscious rejection of the Alan Moore school of writing, a style which, at that point in Moore's career, had been, at least superficially, dependent on literary epigraphs and classical allusions – the villain of *Watchmen*, after all, is named after a Shelley poem. Morrison, though, is not without irony because his mockery (or self-deprecation) about "dignify[ing] some old costumed claptrap" appears only a few panels after he has pretentiously referenced "David Bohm's Implicate Order Theory" to, presumably, dignify some (newer) costumed claptrap.

It's a testament to Morrison's skill that, with all the self-referential distractions, the threat to the Baker family can seem so chilling. Even with all the metafictional playfulness buzzing throughout the series constantly reminding us that these are just characters in a pretend universe, he imparts such personality into the Bakers that we feel concern for their safety. Generally, metafiction pushes the reader away from the text, severing the emotional connection in favor of an intellectual response. Yet Morrison still manages to make us care about Buddy Baker and his family to an almost sadistic degree, especially since he knows what he's going to do to them very shortly.

By the end of the issue, the real Buddy Baker has returned home, and he even encounters his own shadowy self in the final sequence. Nothing is resolved. The ghost cannot communicate with the living. A final, cryptic message "9 27," written on the wet front door of the house, is the only clue about the fate of the Baker family, and we are the only ones to see it as

Buddy obliviously closes the door.

Because this is ostensibly a super-hero comic book, Morrison has to put Buddy Baker back into action, and he does so in issue #15, "The Devil and the Deep Blue Sea." This is another Denny O'Neil-style "social problem" issue, and it's based on the inhumane treatment of dolphins. Thematically, this concern with *animal rights* has dominated *Animal Man* since the issue #1. Morrison obviously feels strongly about the poor treatment of animals in our society, and he uses *Animal Man* as a soapbox to raise awareness every now and then. Unfortunately, the stories end up being the weakest in his run on the title, largely because they don't contribute to the overall narrative progression. Nothing in "The Devil and the Deep Blue Sea" adds to the story of the Baker family or to Morrison's experiments with metafiction. It's not a total loss though, as Morrison revives an old DC hero, Dane Dorrance, "The Sea Devil," and reimagines him as "an eco-terrorist."[84] It's always fun to see Morrison's fresh perspective on stale characters, and this issue is no exception. The story's not worth spending too much time on in the context of this analysis, however, so I'll just leave it at this: "Dolphins good. Humans bad."[85]

At first glance, the following story, in issue #16, "The Clockwork Crimes of the Time Commander," would seem to be as pointless in the grand scheme as issue #15. After all, it's basically a standard super-hero story, as Animal Man joins his Justice League Europe teammates to stop a rogue villain. Unlike the story in issue #15 though, "The Clockwork Crimes of the Time Commander" actually advances the larger story and explores the more interesting themes of the series, such as *the family*, and most importantly, *the role of the hero*.

Family is emphasized in the issue, as Buddy takes Ellen on a trip to Paris. It's an opportunity to show them as a couple, to establish their loving bond, and to see how they interact with each other when they are out in the world. They joke about the silliness of the other super-heroes. They take a

---

[84] Dane Dorrance, leader of "The Sea Devils," first appeared in *Showcase* #27 (1960). The Sea Devils were a generic team of undersea adventurers who would fight giant sea monsters and international spy rings.

[85] This oversimplification of the story leaves out the powerful emotional impact it might have on the reader. Even though I don't have much to say about it, "The Devil and the Deep Blue Sea" is an effective tale about the brutality of commercial fishing and the ethical price we pay for our gluttony.

romantic walk along the Seine. They eat a romantic meal. They talk. "It's all working out, isn't it?" says Ellen, "Everything's going to be all right." They are content with their life, happy with what they have and what the future will bring. It's almost enough to make us forget that bad things are destined to happen. Except Morrison doesn't want us to forget. As Ellen says the lines above, safely within the walls of the restaurant, we see Lennox outside the window. Neither Ellen nor Buddy notice his presence, but even if they did, they wouldn't know anything about him. Only the reader knows how sharply his presence undercuts their happiness. For now, they remain blissfully unaware.

The Buddy / Ellen moments are just the subplot for the issue, as the main plot deals with the attempt to stop the seemingly powerful, though out-of-control, super-villain known as The Time Commander.[86] Morrison revels in the absurdity of such a scenario, giving The Elongated Man[87] dialogue like this: "Time's going crazy! We've just seen German tanks and cavemen chasing Jean Paul Sartre! The French Revolution's happening right around the corner." Sentences like that didn't appear in 1980s comic book stories very often – they seem like remnants of the Silver Age (for which Morrison has continually expressed a fondness) or lines from Morrison's other great comic book series of the 1980s, *Doom Patrol* (which I will analyze later in this book).

While Morrison does have a bit of classic super-hero fun with a villain like The Time Commander, the main thrust of the story is that Animal Man wants to solve the problem without resorting to punches and explosions. As he confronts The Time Commander, Animal Man says, "Just because I wear a costume doesn't mean I enjoy fighting. I'm just a little concerned about what you're doing here. Maybe you should think about it." In the context of the story (and the character), it's a decent and humane thing to say. The Time Commander, after all, is causing temporal chaos, but he's not evil at heart. His goal in the issue is to bring back everyone who ever lived. As he

---

[86] The Time Commander, an obscure villain in the DC Universe, first appeared in *The Brave and the Bold* #59 (1965). Unsurprisingly, he has access to equipment that allows him to alter time.

[87] Elongated Man, Animal Man's Justice League Europe colleague, first appeared in *The Flash* #112 (1960), created by John Broome and Carmine Infantino. Elongated Man can stretch. That's about it.

puts it, "No more sadness! No more bereavement!... Everything is beautiful! And love love love is the clockwork that turns the world." Crazy, yes. Evil, definitely not. Would a punch to the head stop him? Probably. Is Animal Man going to give him one? Nope. Animal Man's pacifism in this story retroactively sheds light on his actions throughout the entire series thus far. It makes his apparent ineffectiveness as a crime fighter into a choice. He wasn't an ineffectual hero in all those previous stories; he was just trying to find a different solution. At least, that's one way to look at it. The other way to look at it is that he *was* ineffectual because he didn't really do anything. Metamorpho,[88] for example, his teammate in Justice League Europe, would probably share that latter opinion. When he comes on the scene at the end of issue #16, he knocks The Time Commander unconscious in front of the disappointed Buddy Baker. Ultimately, Animal Man wasn't given a chance to find out if his way would have solved the problem.

By giving us such a thoughtful, passive super-hero, Morrison subverts all of the typical super-hero conventions, and that's what makes this issue so interesting. It emphasizes exactly what kind of hero Buddy Baker is. It challenges the normal comic book wisdom about what makes a hero (i.e. good punching) and makes us consider that there are other ways to be heroic (i.e. talking things out). Although this may seem like Morrison on his soapbox once again, I think it's different in this case, because Buddy isn't actually very good at talking things out, and his kinder approach to super-heroics may put his family in jeopardy, hardly an endorsement by the author.

Issue #17 brings Buddy Baker back home where he's forced to face the consequences of his unconventional super-hero actions in a story aptly titled, "Consequences." This story begins with a prologue as Mirror Master (whom we've not seen since he invaded the Baker house) and Lennox have a confrontation. We learn that Lennox has been hired by Mirror Master's employers to take over the Baker job, and in case we didn't get the hint that Lennox is going to do something bad to the Baker family, he demands the "layout of Animal Man's house." What happened last time we saw Lennox in someone's house? He ruthlessly murdered a mother and a daughter.

Meanwhile, Buddy Baker has teamed up with some animal rights

---

[88] Metamorpho originally appeared in *The Brave and the Bold* #57 (1965). He can stretch *and* transform into any element. Morrison loves these Silver Age characters, the sillier the better.

activists to rescue monkeys from the University of California labs. Buddy, aiding a criminal act, doesn't wear the Animal Man costume for this mission. As they leave the facility, the activists, against Buddy's wishes, ignite the lab. The next day, a disapproving Ellen confronts Buddy with the news that three firefighters were hurt in the blaze, and one of the men lies critically wounded in the hospital. Even Buddy's friend and manager, Roger, has turned on him. Roger says, "now I don't know whether you're a super-hero or a super-villain." To defend himself and justify his actions, Animal Man agrees to attend a televised debate on the subject of animal testing. The debate seems balanced until Buddy is asked if he's ever broken the law. This question, which he is unwilling to answer, leads him to go on a tirade that ends when he damns his own opinions by saying, "just because I wear a costume doesn't mean I always have to be right!" Later, Buddy confronts the leader of the animal rights activists and tells him, "I'm not even Animal Man anymore. I'm resigning from the JLE [Justice League Europe] and throwing away my costumes."

Clearly, the plot I've described ties in thematically with *the family* and *the role of the hero*. The themes are intertwined as Animal Man's actions in and out of costume have impacted his family (and the threat of Lennox looms over their heads as well) and have forced him to confront his own uncertainty and inadequacy as a hero. Morrison provides depth and complexity in "Consequences" because the monkeys being rescued were clearly tortured (their eyes were sewn shut), and, in saving them, Buddy Baker committed a crime (which injured several humans). It raises the question of moral law vs. criminal law, and Morrison doesn't provide an answer. Buddy Baker's answer is to withdraw from the question entirely. By the end, he has given up even trying to find a solution, given up trying to be any kind of hero.

Undercutting the moral dilemma Buddy Baker faces, Morrison throws some more metafiction into the mix. We see J. Highwater on page 8, driving intensely down the freeway, nearly crashing as his arms temporarily turn into pencil sketches before reverting to normal. Then he appears on the final page of the story, lying on the floor of the Baker house, yelling, "Help! Animal Man. Help me!" He's on the ground because his legs no longer work – they're just pencil sketches. Highwater's appearance, and the indication that he (along with all the other characters) is just a drawing on a page, could severely diminish the complex moral dilemma of the main storyline in "Consequences." While it's true that metafiction normally distances the reader, in this case it doesn't because *to the characters* all the strange stuff that's going on is metaphysical *not* metafictional, and we interpret it at that level as well as we're reading. It's no different than if Highwater's legs had become intangible[89] and he was unable to walk. The only thing that signifies to the reader that something metafictional is going on is that the intangible legs are drawn the way we know penciled layouts look before they are tightened up and inked. Morrison is actually pointing out the process involved in making the comic book, thereby pointing out that it's all fiction, thereby creating metafiction.[90] Even though we know Grant Morrison is writing all of this, as he has repeatedly made us aware, we still tend to think *How is Highwater going to get out of this mess?* and not *How is Grant Morrison going to get Highwater out of this mess?* The reality of the fictional universe is too strong, and we are too conditioned to suspend disbelief, to interrupt our connection with Buddy Baker's moral dilemma (at least at this point – Morrison won't pull out the big metafictional guns until the next couple of issues).

After, presumably, regaining his legs, Highwater brings Buddy Baker to Arizona in issue #18 where they take peyote buttons atop a mesa to try to come to grips with the mysteries of their universe. The story, "At Play in the Fields of the Lord," is the beginning of the end for Animal Man, but Buddy Baker has no idea what's coming. The big metafictional guns I discussed above begin to come out right in the beginning of the story as we get the following caption: "Interior of Baker House. Kitchen. Close-up on Ellen's hand. She is filling a glass of water from the kitchen tap." The very image that's described is shown in the panel. Bad writing? No. It's Metafiction. We are seeing the strings that move the puppets. We are seeing the actual

---

[89] Intangible or invisible objects in comic books are often drawn with a dotted line. When Kitty Pryde of the X-Men phases through objects, she's drawn that way, and Wonder Woman's invisible plan used to be drawn that way as well. The comic book reader knows that the dotted line isn't really representative of what's going on, but it helps to convey plot information in short hand. When Highwater's legs turn into pencil sketches, Morrison shows us that we accept some stylistic devices but not others, even though a dotted line is as much of a contrivance as a pencil sketch.

[90] We don't, however, interpret the dotted lines of Kitty Pryde or Wonder Woman to be metafictional. We just play along, and that's what we end up doing when we see Highwater's sketched legs.

words from the comic book script.

Before Buddy leaves with Highwater, he says goodbye to his family. The farewell seems to have an awkward pause in it. Instead of a single panel, it lingers for a whole page, and the relatively banal dialogue seems to carry some implications of dread. None of the characters know it, and we don't find out until the end of the next issue, but this is the last time Buddy Baker will see his family alive. By devoting so many panels to the moment, Morrison subtly prepares us for what's to come, and he doesn't play any metafictional games right then.

On the mesa, after taking the peyote, Buddy and Highwater hallucinate about the sky opening up. Two totems appear: an eagle to Highwater, which Highwater describes as "a messenger between man and the forces of creation," and a fox to Buddy. The fox takes Buddy on a journey into a cave where they see some primitive paintings. The fox explains that the first painting represents "The Crisis," and we can see the repeated circles which seem to indicate the multiple Earths that once existed. The second painting represents a "second Crisis," but the meaning is uncertain and the fox doesn't explain.

At the Baker house, the doorbell rings, and Ellen answers it (thereby disengaging all the high-tech security installed by the Justice League). It's Lennox.

"At Play in the Fields of the Lord" is just the set-up for the next issue, but it contains a few interesting moments: the excerpt from Morrison's script; the lingering goodbye; the reference to second Crisis; and the horrifying arrival of Lennox. The two totems don't give many answers to Highwater or Buddy Baker, but they are symbolically significant. The eagle symbolizes Highwater's belief system. Kwahu is the Hopi eagle spirit, and "Kwahu" is the name Highwater uses to refer to the totem. The fox symbolizes the author of the comic book universe. It's an allusion to Gardner Fox perhaps, but it's more directly a reference to Grant Morrison himself. One possible derivation of the Scottish name "Morrison" is "son of the fox."

This is all minor compared to the events of issue #19.

Issue #19, entitled "A New Science of Life," is the most significant issue of Morrison's entire run on *Animal Man*, and it still retains its power to shock and surprise even after all this time. The story begins by expanding upon the metafictional opening of the previous issue. Now, though, we are inside Morrison's home, and we "hear" his thinking as he begins composing the very story we're already reading: "The story so far? Animal Man and the physicist, James Hightower, are in Arizona... What happens now? Yes, yes, of course. The secret of the universe." Items in and around Morrison's computer desk include a copy of David Bohm's book, *Unfolding Meaning*, and the page from Grant Morrison and Dave McKean's *Arkham Asylum* graphic novel showing Batman penetrating his hand with a shard of glass.[91] (*Arkham Asylum* had not been released at that point, so readers would not have known what that strange artwork was depicting.) The metafictional madness continues on the pages that follow as we return to Highwater and Buddy Baker on the mesa and watch as their hallucinations turn from the bizarre (everything is red, then a whale appears) to the familiar (but no less bizarre) as the whale's narration is labeled and formatted as an entry from *Who's Who: The Definitive Directory of the DC Universe*. This recap of the origin and brief overview of Buddy Baker's life so far leads into the most shocking use of metafiction ever in a comic book story. Off-panel, a voice says, "That's not the way it happened at all." The voice belongs to the Silver Age Animal Man.

The Silver Age Animal Man, a Buddy Baker doppelganger with a squarer jaw and a shorter haircut, tells Buddy, "I fought crime. Aliens. Simple. I was married. No kids. The radiation sterilized me. And then they changed everything. They wiped out my life and replaced it with yours." Buddy doesn't know how to respond, but as the Silver Age Animal Man shakes him by the shoulders, trying to get Buddy to listen, Buddy cries, "Wait! Who are 'They'? Who are 'They'?" As the Silver Age Animal Man fades away a disembodied voice says, "Do you really want to know the truth? Then turn around. Turn around now. You'll see."

As Buddy slowly turns around, facing the reader, Morrison gives him, and us, a shock. Buddy looks right at us in a full page close-up and shouts, "I can see you!"

He can see us reading the comic book.

Animal Man gasps, "They're watching us." After contemplating what he's seen (us!), he says, "What is God's reality... Heaven, if you like... what

---

[91] David Bohm, *Arkham Asylum*, and *Animal Man*, all converging on the same page. Patterns within patterns. It's all about fractal geometry.

From *Animal Man* #19 – Buddy Baker realizes that we're watching him. Understandably, he's freaked out about it. Art by Chas Truog and Doug Hazlewood. Copyright © DC Comics.

if it's so bad that he had to imagine us to help make His life bearable?" This is a profound statement. It takes the traditional notion of God as creator and then logically completes that analogy. If our creators make universes for entertainment – for the escapist pleasure of readers – then who's to say we are not made for the entertainment of some higher beings. God would therefore not be benevolent and just, but manipulative and cruel. This is literally true for Buddy Baker, and by implication, it may be true for us as well. Morrison has taken metafictional strategies and applied them to do more than make the mechanism of storytelling visible; he's made us challenge our preconception of reality. The significance of that challenge would depend on the strength and bearing of your faith (or lack thereof), but the question of God as creator is certainly raised, and powerfully so.

The sequence also forces discomfort upon the reader for another reason. We've been caught peeping. After reading "A New Science of Life," it's a bit more difficult to remain as impartial observers as we read our comic book stories. Buddy Baker has made us feel a bit like voyeurs. It's creepy to Buddy, as well it should be. It's not enough to make us stop reading though, but it does make us feel more self-conscious about it, as if we're doing something a bit wrong by enjoying the suffering and struggle that we're watching.

This new awareness of Buddy Baker's continues to make him question his own preconceptions about his life. He realizes that there have been a lot of holes in his own story. "A few months ago," he says to Highwater, "or maybe it was a year or more, my wife was attacked and almost raped in the woods... There were four guys. What happened to them?... Why was there no trial?" Buddy is referring to the events of issue #4, and notice how he can't clearly define how long ago they took place. To the reader, it was well over a year before, but to Buddy, living in the fictional world, it happened in some ill-defined past. Either way, he can't recall it clearly because he has no true existence. The reader may have remembered that event and assumed it was dealt with between issues or off-panel. To Buddy, though, there is no such place or time. His whole life has been on-panel. He has done nothing unless we have seen it as we've been reading about him.[92] As Buddy

[92] The idea of comic book continuity relies on the fact that the reality of the comic book world only exists insofar as things happen within a panel. If a character is not shown doing something, or something is not mentioned specifically in the comic

explores these contradictions and inconsistencies, he finds that he is able to move literally outside of the very panel borders that have contained his existence. He looks in at Highwater from outside of the inked border. "Highwater," Buddy asks, "is that you in there?" Because he has become fully aware of his fictional status, he is able to transcend the normal bounds of his reality. Like the ascendant beings in Phase Four of Zenith, his knew awareness allows him to break out of his physical bonds. Then the peyote wears off.

Highwater and Buddy awaken atop the mesa, and they write off their new awareness as a hallucination. This is a necessary plot device because if Buddy Baker didn't return to "normal," he would never feel the need to head back home. Had he not returned home, he, and the reader, would not have seen the tragic final image at the end of the issue:

His family, Ellen, Cliff, and Maxine, lie dead on the kitchen floor. Blood seeps from their gunshot wounds.

The blunt brutality of such an image is haunting. It is one of the most powerful images in any comic book I've ever read. Morrison's genius in this series is that he can, in the same issue, point out in no uncertain terms that these are fictional characters in a fictional universe, and then destroy you emotionally by showing the violent death of characters that you've grown close to. This single page brings all the major themes back together. Buddy will be forever changed because of what happened to his family, and he will have to face the fact that he was unable, as a hero, to do anything to save them. We will soon find out that the cause of their murder was Buddy's very heroism on behalf of animal rights – Lennox's employers didn't like the trouble Animal Man was causing, and this was meant to teach him a lesson. On top of all of that, we, as readers, can't help remembering that a writer, Grant Morrison, as creator of this reality, was the true mastermind behind the execution, and we wonder Can Buddy's quest for revenge possibly go that far?

---

book, then that thing did not happen, according to the laws of continuity. The excuse, "Well, it happened off panel," would not satisfy any avid comic book reader. Especially if the event was significant, the excuse, "Well, it happened off panel," would not satisfy any avid comic book reader.

## Meeting the Maker

A typical revenge narrative is structured like this: Act I, the hero finds his family dead; Act II, the hero seeks out the villain, overcoming various obstacles along the way; Act III, the hero confronts the villain and wins the battle and / or dies trying. The end.

This story is an ancient one. In Western culture, it dates back to ancient Greek drama, continues through Shakespeare (even *Hamlet* follows the structure, it's just that the title character is really *bad* at the whole revenge side of things), and appears in American cinema again and again. (The Steven Segal movies of the late 1980s, for example, all follow exactly the same formula, only with more kicking than *Hamlet*.) It's not quite as common to see the revenge narrative in comic books, though, simply because it resolves things too neatly. Once the killer has been confronted and defeated, everything else feels anticlimactic.

It's a structure that certainly wouldn't work for a continuing series, because the character's whole reason for action (revenge) wouldn't exist after the first storyline resolved (unless the story was unnecessarily dragged out – which wouldn't be very satisfying at all). Two huge exceptions exist, however, in the form of Batman and Spider-Man. These two characters are based on the revenge narrative, and their whole existence as heroes is predicated on the idea that they lost someone they loved (Batman lost both parents, while Spider-Man lost his uncle). In both cases, confronting and defeating the villain did not conclude the story, but that's easily explained because, unlike typical revenge heroes, Batman and Spider-Man were not adults when tragedy struck, and they both blamed themselves for the death of their loved ones, so the psychological trauma of the events affected them more deeply than it normally would have. They should, according to the traditional narrative, end their quest for revenge after they defeat the men who killed their family members, but they don't because they have transformed their goal from revenge to *redemption*. Batman needs to prove to himself that he is strong and capable, because as a child, he was not strong enough or capable enough to stop Joe Chill from killing his parents. Spider-Man needs to prove that he is responsible because, as an adolescent, he was irresponsible and didn't stop the man who would later kill his Uncle Ben when he had the chance. Both heroes need to redeem themselves for their own inaction, even though no one but themselves would possibly put any blame on them. Their obsessive quest for redemption is linked directly to their young age when the tragic events occurred.

Other comic book revenge heroes, like the Punisher,[93] for example, don't work quite as well conceptually as Batman and Spider-Man because we expect adults to handle things differently. We might root for them to get revenge, but we find it hard to believe, even in a comic book story, that an adult would turn that revenge into a life-long crusade. Yet we accept that a child or adolescent could be so severely traumatized by a tragedy that he or she would be forever altered psychologically. Therefore, Batman is seen as *haunted* by his past and *driven* to bring justice to the world, Spider-Man is seen as using his *great power* to be *greatly responsible*, and the Punisher is seen as *crazy crazy crazy*. The Punisher, as a character (at least as I've seen him written), has been unable to convincingly turn his revenge into a larger quest for redemption.

All of which brings us to Buddy Baker. At the end of *Animal Man* #19, he came home to find his wife and children brutally murdered. That's Act I. That's where the revenge narrative kicks in. So does he, in Hollywood action-hero fashion, grab the nearest weapons and go on a rampage until he kills the man responsible? Does he pull a Hamlet and contemplate the best course of action while pondering the mysteries of existence? Does he, like the Punisher, become a psychopathic vigilante with a cool shirt? Does he act like I would and cry and curl up into a fetal position for a few days? Or does he seek redemption?

All of the above.

Essentially, Grant Morrison, in *Animal Man* #20-26, ends his run on the series with one of the greatest revenge stories ever. It combines almost every possible iteration of the revenge narrative into a metafictional stew, and yet it works as an emotionally satisfying story as well. We *want* Buddy Baker to take revenge, and we get what we want, but we also get a whole lot more.

We get Morrison's final statements on the dominant themes of the series, like the importance of *family*, *animal rights*, *the role of the hero*, and *the nature of reality*.

---

[93] The Punisher becomes a crazed vigilante after his wife and children are gunned down by the mob. Unlike Batman and Spider-Man, he was not a child when this tragic event occurred.

We get The Inferior Five and Sunshine Superman.[94]

We get Morrison honestly explaining his own shortcomings as a writer.

And we get to see a wish granted, even if it is *only* a story.

But, before we discuss the conclusion, we need to take a close look at the steps along the way.

Issue #20, "The Last Enemy," begins the narrative of Buddy Baker's revenge in an unconventional manner. Buddy does not immediately vow to avenge his family's death. In fact, throughout the entire issue, Buddy is portrayed as grief-stricken, immobile, depressed, and finally, suicidal. There is no indication that Buddy will even attempt *any* sort of revenge. He seems to have given up completely. His reaction to the event includes fantasizing that his family is still alive, curling up into a ball on the floor, refusing to eat or acknowledge other human presence, and murmuring "oh no no no no." This is not the reaction of a typical revenge hero. He seems paralyzed by his loss, unable to cope – unable, even, to move.

Morrison drags out Buddy's torment for the entire issue as we watch him wallow in self-pity. It's unheroic, and it seems real. We empathize with Buddy's loss, and we recognize that the pain and suffering he's experiencing here is a more human reaction than we're accustomed to seeing in a comic book. We believe Buddy's reaction, and we aren't surprised when he reaches for the sleeping pills at the end of the issue. On the verge of suicide, however, Buddy answers the phone (revealing, perhaps, that he wasn't quite ready to give up – he could have easily ignored the call if he was totally hopeless). A voice on the other end seems to give him a reason to live: "I've got some names you might be interested in hearing." This sentence, with its promise of providing a target for his revenge is enough to keep Buddy Baker alive a little bit longer, and thus the issue ends.

Mixed into "The Last Enemy," between moments of Buddy's suffering, Morrison furthers two subplots. The first subplot deals with the assassin, Lennox, as he returns to his employers to seek payment and protection from retaliation. His employers tell him not to worry as they reveal the

---

[94] The Inferior Five are a parody super-hero team who first appeared in *Showcase* #62 (1966), and Sunshine Superman is a Morrison creation, no doubt inspired by the 1966 Donovan song of the same name. Morrison mines his childhood nostalgia throughout *Animal Man*, but he never does so with cynical intentions, as this final storyline will attest.

From *Animal Man* #20 – Buddy Baker's thoughts don't immediately turn toward revenge. Art by Chas Truog and Doug Hazlewood. Copyright © DC Comics.

ridiculously named "Bug-Man"[95] exoskeleton, which features enough high-tech weaponry to keep an army of super-heroes at bay (or so they think). They openly challenge Animal Man from the privacy of their sanctum, saying, "Let him try [to track us down], Mr. Lennox. Just let him try."

Meanwhile, the Psycho Pirate, still imprisoned in Arkham Asylum, continues to rant: "I shall make the dead to rise and they will outnumber the living! They're coming! All of them! Coming back! They're all coming back!"

This is classic stuff, almost Biblical in scope. Morrison gives us the wronged hero on a self-destructive path but with a (still unfocused) desire for vengeance. He gives us the *hubris* of the mysterious villains, whose own arrogance will no doubt lead to their downfall. He gives us the mad prophet, locked in his cell, chanting of the apocalyptic future. This is the beginning of the end, and Morrison makes sure we know it.

In contrast to the appropriately slow, agonizing pace of issue #20, *Animal Man* #21, titled "Tooth and Claw," accelerates Buddy's revenge to a sprint. Once Buddy finds out who's responsible for the death of his family, he acts quickly and ruthlessly.

The issue begins from Buddy's point of view. We see what he sees and "hear" his narration in the captions. This is the first time in the series that Morrison has used this technique. We've heard Buddy's thoughts before, but we've never seen things from his perspective. What we see is a sink with some hair and some blood, and the narration reveals Buddy's nihilistic perspective: "I keep thinking about Travis Bickle in 'Taxi Driver.' I suppose it's better than anything else." Travis Bickle, of course, was a deranged antihero at best and a psychopath at worst. When Buddy says, "I suppose it's better than anything else," he seems to be indicating that he is distancing himself from his own situation. He identifies with Travis Bickle because it's easier to play someone else's role than to accept what's happened to him. Buddy continues this ritual of self-transformation by changing his garb: "I put on the leather. Old stuff from when I was a punk. Dress in the dead skin of animals." His halting syntax reminds us of primitive chanting, once again confirming that this is, indeed, ritualistic

---

[95] Another Morrison insect reference. As I claimed in my *Arkham Asylum* analysis, insects in Morrison's work tend to imply inhumanity or corruption. The "Bug-Man" suit implies both. It's grotesque and lethal.

behavior. He is invoking the warrior spirit of contemporary America through the form of Travis Bickle. (Where else would contemporary gods exist if not in the cinema?)

Ironically, in the very moment Buddy Baker is "becoming" someone else, we "become" him by adopting his point of view. Morrison seems to be playing with the tradition of hero identification in this opening sequence, encouraging us to revel in the role of violent avenger, while at the same time, undercutting the glory of such a role by referencing the unstable Travis Bickle.

Page 2 reveals the transformation. He stands before us in a black leather costume, wearing jackboots. The "A" on his chest is in white relief, and his hair is poorly clipped. He looks ready to take action.

This new variation on the traditional Animal Man costume is fully in line with the darker, more violent trends of contemporary super-hero narratives. Morrison once again seems to embrace the culture and comment upon it. It's a "cool costume" and a mockery of that type of "edgy" fashion simultaneously. This new, Dark Animal Man is clearly bent on revenge. You can tell because he's wearing leather.

We discover that the anonymous voice on the phone who saved Buddy from suicide was none other than the new Mirror Master, a man known only as McCulloch. McCulloch, at Buddy's house in "Tooth and Claw," reveals the intentions of his former employers:

> There's three of these guys, right? Corporate high heejins that didn't like the way their business was being hit by all youse environmentalists and greens and what-have-you. So they set up this wee boy's club to help put the wind up people they thought might turn out to be dangerous.

McCulloch admits that he didn't want anything to do with these guys once he found out that they wanted to hurt Buddy's wife and children, and that's when Lennox took over the job.

Buddy had been blaming himself for the death of his family, so finding out that his actions on behalf of animal rights had directly caused their death doesn't impact him at all. It does, however, challenge our preconceptions about Buddy's heroic actions in the past. As passive as he had been in previous issues, he did take strong action on behalf of animals. In retrospect, those actions led to the death of his family. He paid a price for being a hero.

As he tries to piece together exactly how his family died, Animal Man's rage focuses his powers in new ways. He's able to draw upon multiple animal abilities at once and "smell" the series of events that began when Lennox knocked on the front door and ended with the bloody corpses of his wife and children on the kitchen floor. As he relives their murder, Buddy says, on page 5, "I'm going to kill him, Lennox. I'm going to kill them all."

It doesn't take him long to fulfill that promise.

Animal Man kills the first member of the corporate cabal on pages 6-7. The man, relaxing on his yacht (a symbol of wealth and privilege), is unprepared for the attack. Buddy holds him underwater "until he stops kicking." Then Buddy tracks down his second victim on the golf course (another symbol of wealth and privilege), dragging the man underground and killing him by cutting off his air from above.

As an ironic counterpoint to these actions, the scene cuts back to the last surviving member of the cabal, Brumley, as he tells Lennox that "Super-heroes don't kill people. This is America." Perhaps Mr. Brumley hasn't been keeping up on his contemporary comic book stories.[96]

Before Animal Man exacts his final revenge, McCulloch (who's been traveling with Buddy to help him track down the cabal) notices something sharp in Buddy's pocket. "The goodies are worse than the baddies these days," says McCulloch. Buddy's reply shows his absurdist world view: "We're all just characters in a bad story. It's not our fault." What seems like absurdism, or nihilism, is actually true in Buddy's case, and the reader knows it. Morrison justifies Buddy's actions on metafictional grounds. It's not that Buddy is acting in an unheroic way, it's that Morrison is writing him that way, as Buddy has finally accepted. Such a statement actually allows Morrison to give Buddy the revenge he needs and yet takes all the blame off the character. It allows Buddy Baker a greater chance at redemption.

When Animal Man arrives at Brumley's office, Brumley tries to escape in an elevator. Animal Man punches the elevator with such force that the whole thing bursts out of the side of the building, and Brumley falls to his

[96] One of the hallmarks of the "Dark Age" of comics, which ran from the late 1980s through the 1990s, was the abundance of excessively violent super-heroes. Even the already violent Batman was replaced, when his back was broken by the villain Bane, with a new Batman, Jean-Paul Valley (a.k.a. Azrael), who took a more lethal approach to crimefighting. And, of course, the murderous "hero" called the Punisher was popular enough in those days to support multiple continuing series.

death. It's a level of strength and brutality that we've never seen from Buddy, and yet it's what we want to see. We want Buddy to destroy these men for what they did to Ellen, Cliff, and Maxine. We are as complicit in the deed as Buddy (or Grant Morrison).

Buddy Baker's final act of revenge comes as he confronts Lennox himself. Lennox, wearing the "Bug-Man" exoskeleton to defend himself, is no match for Buddy's power.

Lennox is soon defeated but left alive as Buddy pulls out a glove with razor-tipped fingers from his pocket. Our point of view shifts away from the action at this point, and we see only the Seal of the United States Government on the wall as Buddy tortures Lennox out-of-frame.

On the final page of the issue, Buddy reveals to McCulloch what his revenge has accomplished: "I've done terrible things and they're still dead. Ellen. Cliff. Maxine. I feel nothing."

It seems to be the end of the revenge narrative at this point. Buddy Baker has overcome the obstacles and defeated the villains. He has achieved the revenge he desired. What keeps the story going, though, is that he has not yet achieved *redemption.* He is responsible for the death of his family, and the only way (he thinks) he can redeem himself is by bringing them back to life. After all, he is a super-hero in the DC Universe, so he does have some options: "I've had an idea," he says at the end of "Tooth and Claw," "All I need is a time machine. I can fix everything."

The following issue, *Animal Man* #22, entitled "Time in a Bottle," features Buddy Baker's attempt to gain redemption by changing the past. He visits John Starr, a.k.a. The Time Commander, the villain last seen at the receiving end of Metamorpho's fist in issue #16. "I don't know what happened to my life," says Buddy. "I want to get it back." He doesn't accept this new reality and believes he can literally turn back time. Redemption can only be accomplished by returning things to the way they were. Nothing else will satisfy him.

Starr can't help Buddy, though, even if he wanted to, because his hourglass was broken by the Justice League during that previous conflict. Forced to look elsewhere for help, Buddy visits another time traveler, Rip Hunter of the Time Masters.[97] Hunter is initially hesitant, but when Buddy

---

[97] Rip Hunter, and his time sphere, first appeared in *Showcase* #20 (1959). Time

spins an elaborate lie about how desperately the Justice League needs a time machine, Hunter hands Buddy a slightly damaged backpack-sized device. Buddy's lie is not a heroic action, but it is a necessary one. Rip Hunter wouldn't have helped Buddy if he knew Buddy's true intentions to manipulate the present by changing the past.

Meanwhile, in Arkham Asylum, the Psycho Pirate is losing his grip on reality as colors stream from his eyes. In a hallucinogenic sequence, a comic book emerges from his brain. It's a copy of *Flash* #123, featuring "The Flash of Two Worlds," the story that initiated the concept of the DC Multiverse and the story that used the motif of the writer as participant in the comic book reality (even if Gardner Fox is just mentioned in the story, not depicted). Morrison's constant use of the Psycho Pirate subplot reminds us that some kind of apocalypse is coming, and the story of Buddy's redemption will undoubtedly pass through Arkham Asylum.

The bulk of "Time in a Bottle" consists of Buddy using the time-travel device to revisit his past in an attempt to warn his family about their impending doom. Because the device doesn't work properly, Buddy doesn't seem to be able to control the distance of his jumps into the past or their duration. He appears for a few seconds outside his house immediately after the first confrontation with the new Mirror Master (as depicted in issue #8). We see the same events from the end of that story replayed from a new point of view, and we realize that the shadowy Animal Man figure who has appeared in several previous issues was, in fact, this future Buddy Baker traveling backwards in time. Throughout the issue, he jumps farther and farther into his past, unable to communicate with his past self or his family members, leaving cryptic clues. The numbers written on the door all the way back in issue #14 – 9 and 27 – revealed the date, September 27th, on which his family would be killed. We didn't know what those numbers referred to at the time, and the Baker family never even saw them, but as we see the time-traveling Buddy inscribe them on the door in this issue, we understand. We also understand that Buddy is repeating events we've already witnessed, and we can logically conclude that he will not be able to change the course of his life. He will not be able to save his family. Time travel will not be the key to his redemption.

---

travel was quite common in the Silver Age DC Universe, but as the "realism" of the 1980s hit, it became almost obsolete.

The issue ends with three characters who are all, in some way, lost. Buddy Baker is lost temporally, traveling through time haphazardly, unable to impact reality in any way. J. Highwater, who we haven't seen in a little while, is lost metaphysically, as he hasn't dealt with the consequences of what he witnessed on that mesa a few issues back but now finds himself confronted by the mysterious aliens who granted Animal Man his powers. The Psycho Pirate is lost mentally, losing control of his memories of the multiple Earths and desperately crying, "They're all coming back."

*Animal Man* #23 begins with the fallout from the Psycho Pirate's mind. We see him in Arkham, wearing his full costume, his cell decorated with artifacts from worlds that shouldn't exist in post-*Crisis* continuity: a wanted poster depicting Ultraman (a character eradicated from the DC Universe in *Crisis on Infinite Earths*), a "Mondale Wins" newspaper headline (presumably from a parallel Earth), a copy of Alan Moore's *Watchmen* trade paperback. Appropriately, the title for this issue is "Crisis," as it not only deals with the consequences of *Crisis on Infinite Earths*, but it also presents a real and deadly crisis for the characters in the story. It's obviously the "Second Crisis" Foxy referred to during Buddy Baker's peyote dream in issue #18.

Contextually, issue #23 seems to be Morrison's commentary on what was lost after *Crisis* occurred. He populates the story with the forgotten, often silly, characters who once made the DC Universe charming and fun, but now have been relegated to the void where characters go when they're no longer relevant. By having them erupt from the Psycho Pirate's mind, Morrison is clearly telling us that these characters never truly die. They cannot be erased from memory, no matter how much the powers-that-be want to erase them from continuity. He emphasizes this by giving the following lines to the Psycho Pirate as he sees what has erupted from his brain: "You're all so wonderful. Why did they have to remove you from the continuity? You'd have made for such marvelous stories. You will make for marvelous stories." Grant Morrison, through the Psycho Pirate, gives these characters new life and celebrates their quirkiness. The cast of characters he chooses to rescue from the void shows his preference for the odd, the fantastic, and the awkwardly-dated creations of the past. A small sampling of the characters appearing in this issue includes Streaky the Super-Cat, Detective Chimp, and The Bug-Eyed Bandit, as well as Crime Syndicate members like Power Ring and Johnny Quick. These Silver Age characters were removed from DC continuity because they didn't fit in with the grim-and-gritty mid-to-late 1980s conception of the DC Universe. Morrison mocks that decision not only by resurrecting these obscure characters and showing that they might have appeal but also by creating a new character, ostensibly from an alternate universe (but really a pastiche of an existing archetype), called Overman. This character, a grotesque, ultra-violent Superman variant, seems to be Morrison's take on the Frank Miller-style heroes that dominated late 1980s comic books.[98] The Psycho Pirate doesn't want to even think about this hero or the world he inhabits. Unfortunately, he can't hold Overman back, and Overman appears in Psycho Pirate's reality holding a giant nuclear warhead, giggling with madness. When the Psycho Pirate is the voice of reason, you know the world's gone crazy.

Overman's power is so great, he cannot be contained within the panel borders. Literally. He is able to smash through the sides of a panel, causing it to rupture open and allow a white light to pour into their reality. The Psycho Pirate responds by saying, *to the reader*, "We're through! And we're coming to get you!" as his hands gesture out toward us, extending past the borders of the panel that contains him. Even after the revelations of issue #19, in which Buddy Baker noticed our presence as observers, it's still a shock to see the Psycho Pirate not only address us, but threaten us. Unlike Buddy Baker, he sees us as a hostile presence, and he doesn't seem happy about it.

Although the reality-warping events at Arkham take center stage in "Crisis," Buddy is not ignored. He continues his quest through time, now guided by the enigmatic Phantom Stranger, who takes him to see Immortal Man and Jason Blood.[99] The scene between these four characters helps to get Buddy Baker back on track. The conversation is philosophical in nature, and

---

[98] Overman is drawn as a Superman-on-steroids with an American flag for a cape.

[99] All three of these characters (the Phantom Stranger, Immortal Man, and Jason Blood) are immortals who occasionally intervene in superhuman affairs. The Phantom Stranger, wearing a fedora, suit, and regal cape, acts as a kind of Rod Serling for the DC Universe, narrating events that are to unfold, but he also guides heroes toward their destinies. Immortal Man is just a guy in a turtleneck sweater who cannot die. Jason Blood is the immortal human host for the Demon, a creature summoned by Merlin in defense of Camelot. Morrison here introduces the idea that these immortal beings would meet occasionally throughout history to talk shop.

it helps allow Buddy to move on with his life. Jason Blood gives some pertinent advice: "The dead are gone. We who remain in the world must continue and make of our time here a heaven. Or hell." If Buddy is to move past denial and rage to acceptance, he needs to listen to the advice he's given. He cannot change the past, but he can change his present (or his reaction to events in the present) and therefore his future. Immortal Man puts it even more bluntly: "Either you're on the side of life, or you're on the side of death. Which is it going to be?" Both characters present Buddy Baker with a duality: Heaven / Hell or life / death. It might not solve Buddy's problem, but it simplifies them enough to get him back where he needs to go (with a little more help from the Phantom Stranger). He arrives back in the present just as he's needed. "It's okay. I'm here," he says on the final page of the issue, intervening on our behalf just as the Psycho Pirate seems ready to break into our world. Buddy doesn't seem to be talking to us, though. He seems ready to stop the "Crisis" at Arkham, and, therefore, seems to have chosen the side of life, ready to redeem himself the traditional way: by being a hero.

Issue #24, "Purification Day," begins with a reminder that this whole thing is all one big metafictional game. The captions, instead of narrating or providing thoughts of a character, show the words of the script for this very issue. "Establishing shot of Arkham Asylum under a tormented, tortured sky," says one of the captions, and the panels on the page cut back and forth between hands on a keyboard and the "setting of the story" at Arkham.

Page 2 picks up where the events of the previous issue left off. Animal Man, who has arrived at Arkham to save the day, is being shown the rift in the panel wall caused by Overman. One of the yellow aliens who transported Highwater to Arkham refers to the broken panel border as "a breach in the continuum. A door in the impossible." "That light," he says, "represents the middle ground between our reality and the higher world, out of which we are unfolded." His words recall the theories of David Bohm which have been referenced by Highwater and Morrison himself in previous issues, theories which promote the idea that everything is connected to everything else. Morrison also picks up a strand from issue #19 here when Animal Man looks out through the broken panel wall and says, "I can see something. It's vague… like a face… a huge blurred face." He is, of course, seeing us, to which Highwater responds, "They're reading our story! We're just minor characters in a story to entertain... I don't know... the gods, if you like." Ultraman, an evil variation of Superman and leader of the Crime Syndicate of America, cannot bear such a revelation: "Minor characters? No, that's horrible! That can't be right! I'm Ultraman..." Overman attacks, and the metafictional moment is interrupted, but Ultraman tries to stop the battle to point out that the reader is the real threat: "You're forgetting the real enemy! Out there! Don't fight! That's what they want! They want to see people hurting each other! Why do you think the world's the way it is!" If Morrison made us feel like voyeurs in issue #19, he makes us feel like sadists here as we recognize that Ultraman's words are essentially true. Their world is violent because it pleases us.

Morrison, perhaps frustrated by the demands of the super-hero genre, which mandates that every climax includes a fight scene, gives the reader a bit of a slugfest, but the characters' self-awareness turns it into something greater. It becomes, in this sequence, a commentary on super-hero conventions, a commentary on the absurdity of a universe where characters solve problems exclusively through violence. *Animal Man* has been about a non-violent character in a violent world. Yet Buddy Baker was dragged into the maelstrom of violence by the death of his family, and it doesn't appear that his brutal actions have helped him toward redemption.

As Overman and Ultraman battle, Animal Man uses his new awareness to transcend the bounds of his reality. He steps through the broken panel wall and into the white gutter between images. He is now on the outside looking in – not as far outside as we are, he is still trapped by the confines of the page, but he is able to move around between panels freely, even tapping the bewildered Overman on the shoulder. Ultimately, Overman becomes destroyed by the panel itself as it slowly closes in on him, crushing him from all sides.

It's as if Overman's lack of self-awareness is his own undoing. Even as his demise is upon him, he refuses to acknowledge his status as a mere character in a comic book. He stubbornly shouts, "I'm real! I'm realistic! This can't happen to me!" Unlike the unrealistic Animal Man, with his goggles and animal powers, Overman is "realistic" because he's deranged and violent. And he carries a nuclear warhead around. Morrison, in this sequence, demolishes the erroneous (yet popular) notion that comic book characters are somehow more "realistic" when they are dark, cynical, and lethal. Yet only a few issues before, Buddy Baker had turned dark, cynical, and lethal. Morrison reminds us that this new attitude of Buddy's did not make him any more "realistic" than he was before. He is, and always will be, a character in a story. Morrison also reminds us that "realistic" characters and stories are less entertaining than the stories of the Silver Age, a perspective best expressed by Power Ring (another member of the Crime Syndicate of America): "All the fun's gone out of [this world]. Everything used to be bright and now everything is dark... I want to go home."

Meanwhile, Overman's warhead is still active, and the characters seemed destined for destruction. On the verge of annihilation, Animal Man steps in to save the day. "All you have to do is switch it off," he says, a reference to the lesson he learned all the way back in *Animal Man* #6 (when Hawkman intervened to save the world from the Thanagarian fractal bomb). Buddy Baker actually acts like a hero this time, saving the world for the first time in the series. He seems to have grown from his experiences over the past few issues, and *Animal Man* #24 ends with him symbolically shedding his black leather "revenge costume" and adopting his old orange-and-blues. He seems ready for the final stage of the quest for redemption as he knowingly says, "Time for the last adventure."

Buddy Baker's last adventure, beginning in *Animal Man* #25, takes him through a literal Comic Book Limbo,[100] where he encounters a cadre of former members of the DC Universe who have now been written out of continuity, forgotten, or otherwise abandoned. Although, technically, any character not recently appearing in the DC Universe could "exist" in Comic Book Limbo, Morrison populates this land with the silly characters who no longer fit into the dark, post-Crisis "reality."

Animal Man's entrance into Comic Book Limbo is a simple one. He opens the front door of his house and there it is. Right in front of him. Whatever force is controlling his fate (which we know as Grant Morrison, but Buddy doesn't) has decided that it's time for Buddy to learn the whole truth, and crossing Comic Book Limbo is the first stage on the trip. It's the equivalent of a yellow brick road, and Buddy's house transplanted to Limbo

---

[100] Comic Book Limbo, as a metaphorical idea, has existed as long as comic books have been around. Any character who hasn't appeared for a while could be said to exist in "Comic Book Limbo." Morrison takes that concept and turns it into an actual place.

does resemble Dorothy's house transplanted to Oz. Although Buddy doesn't have a loyal terrier by his side, he does meet some bizarre characters who help him on his quest.[101]

Juxtaposed with images of Buddy's journey, we see panels of a monkey typing a script on a verdant hillside. At first, he types lines from *The Tempest*, recalling the infinite monkey theorem, which postulates that an infinite number of monkeys with an infinite number of typewriters will, at some point, type the complete works of Shakespeare. Later in the issue, though, the words he's typing seem to be the actual script for this very issue of *Animal Man*. The title of the issue, "Monkey Puzzles," seems to indicate that the monkey (and his typing) may somehow be the key to the whole mystery of Buddy's existence, but first Buddy has to complete his journey.

In Limbo, Buddy meets Merryman, the buffoonish leader of the Inferior Five. Merryman explains the rules of Limbo, telling Buddy that characters come and go, and that Animal Man himself was in limbo not too long ago, but Buddy wouldn't remember because characters have no memory of the place once they are written out of it. Animal Man, in his search for answers, asks, "Who's writing the story? Who killed my family?" Questions which Merryman is not able to answer. As they continue the journey, they pass a foreboding inscription written above two stone columns: "facilis discenus Averno," which translates as "The road to Hell is easy," a reference to Dante's *Inferno*. Morrison, it seems, casts Buddy Baker in the role of Dante, the seeker, the man who wants to regain his beloved, and Merryman is Virgil, the guide.

In the middle of Animal Man's quest, Morrison pulls us out of the narrative, seemingly to comment on his own thought process. On page 12, instead of following Buddy and Merryman, we see panels of hands typing on a keyboard. The captions, which use a courier font on this page, instead of the normal hand-lettering, reveal the inner workings of the author's mind:

> It's stupid, I know, but I care. All the things that meant so much when we were young. Under the blankets late at night, listening to long-distance radio. All those things lost now or broken. Can you remember? Can you remember that feeling? Perhaps I ought to go to a doctor.

---

[101] Buddy follows the same path as every monomythic hero. Just as I explained in my analysis of the Joseph Campell structure in *Arkham Asylum*, the hero undergoes a descent into Hell and then a rebirth.

It's Morrison's rejection of cynicism. He admits that he cares about the foolish things that we're all supposed to grow out of. He embraces the memories of that innocent time. To him, the Silver Age comic books, with their ridiculous "science-based" plots and characters with animal powers, represent the best things in life, and he wants all of us to recall that innocence we once shared. Notice how he ends his internal monologue with the statement, "Perhaps I ought to go to a doctor," as if there's something wrong with him for caring about innocent times in today's corrupt, cynical world. Ultimately, the secret story of *Animal Man* is the story of what happens when innocence meets experience, when Silver Age naiveté meets postmodern cynicism. In this series, those two worlds could never be reconciled, so Morrison turned to metafiction to deal with the inconsistencies.

When we return to Buddy Baker's quest, we find Merryman giving directions on how to reach the City of Formation (where all stories derive): "Head east, past the great ruined cities of Atlas and Warren." Atlas and Warren were, of course, comic book publishers from an earlier age.[102] Eventually, Buddy discovers that his path has been circular. He returns to his own home, where he finds that the monkey (the one who had been typing earlier in the issue) has died. Buddy wrests the papers from the dead monkey's paw and begins to read the script for the issue which we're now reading. He sees the words on the page reflecting what he's just experienced, and when he gets to the page where he's reading about himself reading about himself (*ad infinitum*), he refuses to do what the script indicates he will do next. "I won't go," he says. Immediately, he changes his mind: "Or maybe I will [go]," he says. He gives in to fate, cuts the pages of the script to fashion a crude skeleton key, opens the door in front of him, and finds himself walking through an uninhabited city. He soon reaches the front door of a pale young man, who says, "I'm Grant. You coming in?"

His quest for redemption has brought him face to face with his god, and *Animal Man* #26, Morrison's final issue, is aptly titled "Deus Ex Machina." If Morrison's run on the series has been a strange one, alternating between a straightforward attempt to update Animal Man for the late 1980s and a self-referential mediation on comic book reality (and it has) then the final issue is perhaps the only appropriate way to wrap it all up. By allowing himself to

---

[102] Atlas was the company that would become Marvel Comics in the 1950s. Warren was the publisher of black and white horror titles like *Creepy* and *Eerie*.

become a character in Animal Man's story, Morrison can provide a critical overview of his own work and give Buddy Baker one last chance to redeem himself by convincing "God" to set things right.

Throughout *Animal Man* #26, color cues are used to indicate the break between the "real world" of Grant Morrison and the comic book world inhabited by Animal Man. The "real world" is colored with desaturated hues, lots of tans and dull greens and browns (and Morrison's face and hands are white – not flesh-colored), while Animal Man is his normal, garish orange and blue. This technique indicates that Morrison inhabits a different plane of reality than Buddy Baker, and it once again emphasizes the contrast between the starkness of reality and the brilliant colors of fantasy.

The vast majority of the issue is a dialogue between Morrison and Buddy Baker in which Morrison explains the nature of the comic book reality which Buddy inhabits. When Buddy asks if Morrison is God, Morrison replies, "I'm more of a demiurgic power. Someone else creates you to be perfect and innocent and then I step in and spoil everything. It's a little bit Satanic, I suppose." When Animal Man explodes in a fury of violence directed toward this malevolent god, Morrison points out how well he knows Buddy's inner character: "You're not really violent, are you? You've never really been one of those horrible characters with a gun in every pocket and too much testosterone. You've seen the futility of violence, haven't you?" This is Morrison coming to terms with his own treatment of Buddy's character (after all, he did make Buddy take brutal revenge against Lennox and the cabal), and it's pointing out to the reader that Animal Man's whole problem is that he has been displaced. He is a pacifist in violent times. He is not the Punisher, nor was he meant to be.

When Buddy finds copies of previous *Animal Man* issues lying around Morrison's house, he flips through to see the gruesome image of his slaughtered family. Aghast, Buddy says, "Do you know what you've done to me?" "Of course I know," Morrison replies, "I wrote your grief and your rage and your acceptance. It added drama. All stories need drama and it's easy to get a cheap emotional shock by killing popular characters." Morrison's words are both an explanation of his own technique and an indictment of the way that writers can manipulate the emotions of their audience.

Morrison later explains, "I've been planning this meeting for nearly two

From *Animal Man* #26 – Animal Man meets his maker as Grant Morrison explains it all. Art by Chas Truog and Mark Farmer. Copyright © DC Comics.

years. I had so much to say. It was going to be a really good story. But there's not enough space." Buddy responds by asking, "Am I real or what?" Morrison replies, "Of course you're real! We wouldn't be here talking if you weren't real. You existed long before I wrote about you and if you're lucky, you'll still be young when I'm old or dead... You're more real than I am." Their conversation continues after Morrison displays his ability to conjure things from his mind and turn them into images in Buddy's world, leading to the following discussion.

In this simple exchange, Morrison destroys David Bohm's Implicate Order Theory. In Buddy Baker's universe, everything isn't connected, as much as the writer might want it to be. Furthermore, Morrison explains his predisposition for anticlimax, which has been a staple of his comic book stories since *Zenith*, as one of his flaws as a writer, blaming it on a life filled with anticlimactic events. In many ways, *Animal Man* is the antithesis of *Zenith*, though. *Zenith*'s four phases ultimately were connected intricately, and the anticlimaxes were effective to undermine the conventions of heroic sacrifice. In *Animal Man*, the only real connection between events is that Grant Morrison himself has been pulling the strings all along, and the themes of *family* and *heroism*, though dominant, don't provide enough of a structural framework to tie everything together. *Zenith* may have been Morrison's comment on pop culture super-heroics, and *Animal Man* is his comment on the comic book medium. Therefore, it's difficult to analyze the stories on a character or thematic level in a truthful way because *Animal Man* is about the process of creation as much as it's about the thing actually created.

As Morrison (the comic book character) explains, "Life doesn't have plots and subplots and dénouements. It's just a big collection of loose ends and dangling threads that never get explained." These types of explanations do little to satisfy Buddy Baker, of course, so he asks the big question: "If you can do anything... if you can... will you bring my family back?" It's the final stab at redemption – requesting a boon from his god. Unfortunately, Morrison is bound by the conventions of his time, and he says, "Sorry. It wouldn't be realistic. Pointless violence and death is 'realistic.' Comic books are 'realistic' now." He seems to lament this fact, but, even as a creator, he is unable to change the larger social forces that determine how comic books "should" be written. It reflects Morrison's own frustration at the expectations of the comic book marketplace and once again points to the loss of innocence that has burdened the medium between the first appearance of Animal Man and his most recent incarnation. Morrison, like Buddy Baker, would no doubt like to turn back time to an earlier era, but he knows that innocence can never be regained. Yet, while it cannot be regained, Morrison wants to remind us that it should not be forgotten either.

Thus, he ends the series with a strangely satisfying conclusion. Although everything we've learned in *Animal Man* has prepared us for the "reality" of Buddy Baker's family never coming back, Morrison tells Buddy to "go home," where, sure enough, he finds his wife and children alive and well.

I say it's "strangely satisfying" because we want to be able to regain that innocence once lost, and yet we have been told time and again within the series that these are just fictional characters under the control of a manipulative writer. How could their fate possibly matter to us if the illusion of their reality has been constantly disrupted? The answer, as Morrison has already explained, is simple: Buddy Baker is real. More real, even, than Grant Morrison. Buddy exists in our minds, because we have, as readers, participated in his life. No matter what metafictional tricks Morrison has played on us, we have seen things as Buddy sees them. It's been his journey we've followed, his side we've rooted for, even when he wasn't the best example of a hero. That's the strength of storytelling. Fictional characters are more real than flesh-and-blood humans, Morrison implies, because they endure.[103] Fashions and trends and contexts may change, but characters live on, in our memories, in our hearts. By the end, has Buddy Baker gained redemption? His family is alive once again, and that's all the redemption he needs.

The epilogue of "Deus Ex Machina" leaves the newly reunited Baker family behind to show us a bit more of Grant Morrison as he provides the coda to his run on the series. In the final few pages, he describes how, as a child, he used to signal to his imaginary friend, Foxy (who, you may remember, guided Animal Man through his hallucinations on the mesa earlier in the series), with a flashlight. Foxy would apparently signal back from the distant mountainside, but as Morrison grew older, he realized that it was not Foxy signaling back, it was just the headlights from passing cars rounding a turn miles away. *Animal Man* #26 ends with the adult Morrison trying once

---

[103] Morrison has been known to say that "Superman is realer" than we are because, as a fictional character, he will outlast us all.

more to signal to his former imaginary friend, and this time there is no light in the distance providing a response. It's only as he turns away that a beacon appears, but it's too late; Morrison has given up and doesn't see the reply. Morrison, by ending his run on *Animal Man* with this bit of himself, reminds us that the series has been about trying to recapture a more innocent time. It's been about memory, and loss, and growing up to face the harsh realities of life (and all the choices, heroic or not, that we must face). But it has also been about that glimmer of hope in the distance, the recognition that Foxy may be gone (he may not have ever existed) but not forgotten. By bringing back the absurd, ridiculous characters from an earlier era (from B'wana Beast through Ultraman) and showing us, with sadness, how great the universe was when characters weren't always so grim and gritty (while, at the same time, showing the futility of violence and destruction), Morrison does more than just criticize the comic book industry – he reminds us all to celebrate the things that mattered to us when we were young. "Realistic" super-hero comic books are no less ridiculous than super-pets or Merrymen; they're just less fun.

In his 26 issues of *Animal Man*, Grant Morrison gave us a chronicle of his struggle trying to reconcile his sense of wonder about the past with his responsibilities as a contemporary comic book writer. Early in the series, he gave in to the temptation of "realism" and "relevance," and the rest of the series was his attempt to reject those very notions. By the end, the series became *about* the inner conflict that Morrison faced until he had no choice but to wrap it all up in a final conversation between a man and his creator. As schizophrenic as *Animal Man* is at times, it may be, paradoxically, Morrison's most complete work. Its flaws become its beauty in many ways, showing us a talented mind struggling to say something new about a tired old genre. In *Animal Man*, Morrison peels back the curtain to show us the wizard in all of his failure, and the honesty with which he does that is worth as much, if not more, than all the slick, tightly plotted, "successful" comic books of his contemporaries. If Morrison's autobiography is written across all of his comic books, and *Zenith* was representative of his rebellious teenage years, and *Arkham Asylum* is his youthful obsession with symbols and meaning, then *Animal Man* is his struggle to grow up, to leave his overt influences behind, and begin to have fun on his own terms, and it's exhilarating to see.

# *Batman: Gothic*

In the midst of Grant Morrison's extended run as writer of both *Animal Man* and *Doom Patrol*, he returned to the Batman character in a five-issue arc which was originally published in *Batman: Legends of the Dark Knight* #6-10. The story, entitled *Gothic*, was not nearly as ambitious as *Arkham Asylum*, but it does present an interesting perspective on the Batman mythos.

Structurally, *Gothic* is an homage to the traditional stories as seen in the monthly *Batman* or *Detective Comics* serials. In essence, Batman must use his detective skills, his crimefighting abilities, and his gadgets to stop a maniacal villain and save Gotham City. It's not a symbolic psychological struggle like *Arkham Asylum*. It's a relatively standard comic book story with a well-above-average pedigree. For even at his most straightforward, Grant Morrison uses literary devices and stylistic twists that add layers of meaning to the narrative. *Gothic*, for all its super-hero trappings, is, at its core, a dark romance in the classical sense.

The term "Gothic," so inherent in Batman's world that his home city is named after it, can be readily used in relation to two main art forms: architecture and literature. Gothic architecture, of the type widely seen in Gotham City, is based on the design of the pointed arch, which is used throughout the structure. In addition, Gothic architecture employs flying buttresses, ribbed vaults, large windows, and gargoyles. This style would be completely familiar to anyone who's ever read a *Batman* comic book, and it's not surprising that Morrison uses it here. What is unique about Morrison's approach is that he makes Gothic architecture a central plot point in the narrative. The climax of the story isn't just set in a Gothic cathedral, it involves the use of Gothic architectural design for supernatural purposes.

Gothic literature, a tradition which began in 18th century Europe, also involves supernatural elements. Essentially, Gothic literature is an off-shoot of Romanticism. The Romantics rejected industrialization and the rigid conformity of the Age of Reason, and they chose to embrace the wisdom of the past and return to the purity and innocence of nature. Medieval "romances," stories about valiant knights on impossible quests, gave the Romantic poets and novelists the inspiration for their name, and the stories of the courageous heroes of the Medieval romances provided source material for writers in an industrial age trying to recall the glory of earlier days. Gothic literature adds a darker dimension to the stories of the Romantics. A Romantic writer might describe beautiful fairies that inhabit the green forest, while a Gothic writer would describe the hideous monsters and demonic forces that lurk in the murky wilderness. Batman is a questing knight, but he lives in a twisted Gothic world in which supernatural forces conspire to destroy the purity of life. Grant Morrison's *Gothic* implies these ideas in its title and in its execution.

Morrison begins each volume of the five-part *Gothic* story with an elaborately designed frontispiece reminiscent of a Gothic novel. The illustration features an ornate frame made from brambles with a rose at the bottom-center. The rose appears regularly as a symbol in Gothic literature as the embodiment of the Gothic sensibility: its beauty is undercut by the sharp and dangerous thorns. Neither Batman nor any bat-like words or images appear on this opening page. All it says is,

**Gothic**

**a romance**

By Grant Morrison and Klaus Janson[104]

---

[104] Klaus Janson, the artist of the five volumes of *Gothic*, is an appropriate collaborator for at least three reasons: (1) He was Frank Miller's inker on *The Dark Knight Returns*, and his scratchy pen line here evokes the work on that most influential of graphic novels. (2) He is more of an expressionist than a realist. His figures and landscapes are often asymmetrical, and he's not afraid to use black spaces. (3) He seems unable (or unwilling) to draw beautiful people. Even his depictions of Bruce Wayne's childhood show the Wayne family with slightly distorted faces. His characters aren't grotesque, but they look tortured. All in all, the perfect collaborator for a moody Gothic tale.

IN FIVE VOLUMES

"But that I am forbid to tell
the secrets of my prison house
I could a tale unfold whose lightest word
would harrow up thy soul..."
— HAMLET

volume one
**Man Without a Shadow**

The look of the page indicates that the story will be much more literary than the customary Batman tale, and the epigraph comes from Shakespeare's most Gothic play. The quotation from *Hamlet* alludes to the slain king's torment in hell, which not only sets the mood for Morrison's story, it provides a clue about the direction in which the story is headed.

Batman doesn't appear in costume until page 15 – in the first 14 pages Morrison establishes the themes and motifs which will dominate *Gothic*. The first image on page one shows a God's-eye-view of Gotham City before shifting to a close-up on a battered face in panel two. The theme of *violence* is emphasized immediately with this image, and we soon find out that this battered face belongs to a man hanging by his feet from a warehouse ceiling. A larger man with a baseball bat is causing the brutalization while cracking jokes. He says, "You know what they call me? The bat-man, is what. Pretty funny, huh?" So the first "bat-man" Morrison gives us is a fat gangster with a penchant for tank tops and physical violence. Immediately, he undermines our expectations.

Three important motifs are also established in this opening sequence. The first, the *bell* motif, is evoked by a recording of the "Oranges and Lemons" rhyme which the "bat-man," O'Rourke, finds ominously playing on a phonograph in the shadows of the warehouse. The "Oranges and Lemons" rhyme is an English nursery rhyme dating back to the 18th century, if not earlier. It begins, "Oranges and lemons, say the bells of St. Clement's / You owe me five farthings, say the bells of St. Martin's..." and describes the bells of various churches answering each other back and forth. The rhyme ends with the lines, "Here comes a candle to light you to bed / Here comes a chopper to chop off your head," which certainly connects to the theme of violence we've already seen. But it's the bells that really matter, although Morrison doesn't explain why until the final volume of the story. The nursery rhyme also connects to the second motif: *childhood*. Like many Batman stories, and like Morrison's own work in *Arkham Asylum*, Batman is haunted by his past, particularly his childhood and the murder of his parents. The "Oranges and Lemons" rhyme is just the first impression of that motif as used throughout *Gothic*. The third motif, *poetry*, directly implied on the title page, is referenced in the opening sequence when O'Rourke finds a card on the phonograph which bears the words, "Like one that on a lonesome road, doth walk in fear and dread..." The words come from Samuel Taylor Coleridge's famous poem, "The Rime of the Ancient Mariner," the most Gothic of all the Romantic poems.[105] All three of the motifs – bells, childhood, and poetry – tie the mysteries of the story together.

Thematically, while *Arkham Asylum* was about mothers and sons, *Gothic* is about *fatherhood.* The father theme is introduced relatively soon in the story – within the first ten pages. Morrison uses another motif, *dreams*, to establish Batman's memories of his schoolboy days and his sense of loss relating to his father's death. In the first dream sequence, we see a young Bruce Wayne talking to a schoolmate. "It's not a school, it's a cathedral," young Bruce says, adding more than a bit of foreshadowing. It's the end of the dream sequence that connects thematically, though, as young Bruce sees a shadowy figure and screams out, "Father? Oh father, they told me you were dead. Father? Father, I've missed you so much. Speak to me. Please. Please just say..." When Bruce's father turns around, we see in horror that his mouth has been sewn shut. With that image, Batman (as Bruce Wayne, in his mansion) awakens from the dream. Morrison's repetition of the word "father" in the dream sequence shows Batman's obsession with his father's death, and the sealed mouth symbol suggests a secret which Bruce's father was unable to share. As we find out later, Thomas Wayne does indeed have something to tell his son, even from beyond the grave. It is a Gothic story after all.[106]

---

[105] "The Rime of the Ancient Mariner," which tells of a crime against nature, is most effective when it describes the ghastly terror of the voyage. Coleridge is clearly more at home in the parts of the poem that read like a dark opium dream. When the Mariner later blesses the sea creatures as his heart fills with love, the reader senses that Coleridge is trying to shoehorn Romantic idealism into an essentially Gothic poem.

[106] Although Thomas Wayne does not appear as a literal ghost in *Gothic*, his presence is felt in dreams and artifacts (as you'll see) throughout the story. Thus, he

When Bruce Wayne tells his butler, Alfred, about the dream, Bruce says, "It was the same dream," a phrase which he repeats three times as if in disbelief. Unlike *Arkham Asylum*, which used a dream-like narrative throughout the story, dreams in *Gothic* are used much more traditionally: they reveal unconscious understanding and present symbols that the dreamer (and the reader) must interpret. The narrative takes place in the "real world" of Gotham City, but the dreams allow Morrison to emphasize the father theme without the heavy-handed device of placing Batman's internal monologue in captions.[107]

Meanwhile, in that "real world" of Gotham City, bad things are happening. People are being murdered and, in each case, the victim finds a card bearing a few lines of poetry immediately before their death. I mentioned the excerpt from "The Rime of the Ancient Mariner" before, and O'Rourke, who found the poetry, died at the hands of a mysterious man. The second death occurs after the victim finds a verse from John Milton's *Paradise Lost*. The lines in question tell of Satan's fall from grace, and they do more than indicate the presence of a serial killer with a gimmick (giving poems to his intended victims) – the *Paradise Lost* excerpt also provides a clue to the nature of the killer. Batman is a detective, after all, and clues are part of the game. In fact, Morrison plays with all of the pieces of the Batman game in *Gothic*, perhaps because he created such an isolated, claustrophobic mood in *Arkham Asylum*. Here, he makes sure he throws in all the classic Batman traditions, including (but not limited to): Alfred, the Batcave, the bat-signal, Batman's utility belt, and the elaborate death trap.[108] These conventions are part of the fun of a classic Batman story, and Morrison gives them his own unique twist.

In terms of Batman's psyche in this story, Morrison implies more than he

---

"haunts" Batman in typical Gothic tradition.

[107] Besides the overwhelming darkness and "realism" which pervaded the post-*Dark Knight Returns* Batman stories, a tortured internal monologue gained prominence as well. Thought balloons were replaced by narrative captions which revealed the grim, humorless mentality of the Caped Crusader. Morrison avoids that technique entirely in *Gothic*.

[108] Because these traditional Batman elements were so prominent in the campy 1960s *Batman* television show, many writers would be timid about adding them to a serious Gothic narrative. Not Morrison, though. He embraces absurdity and makes it matter.

From *Batman: Legends of the Dark Knight* #6 – Bruce Wayne and Alfred Pennyworth at Wayne Manor before a night on the town. Art by Klaus Janson. Copyright © DC Comics.

states. For example, he doesn't have Batman describe his obsession with his parent's death, and he doesn't write yet another flashback to that fateful walk in the alley. Instead, he simply shows Bruce Wayne sitting in his study. All the clocks in the room show *8:25*. It's a comic book panel, it doesn't move anyway, so the image doesn't indicate that the clocks are stopped, but Alfred mentions Bruce's "morbid introspection in a room full of stopped clocks." No one ever mentions in the story that Batman's parents died at 8:25. We understand because of the context. It's a nice, subtle moment from Morrison that tells us more than enough about Bruce Wayne's inner demons.

As Morrison cuts away from Bruce Wayne in the mansion to the world of decay that is Gotham City, he shows us a bit more about the string of murders. We find out that someone named Mr. Whisper is killing these people, and we also learn that it involves the organized crime families in Gotham.[109] Morrison gives us just enough to know that Mr. Whisper is getting revenge for something, and we see another character die at his hands without knowing anything about his motivation. Besides the abundance of death, Morrison also includes another Gothic feature at this moment when one of the characters mentions Mr. Whisper and says, "How many other guys have no shadow? It's him!" Since Mr. Whisper does not, in fact, cast a shadow, that places him in the realm of the supernatural. It also establishes him as Batman's antithesis, since Batman, in effect, is all about casting a shadow.

Another supernatural element is jokingly introduced by a newscaster who, when flubbing a line in a broadcast, blames the "gremlins" or "gargoyles." His joke reminds us of the Gothic elements of the story, but his scene is important for another reason: he provides exposition about the reopening of Gotham Cathedral, which has just undergone five years of restoration. The cathedral is a dominant Gothic element that's central to the

---

[109] Although Morrison includes nearly all of the traditional Batman trappings in this story, he completely avoids any mention of Batman's rogues gallery. The in-story conceit for this is that *Gothic* takes place early in Batman's career, although just how early is never clearly established. But in *Batman: Legends of the Dark Knight*, the comic book in which it was printed, the story was designed to showcase Batman's early years, so one might assume that Batman had not been introduced to many costumed villains at that time. The other likely possibility is that Morrison had already explored Batman's relationship with his evil counterparts in *Arkham Asylum*, and he didn't want to cover the same ground again.

story.

As mentioned earlier, when Batman finally springs into action, in costume, diving from the rooftops to the streets below, we're already fifteen pages into the story. Batman's targets are two violent, knife-wielding adolescents, reminiscent of the droogs from Anthony Burgess's *A Clockwork Orange*.[110] They harass an elderly business man, saying, "We don't want your money. We just want to cut you into little bits." Batman lurks in the shadows, whispering, "We are all in Hell," before leaping into view and shouting, "I am the King of Hell!" Such overt references to the torment of the underworld fits perfectly into the Gothic atmosphere of the story, but it is still quite unusual to see Batman compare himself to Satan.

Meanwhile, Mr. Whisper appears again in a scene intercut with Batman's quick battle with the two young street thugs. In an opera house, during a performance of Mozart's *Don Giovanni*, Mr. Whisper leaves his seat and drops off a box of chocolates with the usher and tells him to deliver them to Mr. Graziano. The usher asks if Mr. Whisper had been unhappy with the performance, and Mr. Whisper replies, "On the contrary: 'Don Giovanni' is one of my favorites. It's just the ending, you see. I don't like the ending." *Don Giovanni* ends with the title character, refusing to repent his sins, getting sucked down into the depths of Hell. As the opera reaches its climax, the box of chocolates explodes, sending a blast of fire into the night sky. The *Don Giovanni* reference and the line from Batman with the adolescents are just two of many mentions of the *Hell* motif Morrison uses throughout *Gothic*.

Because of Mr. Whisper's murder spree, the organized crime families, out of fear, resort to extraordinary tactics, and as the first volume of *Gothic* ends, Batman, perched on a rooftop, looks out onto the city to see an inverted bat-signal blazing in the sky – a sacrilegious cry for help from the crime bosses.

Volume two of *Gothic*, entitled "The Death Ship," opens with the same title page design as the first volume, but the epigraph has changed. This time it reads, "How fast she nears and nears! / Are those her sails that glance in

---

[110] They bear no resemblance to actual teenage criminals from our world or the traditional "reality" of Gotham City: They have masks over half their faces and wear kneepads. They seem to be from some unhappy future reality. No explanation is ever given for their strange appearance.

the sun, / Like restless gossameres?" This excerpt, from Samuel Taylor Coleridge's "The Rime of the Ancient Mariner," refers to the ship of death which visits the Ancient Mariner during his nightmare voyage, connecting the title of the volume and the epigraph. The ship of death will literally appear in *Gothic* before the story is over, and the reference here foreshadows events to come and reinforces the darkly romantic mood of the narrative.

In "The Death Ship," Batman confronts the men who summoned him with the inverted bat-signal. Batman demands that they never use that symbol again as they plead for his help. They offer to suspend their illegal activities, "keep the streets clean," until he finds Mr. Whisper. "You want to bargain? With me?" asks Batman. His use of the word *bargain* is indicative of Morrison's intent with this scene. Morrison invokes a classic element of Gothic storytelling, the *Faustian bargain.* If Batman is the king of Hell, then the men are trying to make a deal with the Devil in the tradition of the Faust legends.[111] Such a bargain parallels the one apparently made by Mr. Whisper, who, according to the mob bosses, died twenty years earlier. "We killed him and he won't stay dead," one of them says. The supernatural motif of the dead man rising up to avenge his death is nothing new in literature, and Morrison plays with this Gothic convention to provide Batman with an enemy who is more than just a deranged cartoon character.

Morrison returns to the dream motif in this volume as Batman dreams of death ships, school rooms, "Ring Around the Rosie," and his mute father scrawling "Unlock the Rose" in the sand. Although these recurring dreams seem abstract and disjointed, Morrison uses the themes and ideas from these dreams throughout the story. In a highly structured manner, the dreams are suggestive of the larger plot. Everything Batman dreams about in these early nightmares will make sense when the true nature of Mr. Whisper is revealed. Batman realizes this during his waking hours, but his logical, deductive mind is incapable of interpreting such symbols. He tells Alfred, "I feel as though I'm trying to do a jigsaw puzzle in the dark." Unlike Morrison's use of symbolism in *Arkham Asylum*, where the symbolism was the meaning of the entire work, Morrison uses the symbolism in *Gothic* to provide plot clues. The symbolic dreams are not the point of the narrative here, just one aspect

[111] According to legend, Faust sold his soul to the devil to gain power. This is one of the archetypal stories throughout literature – the tale of a man who literally, or metaphorically, gives up his soul for personal gain.

of the journey.

Batman does piece some of the puzzle together rather quickly, though, since he has heard Mr. Whisper referred to as a man with no shadow. As a boy, Bruce Wayne knew a man without a shadow: his old schoolmaster, Mr. Winchester. Batman recalls his terrible school experiences and the abuse he received at the hands of this sadistic monster. Batman also recalls that his schoolmate may have been killed by Mr. Winchester, but young Bruce Wayne was more traumatized by fact that the schoolmaster lacked a shadow. Morrison doesn't use Batman's past here as an excuse for deep psychological inquiry, like he did in *Arkham Asylum*. Instead, he uses it as just another plot point and, thematically, as a way to connect a father figure, the old schoolmaster, with Batman's current elusive nemesis.

The remainder of volume two picks up the pace, as Mr. Whisper attempts to continue his revenge killings and Batman attempts to stop him. Morrison actually gives the reader an action sequence in the final half of "The Death Ship," with the apparently immortal Mr. Whisper escaping Batman's attempts at capture. This sequence is atypical Morrison in that it's relatively straightforward (except for Batman almost choking to death from getting his cape caught on a cherub statue), but action sequences are just one of the many Batman traditions that Morrison willingly goes along with in *Gothic*. As I've said earlier in this analysis, Morrison employs all the famous Batman conventions in this story, and the chase-and-escape is just one of them.

Volume three, "The Burning Nun," again opens with the same title page design, and the new epigraph comes from Charles Baudelaire's "The Evil Monk" (although Morrison gives us the title and verse in the original French). Translated by Lewis Piaget Shanks, the lines read, "my soul's a tomb, which – wretched friar! – I / have paced since Time began, and occupy; / bare-walled and hateful still my cloister stands." Self-loathing, immortality, religion, imprisonment, corruption – these concepts are implied in the epigraph and realized more fully in the text of *Gothic*.

The plot of volume three features a deeper investigation into the mysteries surrounding Mr. Whisper. Batman, as Bruce Wayne, visits his old prep school to retrieve tapes of his old schoolmaster reading Romantic poetry. After seeing Mr. Whisper up close during the pursuit in volume two, Batman is convinced that the man he knew as Mr. Winchester is the same man who is terrorizing the Gotham City underworld. By listening to the tapes, he hopes to gain an understanding of Mr. Whisper and identify his origin. The computer identifies the accent as Austrian, but when Batman attempts to cross-reference the audio with tapes of regional dialects, he hears a surprising voice: his father's. Batman has misfiled the reference tapes and accidentally listened to a recording of himself and his father made when Bruce was a child. On the old recording, Thomas Wayne talks about a possible vacation spot for the family: "the beautiful Lake Dess with its famous drowned monastery." Although Alfred is skeptical about the "tenuous" connection between his father's words, as recorded decades before, and the current case, Batman takes it as a clue and rushes off to visit Lake Dess personally.[112] Notice how Batman's father continues to haunt him, metaphorically speaking, and how quickly Batman takes the words of his father to heart.

Morrison, as he does throughout *Gothic*, includes classic Batman tropes in this sequence, as he shows Batman using his high-tech bat-computer to provide voice analysis on the tape recording before uncovering the bat-gyro (the helicopter / plane with scalloped wings) and flying across Gotham City, silhouetted by the moon. These conventions of the Batman mythos appear in hundreds of stories, and Morrison includes them as essential elements of the tale he's telling. He doesn't throw them in as an inside joke to comic fans. He's trying to tell a Batman story, and what would a Batman story be without all the cool bat-gadgets? It's yet another example of Morrison's disdain for the grim-and-gritty "realism" of the time. He's giving us a serious Batman story, but he doesn't strip away the fantastic mythology to do so. Instead, he embraces the ridiculous conventions and makes them integral to the character and, thus, the narrative.

When Batman arrives in Austria, his quest to find Lake Dess leads him to an Abbot who holds an illuminating story for Batman. The Abbot tells a tale from centuries earlier about a monk named Brother Manfred who was "drawn into that darkness from which there is no return." Manfred swayed his brothers toward the evil path, and they lived lives of debauchery until the

---

[112] As a clue, the fact that Bruce Wayne's father mentions a lake in an old recording is useless. It's irrelevant, logically speaking. It's just a random thing his father said years and years ago. But in Morrison's tale, and in Gothic fiction, their are no coincidences. A random statement in an old recording is as valuable as a fingerprint according to the dream-like logic of a Gothic narrative. It's not out of place in Morrison's work, echoing, as it does, the idea of a pattern beneath the chaos.

black plague struck. Then, according to the Abbot, Brother Manfred "called upon the fallen angel and pledged his soul to hell, in return for release from the plague and three hundred years of life." The Devil apparently accepted the terms of the bargain, for Brother Manfred was cured. "There was to be no escape from God's judgment," for Manfred's brother Capuchins,[113] however, as the river Dess tore through the hillsides and purified the monastery. The Abbot described Manfred and his men surviving the event, piloting a "spectral death ship on an endless nightmare voyage."[114] This piece of evidence, providing an explanation – one steeped in Romantic legend – for Mr. Whisper's apparent immortality, gives Batman the answers he seeks, but he's not done in Austria yet. He visits the drowned monastery and sees the burning nun, a glowing figure who haunts Lake Dess in memory of her torture at the hands of Manfred and his brothers. This ghost, who Batman seems to regard as a trick of the light, leads him toward a secret panel in a wall. He remembers a clue from the dream of his father: "Unlock the rose." As he twists the rose engraving, a secret chamber reveals a blueprint for Gotham Cathedral.

*Gothic* is more plot-driven than any other Morrison story from this period, and many of the scenes simply work together to drive the narrative forward, but Morrison ties everything together with a tight structure. And, unlike *Arkham Asylum*, which was full of symbolic patterns, *Gothic* is full of mood and texture. It's much more literal than any other Morrison work at the time, but it still maintains a certain dream-like quality with its reliance on coincidence and supernatural elements. Batman follows the clues, but he never seems to be totally in control of his fate as he pieces the puzzle together. He just happened to accidentally listen to his father's old recording, which leads him to an Abbot who happens to tell him about a three hundred-year-old legend that explains everything about Mr. Whisper, and the ghost of a dead nun just happens to lead him to Mr. Whisper's three hundred-year-old plan for a cathedral of evil, which just happens to be

---

[113] Manfred and his fellows are identified as members of the Capuchin order, an offshoot of the Franciscan monks.

[114] Klaus Janson's illustration which accompanies these words shows a death ship which bears more than a little resemblance to the ship described by Coleridge in "The Rime of the Ancient Mariner." If it is the same ship, then Coleridge's poem can be considered part of DC continuity.

opening in Gotham later in the week. Yet all of these plot points, and the scenes in which they occur, evoke the feeling of a dark romance, and that's the point of the story.

Volume four, "The Hangman's Tale," opens with the same illustrated title page as the other volumes but with an epigraph from Thomas de Quincey's *On Murder Considered as One of the Fine Arts*, which features the line, "All perils, specially malignant, are recurrent." On that dark note, which seems to allude to the return of Mr. Whisper, Batman returns to Gotham, just in time to stop a gunman from hurting a young hostage. The scene has no bearing on the Mr. Whisper plotline, but it establishes that Batman is back home, and the terror of the gunman, who screams "Nooooo," as he cowers before Batman's stoic form, emphasizes the terrifying, demonic aspect of Batman himself. Morrison reminds us that Batman is no white knight, but rather a dark figure who lives in a tainted world. The literal Faustian bargain made by Brother Manfred three hundred years ago is echoed in the character of Batman, who has renounced his humanity for the sake of his own vengeance. As in all Gothic tales, no true goodness exists, just varying degrees of corruption.

Batman confronts Morgenstern, a crime boss, to find out more about Mr. Whisper's connection with the Gotham City underworld. Morgenstern admits that he and his men tried to kill Whisper twenty years before, going so far as to hack him up with an axe, but as he explains, "It was like his body just kept fixing itself and all the time Whisper kept screaming that he'd get us, he'd make us pay." Ultimately, the men dumped Whisper in the river with an anchor tied around his waist. Morrison emphasizes the nightmarish nature of *Gothic* as Morgenstern concludes by saying, "Bad dream over... We all woke up, we all got old, and all the time, he was waiting."

Back in the Batcave, Batman searches for the connection between all the clues. "I wish I knew a little more about sacred geometry," he tells Alfred, before going into expository mode. "I read somewhere," Batman explains, "that the term 'Gothic' might possibly be derived from the word 'goetic' – *goes* in the Greek – meaning 'magical.'" Yet he can't make sense of everything he's discovered. "A man with no shadow who's lived for over three hundred years. Dreams. Ghosts. Murdered children and occult architecture. How does it all connect?" he wonders. Then he shifts into deductive mode, providing, for himself, Alfred, and the reader, an indication of Mr. Whisper's plan. He explains that the architecture of any Gothic cathedral is based on an arch called the *ogive*, which would direct all the forces of the building upward. Batman says, "The cathedral became a transmitter, aimed toward God." He realizes that the Gothic cathedral is a mechanism which focuses spiritual power and wonders if such an instrument could be used for evil.

Batman's revelation is important, and it foreshadows the climax of the story, but what's interesting about it isn't just the pseudo-scientific explanation of the power within a cathedral, it's the way Morrison juxtaposes this exposition with a sequence of panels showing Alfred and Batman eating sandwiches as they discuss these ideas. It grounds the fantastic elements of their conversation with domestic reality. And Morrison's use of sandwiches (as opposed to caviar or steak) indicates the casual family bond between Alfred and Batman. They are like co-workers on their lunch break, or, more accurately, Batman is the child figure, taking a break from playtime, and Alfred is the patient and devoted father figure who makes the comfort food.

The theme of *fatherhood* should not be overlooked in this story, and Morrison connects the idea even further by transitioning from the lunch conversation to a flashback of how young Bruce Wayne escaped the torment of his demented schoolmaster. Batman, in the present, describes how his father, "arrived the next day [after a beating by Mr. Winchester / Mr. Whisper], like a knight in shining armor." Batman reveals that he was just glad that his father was taking him home, but he ends the memory by alluding to the most fateful night of his life, indicating that his father wanted to celebrate young Bruce's return home by going out to a movie. Morrison doesn't tell us any more than that, but Batman's parents were gunned down after leaving a movie theater, so he's implying an indirect connection between Mr. Whisper and the death of Batman's parents. If young Bruce hadn't needed to be rescued from the school, and if they hadn't all gone out to celebrate that night, Batman's parents might never have died. Thus, Mr. Whisper is bound up in Batman's memories of his parent's death.

Volume four ends with an extended climax, in which Batman, investigating the interior of Gotham Cathedral, finds dozens of dead bodies hanging from the rafters. Mr. Whisper soon appears, and Morrison throws in another Batman convention as Batman tosses an ineffective batarang in Whisper's direction. Since Whisper can't be hurt or killed, the battle ends quickly, and Batman soon finds himself in another conventional situation: caught in a death trap as the villain provides exposition.

Whisper reveals that young Bruce Wayne[115] would have been his eighth victim if Batman's father hadn't intervened. But Whisper points out that Thomas Wayne never got a chance to expose him because of the Wayne's tragic death. Whisper provides a cruel, but unsurprising, perspective on Batman's psyche, saying, "you were plunged into the darkness. You're still little more than a brutalized child for whom the world is all shadows and fear. I pity you. I suppose it's a kind of hell." But Whisper is going to relieve Batman from his psychological torment because he plans to unleash a "refined killing elixir – a pestilential brew" which will kill the inhabitants of Gotham. When the bell strikes midnight,

> its tone will reverberate through the cathedral, shattering the glass that contains the plague. Twenty-four hours later, the citizens of Gotham will all be dead, their souls trapped within the structure of my cathedral. And those souls I will offer as a gift to Satan, in lieu of my own. I will cheat the Devil.

After revealing his plan, in typical super-villain-who-has-the-hero-in-a-fatal-trap manner, Whisper leaves the cathedral on the final page of volume four and shouts, "Out, brief candle!" – in reference to the candle which will set the death trap in motion when it burns out. It's also an allusion to Shakespeare's *Macbeth* and the famous words Macbeth says upon learning of the death of his wife:

> To-morrow, and to-morrow, and to-morrow,
> Creeps in this petty pace from day to day
> To the last syllable of recorded time,
> And all our yesterdays have lighted fools
> The way to dusty death. Out, out, brief candle!
> Life's but a walking shadow, a poor player
> That struts and frets his hour upon the stage
> And then is heard no more: it is a tale
> Told by an idiot, full of sound and fury,
> Signifying nothing.

Morrison's reference to *Macbeth* ties in the poetry motif once again, but it also provides a clue about how *Gothic* will conclude, after all the "sound and fury" is over.

The final volume of the five-part story begins with a red-saturated title

---

[115] Whisper easily recognizes that Batman is Bruce Wayne, just as Batman easily recognized Mr. Whisper as the man he once knew as Mr. Winchester.

page featuring an epigraph from Christopher Marlowe's *Doctor Faustus*: "The stars move still, time runs, / the clock will strike, / The Devil will come / and Faustus must be damn'd." Morrison, through Marlowe, reminds us that every Faustian bargain ends with the Devil getting his due, and this volume, entitled "Walpurgisnacht" in reference to the pagan fertility ritual mentioned in Goethe's *Faust*, reveals the outcome of Whisper's plan to escape his fate.

"Walpurgisnacht" opens with three pages of rigid nine-panel grid layouts, systematically showing each step of the death trap as it triggers, coming closer and closer to killing Batman. In the final panel of the third page, Batman is shown standing outside the panel borders, symbolically indicating that he's free from the contraption. "Nice try," he says, looking at the burning, demolished trap. Morrison, or more accurately, artist Klaus Janson, doesn't break panel borders for metafictional purposes here.[116] It's simply a way to emphasize a dramatic moment and to add the illusion of depth to a scene.

Whisper, meanwhile, unaware of Batman's escape, has brought a young victim, a wayward nun (who has appeared throughout the storyline at various intervals, for no apparent reason) into the cathedral. As the girl ominously, and deliriously, sings verses from "Ring Around the Rosie,"[117] Whisper explains his plans once again before coming across a card inscribed with poetry. The lines, "My hour has almost come when I to sulph-rous and tormenting flames must render up... myself," come from Shakespeare's *Hamlet*, and Whisper realizes that Batman must have left the message for him. The choice of verse is particularly appropriate, for not only is *Hamlet* the most Gothic of the Shakespeare plays, as I indicated before, but it deals with vengeance on behalf of a father – and what could be more appropriate to this story, and Batman in general, than that?

Batman makes a grand entrance, and the final battle lasts for twelve pages of the story as he pursues Whisper throughout the cathedral. In the

---

[116] In Morrison's run on *Animal Man*, characters who became self-aware could escape the confines of the panel to see their reality from a new perspective. Traditionally, though, when a figure, or object, breaks the line of a panel border, it merely indicates that something important is happening on the page. It's an illusion of a 3-D effect. Morrison and Janson use it in *Gothic* without any ulterior motive.

[117] "Ring Around the Rosie" appears more than once in the story, which is appropriate considering it connects the Gothic symbol of the rose with the evocation of the black plague.

midst of their confrontation, the floor of the cathedral crumbles, symbolically sending them down into the depths. Here, after being run over by a subway train (to no lasting effect), Whisper quotes some more poetry – Keats, this time – as he strikes Batman. When another train barrels toward them, Batman sends Whisper flying through the windshield, causing the train to drag Whisper away from the cathedral so Batman will be able to stop the bell from ringing in time to save the city. Morrison prolongs the suspense here by showing the bell, the clock nearing twelve, then two more panels of the bell, before pulling back to show that Batman has dismantled the bell by removing the clapper inside. The bell will never ring. The panels are silent until the end of the page, when Batman makes a humorous call to Alfred: "Gotham Cathedral. Now," he says, "And bring a band-aid." Corny jokes are also part of the Batman mythos – part of the campy tradition that post-*Dark Knight* narratives avoided exclusively – and Morrison structured the story to include just such a corny joke after the appropriate climax.

Mr. Whisper, thwarted by Batman, receives his ultimate punishment in the form of the young nun he had taken hostage earlier in the story. When Whisper recovers from the subway ride and returns home, he finds the girl waiting for him in his apartment. She says, "Three hundred years ago we made a bargain, you and I," revealing herself to be the Devil in disguise. "Resign all hope of pardon," she says. "Come with me and die forever." And that's the end of Mr. Whisper.

In the epilogue, Bruce Wayne, recovering at Wayne Manor, finds a package wrapped in a golden cord that once belonged to Mr. Whisper. Inside, he finds a human heart – presumably Whisper's. Alfred tries to undercut the horror of the discovery with a joke: "Shall I alert the Tin Man, sir?" he asks. But Batman has a better idea.

He returns to Austria, to the drowned monastery at Lake Dess. "I myself am far from being a superstitious man," Batman narrates,[118] "but some of the brothers here claim to have heard things. Seen things... [they say] that the young nun who was sacrificed on Manfred's pyre still haunts the submerged corridors. In her hand she bears a lantern, ceaselessly searching for her tormentor." He throws the heart into Lake Dess and says, in a word balloon,

---

[118] This is the only time Batman reveals any kind of internal monologue in *Gothic*, and it's not the type of tortured inner voice seen in other Batman stories of the time. It's more like poetic exposition here.

From *Batman: Legends of the Dark Knight* #10 – Batman throws Mr. Whisper's heart into the depths of Lake Dess. Art by Klaus Janson. Copyright © DC Comics.

"You're free. Go in peace." The story ends with this scene, showing Batman freeing a lost soul, granting her the freedom that he can never have – the freedom from vengeance.

*Gothic* isn't as grand as *Zenith* or as packed with heavy symbols as *Arkham Asylum.* It's not as metafictionally playful or emotionally powerful as *Animal Man.* But it is a successful attempt to tell a standard Batman tale with overt Gothic trappings, and it does have mythic undertones, with the vengeful son and the pact with the Devil. Morrison may not have broken any new ground with *Gothic*, but he reinvigorates the Batman milieu by bringing back some of the fun aspects of the old Batman stories and packaging the whole thing together in his own unique way. It's a literate super-hero story that explores Batman as part of a much larger narrative tradition.

# *Doom Patrol*

Grant Morrison's *Doom Patrol* must be examined differently than his work on either *Zenith*, Batman, or *Animal Man* because, in this case, he was asked to revamp a series already in progress. It was not a new creation like *Zenith*, nor was it a self-contained piece like Morrison's Batman work, nor was it a re-imagining of an underdeveloped character like *Animal Man*. *Doom Patrol* was a fondly-regarded series from the 1960s and was in the midst of an unsuccessful[119] relaunch when Morrison was assigned the title. Morrison's approach was to return the team to its original purpose, as he explains in the letter column of *Doom Patrol* #20 (his second issue):

> I decided straight away that I would attempt to restore the sense of the bizarre that made the original Doom Patrol so memorable. I wanted to reconnect with the fundamental, radical concept of the book–that here was a team composed of *handicapped* people. These were no clean-limbed, wish fulfillment, super-adolescents who could model Calvins in their spare time. This was a group of people with serious physical problems and, perhaps, one too many bats in the belfry.

## Wreckage of the Past

The original Doom Patrol first appeared in *My Greatest Adventure* #80, cover-dated June 1963. Created by Arnold Drake (with help from writer Bob Haney) and artist Bruno Premiani, the team consisted of the Chief (Niles

---

[119] Critically unsuccessful, anyway. It sold well enough to avoid cancellation, but it was not a well-regarded series before Morrison took over.

Caulder), a wheelchair-bound genius; Elasti-Girl (Rita Farr), a former actress with the power to grow or shrink her body at will; Negative Man (Larry Trainor), an ex-pilot, fully covered in bandages, with the power to release an energy being from inside his body; and Robotman (Cliff Steele), a former racecar driver whose brain was transplanted to a robot body after a terrible crash. This team of self-proclaimed outcasts dedicated themselves to protecting the world from all types of strange threats, like the Animal-Vegetable-Mineral Man, General Immortus, and the Brotherhood of Evil, led by a disembodied Brain and the talking gorilla known as Monsieur Mallah.

The original *Doom* Patrol was weird and just plain different from everything else in the DC Universe. Regarding the 1960s incarnation, Morrison admits,

> I hardly *ever* read DOOM PATROL; that comic *frightened* me and the only reason I read any of the stories at all was that there was a certain dark and not-altogether-healthy glamour about those four characters... Back in the 60s, when DC super-heroes still sported right-angled jawlines and Boy Scout principles, the Doom Patrol slouched into town like a pack of junkyard dogs with a grudge against mankind.

Another aspect that distinguished the original *Doom Patrol* from other series of the time was that it actually came to a conclusion. In *Doom Patrol* #121, cover-dated September-October 1968, the team sacrificed their lives to save a small village. Unlike other heroes of the time, the members of the Doom Patrol *died*. And, unlike other heroes of *our* time, they stayed dead (at least for a decade or so).[120]

In *Showcase* #94, cover-dated August / September 1977, Paul Kupperberg and artist Joe Staton relaunched a new Doom Patrol team featuring a revived Robotman, along with three new characters: Celsius (Arani Desai Caulder), a mistress of heat and ice who claimed to be the Chief's widow; Tempest (Joshua Clay), who could fire energy blasts from his hands; and Negative Woman (Valentina Vostok), who had gained possession of the energy being that once resided in Larry Trainor's body. The team was featured in only a few issues of *Showcase* but didn't catch on with readers and appeared infrequently over the following decade.

---

[120] In comic books, nobody stays dead forever. Even if you see the body, and the character is confirmed as dead, some writer in the future will resurrect that character. It's inevitable. The original Doom Patrol members stayed dead longer than most.

Ten years later, in October 1987, Paul Kupperberg again tried to resurrect the team, this time with artist Steve Lightle in the first-ever *Doom Patrol* #1.[121] The series initially featured the same team from Kupperberg's earlier *Showcase* run, but this new incarnation was a bit darker, with more angst and less costumed hijinx. Kupperberg attempted to inject some strangeness into the proceedings by furthering the mystery of Arani Desai's relationship with the deceased Chief and creating new villains such as the insect-like Kalki, but the series soon reverted to traditional mid-1980s super-heroics with plenty of hysterical shouting, ponderous thought balloons, and punching.

Kupperberg's work on the title was enhanced by the detailed pencils of Steve Lightle, and the series was not without its charms for the first few issues. Things began to take a downturn, however, with the introduction of some new, youthful members of the Doom Patrol. Lodestone (Rhea Jones), Karma (Wayne Hawkins), and Scott Fisher (no super-hero name given) were probably brought in to re-invigorate the team, but they, with the help of cartoony new visuals from replacement artist Erik Larsen, took the team even farther away from its original conception and turned it into a silly, punchline-laden atrocity.[122]

Luckily, Grant Morrison was waiting in the wings. In Kupperberg's final issues, and in the *Invasion* mini-series, the Doom Patrol was dismantled. Arani Desai was revealed to be a fraud and died attempting to redeem herself, and the new younger characters were killed, incapacitated, or removed to places where they would never be seen again. Kupperberg practically wiped the slate clean for Morrison's arrival and *Doom Patrol* #19, thankfully, introduced a new era for the team. In addition to better paper-quality and fancier printing (the series moved from newsprint to the "New Format" with issue #19 to mark the new beginning), the team received a new artist as well, in the form of Richard Case.[123] Unlike Larsen and Lightle,

---

[121] Because the original Doom Patrol series began in *My Greatest Adventure*, DC just continued the numbering when the name of the comic book was changed to *Doom Patrol* with issue #86. Hence, until the 1980s, no *Doom Patrol* #1 had ever existed.

[122] The less said about this incarnation of the Doom Patrol, the better. I will say this: It was quite bad.

[123] Richard Case, while not quite as good with facial features as Steve Yeowell, comes from the same artistic tradition. Both artists use geometric compositions and

Case was not a traditional super-hero artist. He was a good choice to illustrate the new perspective Grant Morrison brought to the series.

Morrison's intention with the series was to "break away from the massive influence that the Claremont / Byrne era *X-Men*[124] continue to exert over the whole concept of a comic-book super-team and to forge a new style that would look forward to the '90s." He certainly lived up to his intention, a fact which became immediately apparent before the first storyline was completed. His inspiration for his run on *Doom Patrol* (besides the work of Drake and Premiani on the original series) varied from the films of people like Jan Svankmajer, Kenneth Anger, and Maya Deren, to the mathematics of *Godel, Escher, Bach*, to the multiple-personality account of *When Rabbit Howls*, to the fiction of Jorge Luis Borges, to the actions of avant garde poster-boy Tristan Tzara, and beyond.[125] Morrison brought all of these influences into the series just as a starting point and expanded the Doom Patrol universe from there.

In a 1995 interview with *The Comics Journal*, Morrison reflects on his *Doom Patrol* issues and explains that readers misunderstood the apparent complexity of the series:

> People seemed to pick up on all the wrong elements of it, and feel that there were things which they couldn't understand, when they were basically things which they didn't have to understand. There weren't any secrets in it, nothing was symbolic in *Doom Patrol*.[126]

---

stark blacks. Case, though, is blockier where Yeowell is elegant. This blockiness gives *Doom* Patrol a certain clumsy, awkward look that's more than appropriate for the direction in which Morrison took the comic book. Case illustrated the vast majority of *Doom Patrol* stories during Morrison's run, and although other artists occasionally filled in, Case created the look and visual texture of the series.

[124] The 1980s incarnation of the X-Men, which reached its apotheosis with the work by writer Chris Claremont and artist John Byrne, established the rules of a contemporary super-team. These rules can be summarized as follows: (1) the team is like a family; (2) the team must argue dramatically whenever possible but must come together in times of crisis; (3) the team must contain a good mix of men and women for maximum sexual tension; (4) the team must contain a good mix of young and old so you can get the "coming of age" storylines along with the "wise mentoring" subplots; and (5) the team must be cool and tough, or at least act like they are.

[125] The only thing these artists and writers have in common is that they pushed the boundaries of their art form. That's why they interest Morrison so much, and that's why he uses them to inspire his *Doom Patrol* work.

[126] There is plenty of symbolism in *Doom Patrol*, contrary to what Morrison says,

From Morrison's perspective, "*Doom Patrol* was a very simple comic." Morrison is reacting to the critics of the series, who dubbed it "pretentious" and castigated it for not making any sense. His work on the series, does, however, make a great deal of sense. It's strange, certainly, and unique, definitely, but it is logical in its own way. It's certainly no less logical than a giant purple-clad planet devourer or men made out of rocks, fire, or rubber.[127] It's basically a straightforward action series with an odd cast of characters, and unlike, say, *Arkham Asylum*, *Doom Patrol* is not laden with Jungian symbolism that demands interpretation.

This does not imply, however, that *Doom Patrol* is without meaning. Its meaning lies in its formal experimentation and in its thematic focus which, at least for the first six issues written by Grant Morrison (*Doom Patrol* #19-24), revolves around a major idea: *revision and transformation.*

Just as Morrison revises the Doom Patrol for a new generation, a new decade, the text of *Doom Patrol* itself is all about revision. Revision of character, revision of self, revision of reality, revision of the past, revision of images, revision of art, and revision of our concepts of right and wrong all play a role in Morrison's stories in this series.

If revision is part of the act of creation, it's also an act of destruction, as Morrison indicates in *Doom Patrol* #19, which is part one of the four-part story arc titled, "Crawling from the Wreckage." Morrison has to destroy the foundation of the Doom Patrol – the fetid, stagnant foundation of the Kupperberg series, anyway – before he can rebuild and revise. As Morrison points out in the letter column of issue #20, Kupperberg was kind enough to help him clear the way: "[Kupperberg] kindly agreed to kill or maim most of his characters and leave the field clear for me to introduce a Doom Patrol that was a little less comfortable, a little more unsettling." When issue #19 begins, Cliff Steele (who, for the remainder of Morrison's run, will no longer be referred to as "Robotman,") is recovering in a mental institution, Larry Trainor is in the hospital, Joshua Clay (who has not only forsaken his super-

---

but it's not symbolism of the type seen in *Arkham Asylum* and it's not allegorical symbolism either. *Doom Patrol* does not mean anything other than it seems to mean. It's a super-hero comic book with a lot of outrageous ideas, that's it. But the ideas are so outrageous that some readers become baffled by the stories.

[127] Galactus, the Thing, the Human Torch, and Mr. Fantastic, respectively, from Marvel's *Fantastic Four.*

hero name, "Tempest," but also his costume and powers) is aimless, Rhea Jones (no longer called "Lodestone") is in a coma, the rest of the new additions to the team are dead or gone (never to be mentioned again), and Niles Caulder (who is not seriously called "Chief" in Morrison's issues) is trying to pick up the pieces. By "re-damaging" these characters, Morrison returns them to their original purpose. They aren't idealized, perfect heroes. They are flawed and disturbed and strange. Just like they're supposed to be.

Although Morrison will physically transform Cliff Steele over the course of the series, in the initial few story arcs, Morrison deals more with Cliff's mental transformation. Morrison establishes early on in "Crawling from the Wreckage" that Cliff *suffers* because of his robotic body. Cliff says, to Doc Magnus[128] (a visitor at the mental institution – and the inventor who originally designed Cliff's body), "You know, they say that amputees feel phantom pains where there limbs used to be. Well, I'm a total amputee." In that one sentence, Morrison imbues more characterization into Cliff than in the entire 18 issues which preceded it. That statement tells us what Cliff suffers from, and explains his rage and self-loathing as he continues: "How can I destroy myself?... I. Can't. Feel. Anything." He repeats these last words as he literally slams his own head against a brick wall. Cliff's humanity, his need to connect with others, is bound inside his insensitive body. He is a displaced man in every sense of the term.

Meanwhile, Larry Trainor, rendered powerless by previous events, is contacted by the disembodied Negative Being which was once inside of him. This time, though, the Negative Being fuses Larry Trainor with Dr. Eleanor Poole before inhabiting this new, hermaphroditic shell. This new being, now fully wrapped in bandages, refuses to answer as either Larry or Eleanor and calls itself Rebis, which, as Niles Caulder points out, refers to "a term used by the medieval alchemists to identify the result of a chymical wedding" between sulfur and mercury (such a combination is literally referred to as a "hermaphrodite" in alchemy as well). Therefore, Morrison gives us a displaced man in Cliff Steele, and a dual-gendered energy being in Rebis

---

[128] Doc Magnus, in DC continuity, created "The Metal Men," a group of super-powered robots made from various elemental metals. His appearances in Morrison's *Doom Patrol* generally set him in opposition with Niles Caulder, since both he and Caulder have different approaches to building robots and each thinks the other is an idiot.

before he's even halfway done with the storyline. To mirror the composition of the original Doom Patrol, now that he has his "Robotman" and his "Negative Man / Woman," he needs a replacement for Elasti-Girl. In her place (since Rita Farr is thankfully allowed to rest in peace), Morrison delivers an unorthodox variation on the typical female team-member. Unlike Rita, with her short skirts and her apparent lack of oddness (it was easy to see why a metal man or a mummy-looking guy were seen as outcasts in the original series, but it was much harder to see why the beautiful ex-actress was such a freak just because she could – gasp – grow or shrink at will), Morrison's new addition to the group is as damaged as the rest: Kay Challis, a.k.a. Crazy Jane, a mental patient who has 64 multiple personalities, each with its own name and a super-power that comes with it.[129]

These three, along with Joshua Clay as medical support and Niles Caulder as leader, comprise Morrison's revised Doom Patrol. Notice, though, how masterfully he has updated the concept for the postmodern era while maintaining the essential weird-ness of the original team. The original team was strange because they were, largely, unattractive and unglamorous, yet they fought the good fight. They clearly embodied the ethics and obsessions of the mid-20th Century and had become conceptually outdated. Robotman was a symbol of post-war innovation – a mechanical man who was better than human. Negative Man was a symbol of the danger and power of nuclear energy – something that could be harnessed to great effect but at a great risk. Elasti-Girl symbolized the all-American girl who seemed perfect, yet struggled with her own inner demons. The Chief, in a Dr. Strangelove-ian[130] way, symbolized rationalism and science as solution to world problems. These were heroes for the atomic age, surely, but not for the post-Reagan era.

Morrison realized that previous writers' adherence to the original cast, and misguided attempts at revitalizing the team with new members, had caused the team to lose its focus – by the time he took over, they represented nothing more than typical Marvel mutants[131] – they were just generic heroes

---

[129] Morrison claims that Crazy Jane was inspired by Trudi Chase, who wrote *When Rabbit Howls* (1987), a memoir "narrated" by her multiple personalities.
[130] Meaning: creepy and emotionless. In reference to Stanley Kubrick's *Dr. Strangelove, Or: How I Learned to Stop Worrying and Love the Bomb* (1964).
[131] By the mid-to-late 1980s, the mutant (super-humans born with powers which

who were feared and hated by society (unconvincingly feared and hated, to make matters worse). Morrison's revised Cliff Steele, then, is no longer a post-war innovation, but a postmodern train-wreck – a mechanical man who feels like he no longer fits into the world. His Rebis is not a symbol of nuclear energy, but of spiritual energy – of the essential powers of both man and woman. His Crazy Jane is a contemporary representative of psychosis – a depressed beauty queen is old news by now, so he ups the ante by providing a psychological problem 64 times worse than Rita Farr's. His Niles Caulder is esoteric and distant, using occult knowledge that is as strange and exciting for us as science was generations before. Morrison's Doom Patrol works where Kupperberg's failed because it, like the original Doom Patrol, reflects the essential concerns and disillusionment of its era, while Kupperberg's reflected nothing more than other popular super-hero comics.

The first mission the new Doom Patrol tackles further emphasizes the themes of revision and transformation and shows that Morrison is not shy about borrowing ideas from other sources. The plot of "Crawling from the Wreckage" (which kicks in as the new team is being "assembled") deals with a fictional world, called Orqwith, overtaking reality, replacing city streets with spires of bone as it spreads like an infection. It recalls the metafictional games Morrison so prominently played in *Animal Man*, but it more directly alludes to the story, "Tlon, Uqbar, Orbis Tertius," by famed Argentinean writer Jorge Luis Borges. In Borges's tale, the narrator learns about the history and culture of a fictional world before becoming increasingly disturbed as he finds artifacts from this unreal world permeating our own. By the end of the story, the narrator describes how, "Contact with Tlon, the *habit* of Tlon, has disintegrated this world... already a fictitious past has supplanted in men's memories that other past, of which we now know nothing is certain – not even that it is false." In "Crawling from the Wreckage," Crazy Jane, after using her Mama Pentecost persona to translate a mysterious text, reveals that,

---

manifested in puberty) population of the Marvel Comics, as seen in *Uncanny X-Men*, had become synonymous with persecution. The mutants were outcasts who were hated because they were different. Although writer Chris Claremont sometimes used the treatment of mutants to explore civil rights issues, more often than not the mutant heroes just complained about how they risked their lives to help the very people who despised them.

> the whole book [she just translated] is a kind of metafiction; a self-referring text. Basically it tells the story of a group of philosophers who decide to create a book which will radically alter human thought. They propose to fill the book with parasite ideas which will enter human consciousness and transform it.

The book's potency is so great that it actually transforms physical reality as well, and the Doom Patrol members soon find themselves facing the bizarre threat of the Scissormen, emissaries of Orqwith, who use their giant scissor-hands to "cut" humans out of the world (which, presumably, then transports these hollow people to Orqwith). One of their own support-team members, Joshua Clay, falls victim to the Scissormen. His absence is depicted as if he's been cut out of the comic book panel.

The Scissormen speak in nonsensical phrases and can revise reality with their blades, but Morrison doesn't treat this as a metafictional commentary on the art of narrative in *Doom Patrol*. Here he plays it straight – the Scissormen are freaky, and the infection of Orqwith on reality must be stopped. (Morrison admits that he was inspired to create their nonsense language when he was playing around with the spellcheck function on his computer and noticed all the strange words that the computer would suggest for a misspelled word – the Scissormen, therefore, or their words, anyway, are literal products of the revision process.)

Just as Zenith posed a paradox to stop the bombing of London in *Zenith*'s Phase Two, the Doom Patrol pose a paradox to force Orqwith to collapse upon itself. (It's yet another example of Morrison's use of *inaction heroes* – even with the Doom Patrol who kick and punch their way to the climax of the story, he has the characters employ words, not fists, to deliver the final blow.) Rebis confronts the leaders of Orqwith, two priests – one in white, one in black – and finds out that one is honest and one is a liar. By getting the priest in black, the liar, to say, "There is something instead of nothing," the entire unreality of Orqwith comes crashing down. Since he lied about Orqwith being "something," it must, therefore, be nothing. So it disappears.

Although Morrison stated that nothing is symbolic in these *Doom Patrol* stories, the Orqwith plot clearly reveals his fascination with the line between fiction and reality and the possibility of crossing the line between the two worlds. *Animal Man* dealt with this extensively, and Morrison's later work, most notably *The Invisibles*, hinges on the idea that a portal (or "fiction suit")

From *Doom Patrol* #21 – Niles Cauler, Crazy Jane, Cliff Steele, and Rebis find that Joshus Clay has been taken by the Scissormen. Art by Richard Case and Scott Hanna. Copyright © DC Comics.

could allow the wearer to travel from fiction to reality. Yet in "Crawling from the Wreckage," Morrison portrays the crossing over as a negative action, and the Doom Patrol are unheralded saviors for defeating the spread of Orqwith.

## Revision and Red Jack

Morrison continues exploring the themes of *revision and transformation* with the second storyline, beginning in *Doom Patrol* #23. This two-part story, the "Red Jack" narrative, begins with Niles Caulder explaining chaos theory to Joshua Clay (while showing him a depiction of a Lorenz Attractor): "a catastrophic cyclone in Bangladesh can be traced back to something as simple as the tiny perturbations made in the air by the wings of a butterfly in South America." Chaos theory has appeared in nearly everything I've analyzed in this book so far: in *Zenith* the chaos bombs destroy the oppressive order of the dark gods; in *Animal Man* the Earth is nearly destroyed by a Thanagarian chaos artist; and in *Doom Patrol* chaos theory is explained but not addressed until later (and then, only implicitly). Yet chaos naturally leads to change which sounds a lot like revision and transformation, doesn't it? See, it's all connected, even if Buddy Baker says it's not.[132]

Revisions are abundant in *Doom Patrol* #23. The team members sport their new, Brendan McCarthy-designed[133] costumes for the first time in this issue. The matching jumpsuits of the Kupperberg (and earlier) era are replaced by leather jackets (a shock, I know, especially after seeing Zenith and Animal Man clad in similar garb), and Cliff Steele no longer prances around in his "naked" robot body – he gets to wear jeans (or are those leather pants?) now too. Also, we meet a new addition to the team: the simian-like Dorothy Spinner (who first appeared in a Kupperberg issue) shows up at Doom Patrol headquarters, apparently summoned by Niles Caulder, because she has begun to manifest superhuman powers; she now has the ability to generate illusions which *transform* people's perceptions.

The plot of the "Red Jack" storyline provides more opportunities for

---

[132] Buddy, remember, says that his life has just been a series of random events at the end of Morrison's run on *Animal Man*, but even if that seems true to Buddy, he, as a Morrison creation, is part of a much larger fictional structure.
[133] Just as he did with *Zenith*, Brendan McCarthy contributed character designs to *Doom Patrol*, updating their look for the new era.

revision and transformation as Rhea Jones, who's been in a coma since Morrison took over, is kidnapped. Crazy Jane, using the William S. Burroughs cut-up technique of taking scissors to pages of books and seeing what new combinations of words arise on the floor, divines the whereabouts of Rhea (and the identity of her captor – a being who calls himself, variously, Red Jack, Jack the Ripper, and God, among other names). To create a doorway into Red Jack's world, she begins to chant the names of the prostitutes who were killed by Jack the Ripper, causing the hospital door to transform into a portal to Red Jack's palace. The team, with no help from Caulder (who doesn't even know where they've gone), finds that Red Jack has taken the comatose Rhea to be his bride. After Red Jack reveals his various alter egos to Cliff, Crazy Jane, and Rebis, he describes the motives for the deeds he committed a hundred years before as Jack the Ripper in the streets of Whitechapel:

> I had a plan, you understand. The old urge to create was still strong. So I cut them up... They were nothing. Cheap harlots and sleepwalkers... I thought that if I cut them up an reassembled the flesh in new configurations... Well, I thought that I could create a beautiful new form of life. Something better than human. Plan didn't work. Typical.

This scene reveals the emphasis on revision and transformation but shows how disappointing the final result can be (especially when attempted by a madman).

Ultimately, Red Jack is just another megalomaniacal super-villain attempting to take, by force, something (or someone: Rhea) that doesn't belong to him. He may look different – he may dress like a dandy and have a head like a playing-card character, and he may have different hobbies – he collects butterflies (Rhea is a human butterfly, though we don't know it at this point, ready to burst forth with new life from her cocoon / coma), but he's still defeated by the old knife-in-the-back trick. Rhea awakens and stabs him in his moment of triumph, leading him to say, with sadness, "I thought I was part of the grand story... the story that... would at least give meaning to this senseless trajectory... this loop and spin of being... instead I have learned the horrible truth of... existence... some stories have no meaning." Red Jack vanishes with that existential thought.

Contrary to Red Jack's final words, the "Red Jack" storyline seems to serve several purposes. It sets up future plot threads, as we have this foreshadowing of Rhea as a butterfly, and we wonder what she'll transform into. It establishes the unity of the new Doom Patrol team (at least the core team – the support team was unconcerned and unhelpful), if not its effectiveness – they seemed destined to lose if not for Rhea's timely awakening. (And if the chaos stuff and the leather jackets weren't enough to link *Zenith* and *Animal Man* and *Doom Patrol* together, could we get a more useless group of heroes? Combined, they are almost completely ineffective in every situation.) It also sets *Doom Patrol* up as a traditional super-hero comic book. Even though Red Jack was strange and enigmatic, he provided a standard villainous threat and his defeat provided the climax of the story. Morrison is signaling, at least at this point in his run on the series, that he's not out to challenge the structure of comic book narratives as we know them – he's interested in telling stories that follow standard super-hero conventions. It's just that his heroes are bizarre, and his villains sometimes claim they are God. But are the battles between the Fantastic Four and Galactus really any different? (Answer: yes, but not in theme or content; they differ only in the way in which they are told.)

A final comment: the "Red Jack" story begins and ends with two similar pages. At the very beginning of *Doom Patrol* #23, Red Jack walks out onto a white, tiled floor where we see, from a high perspective, a butterfly flapping its wings helplessly. Red Jack pokes it with his finger, saying, "Did you think you could ever escape? Do you dream of an end to pain? There is no way out. There is no end," before walking away. In the final pages of *Doom Patrol* #24, after Red Jack has been defeated, we see this same butterfly on the white, tiled floor again. This time, though, we are at ground-level, looking at the butterfly up close as it tries to move. In the background, Cliff, Jane, and Rebis (with Rhea in its arms) walk toward us. Cliff says (and this is "translated" because his slightly damaged motors cause him to sputter and crack as he speaks in this scene), "We never see the things that are right under our noses, do we? Still... that's life, I guess." As he says these last words, he steps right on the butterfly and squashes it. Does this mean that the Doom Patrol members are obtuse and unaware and that's the joke? Or does it mean that they are saviors without even knowing it – freeing the butterfly from its torment? Or does it mean that we are the struggling butterfly and life will squash us? Or does it mean all of the above? Or none of the above? I think it all connects back to Caulder's butterfly reference back at the beginning of issue #23: the smallest things can have catastrophic effects – i.e. even butterflies are important. Morrison once again indicates that everything is connected, and we will soon learn what type of metaphorical butterfly Rhea will transform into. So I think it means all of the above, but for now, it's enough to say that Morrison teases us with butterfly imagery to hint at what he has in store.

## The Yellow Brick Road, Mr. Nobody, and Driver 8

As previously mentioned, Grant Morrison brought Dorothy Spinner, a character who appeared briefly in Paul Kupperberg's run, into the Doom Patrol fold by having her show up at the headquarters with newly developed illusion-casting powers. I didn't point this out at the time, but Morrison uses Dorothy to complete the *Wizard of Oz* motif he's established for the revamp. Cliff Steele, a man of metal, is an obvious stand-in for the Tin Man. Rebis, a hollow creature, is the Scarecrow, and Crazy Jane, who is emotionally damaged and withdrawn, is the Cowardly Lion. Dorothy Spinner, who, when we first meet her on the plains of the Midwest in *Doom Patrol* #14, is wearing a blue dress just like Judy Garland, is a not-so-subtle Dorothy Gale doppelganger (although, in typical *Doom Patrol* fashion, she is ugly instead of beautiful).

This *Wizard of Oz* conceit of Morrison's is never explicitly stated and never fully developed into a significant storyline, but it underlies the basic structure of the team. It provides a shorthand for their assumed desires. Cliff, like the Tin Man, wants a metaphorical heart – he wants to be able to feel again. Rebis wants a brain – a sense of identity and self that it has been unable to fully reconcile. Jane wants to heal her fractured psyche and gain courage to return to the company of men. (Note how impotent the Doom Patrol team is, by the way, in contrast to other, virile super-teams – this team features a wheelchair-bound cripple, an emasculated robot, and a hermaphroditic being wrapped in bandages – all of whom pose no sexual threat to Jane. Dorothy wants to find her "home," which, in her case, is not her literal home, but somewhere she'll be accepted for what she is – a place like Doom Patrol headquarters.

In *Doom Patrol* #25, "Imaginary Friends," Dorothy's character gets the spotlight, along with Joshua Clay, while the other members of the team finish their battle with Red Jack (as described in the previous two issues). In this issue, we learn more about Dorothy's strange childhood, where her imaginary companions taught her "how to read and write and all kinds of stuff." Unfortunately for Dorothy, her newfound illusion-casting powers, accidentally amplified by a nearby "Meterioptikon"[134] (a left-over artifact from when the place was the headquarters of the Justice League), cause her imaginary friends to come to life. She is tormented by these beings throughout the issue, culminating in a horrifying sequence where Dorothy says, "Darling-Come-Home said that I couldn't have ruby slippers... only red shoes... like Hans Christian Andersen." The ruby slippers, which would have transported her to safety and shelter, are cruelly replaced by the red shoes of the famous fairy tale, which told the story of a girl who was compelled to dance in the shoes until she was forced to have her own feet chopped off. *Fairy tale* motifs, like the red shoes, are quite common in horror fiction. Morrison uses that strategy to bring a sense of unease to *Doom Patrol*, a title that, as I pointed out in the last column, had become a generic super-hero slugfest before he took over. Morrison adds a sense of dread that is appropriate for the title, but he ends with a hopeful scene, tying the *Wizard of Oz* theme into the story after the Materioptikon is destroyed: "You put on the red shoes?" Joshua Clay asks. "The ruby slippers, Mr. Clay. They were ruby slippers all along." Then, she clicks her heels together, smiles, and says, "There's no place like home."

Dorothy plays a minor role in Morrison's early issues, but the emphasis on her in this issue reminds us that the Doom Patrol, as bizarre as it is, can be a haven for people who have been cast out by society.

The next storyline, which begins with *Doom Patrol* #26, "Nowhere Man," features a striking cover by Simon Bisley;[135] it's the first cover with the new logo design, and it features the Brendan McCarthy-designed Brotherhood of Dada.

---

[134] The Materioptikon, created by Justice League villain Dr. Destiny, whom you may recall from his brief cameo in *Arkham Asylum*, gives the user the power to turn dreams into reality. Such an invention fits perfectly into the dream-like structures Morrison likes to use.

[135] Simon Bisley, best known for his work on *Lobo* in the 1990s, splashed onto the American comic book scene with this *Doom Patrol* cover. His style, a conflagration of the dynamic anatomy of Frank Frazetta and the hyper-sylized look of Bill Sienkiewicz, helped to promote the new direction of Morrison's *Doom Patrol* and set it apart from everything else on the comic book racks.

It's an appropriate cover to signal a new beginning for the Doom Patrol. By this issue, Morrison had introduced the new Doom Patrol team, established the odd milieu of the setting, ironed out some rough spots (the issue featuring Dorothy, as interesting as it was for the *Wizard of Oz* / fairy tale motifs, was not one of Morrison's stronger tales), and could now unleash his full creative fury. He does so without hesitation.

He begins the issue with the preposterous situation of a Japanese costumed hero, Sunburst,[136] being followed by television cameras as the star of the popular reality show, "The Adventures of New Sunburst." It doesn't sound preposterous at all now, does it, with our abundance of reality TV? Even Marvel's *Civil War* crossover event used the conceit of a super-hero reality show to propel the story. *Doom Patrol* #26, though, was published in 1989, a decade before even *Survivor* hit the airwaves. Morrison enjoys predicting pop culture trends; he must have seen what the future would bring, and he satirizes reality television in the persona of Sunburst years before the trend even catches on.

Morrison also continues with the *revision / transformation* theme (and *butterfly* motif from previous issues) as he shows Niles Caulder studying the comatose body of Rhea Jones. Caulder explains, "I believe Rhea has entered a chrysalis state... and I believe her body is about to undergo some kind of metamorphosis." This is obvious foreshadowing, but Morrison's in no hurry for the metamorphosis to occur. It is important to note, however, that this scene with Rhea in a coma is one of only four pages out of the entirety of *Doom Patrol* #26 which features the actual members of the Doom Patrol; the remaining 20 pages focus on something else entirely: the Brotherhood of Dada.

The original Doom Patrol, of course, had opposed the Brotherhood of *Evil*, an organization most famously comprising the Brain, Monsieur Mallah, and Madame Rouge. In Morrison's *Doom Patrol*, the new leader of the Brotherhood, Mr. Nobody (formerly a forgotten member from the early days known as Mr. Morden), explains, "'Good!' 'Evil!' Outmoded concepts of an antique age... The Brotherhood of Evil is dead... Long live the Brotherhood of Dada!" Mr. Nobody's group name is a reference to the Dadaist art movement of the early 20th Century, a movement that was

---

[136] The previous Sunburst, a Japanese actor-turned-super-hero, died in *Crisis on Infinite Earths*. This new Sunburst, a television star, is a Morrison creation.

deemed "anti-art," a movement that was about rejecting aesthetic values, a movement that was about absurdism and nihilism, a movement that would have hated to be called a movement. The Brotherhood of Dada is the perfect counterpoint to the Doom Patrol. The Doom Patrol, as strange as it is, still works to establish order in a chaotic world. For the team, it's not about goodness fighting against evil; it's about solving problems and straightening things out. The Brotherhood of Dada represents the exact opposite; for them, it's about nonsense and chaos, fun and frivolity, disruption and ridiculousness. To Mr. Nobody, the members of the Brotherhood represent the future, and as he recalls his origin he bombastically declares that he personally "had become the spirit of the Twenty-First Century." Physically, he is almost non-existent – a slight mass of black shapes in a vaguely humanoid pattern. He is a silly-looking villain – appropriate for such a ridiculous team.

The other members of the Brotherhood of Dada are equally ridiculous: Sleepwalk, who has great strength when somnambulating; the Fog, who can turn into a gaseous form and absorb others into himself (but is forced to hear the squabbling voices of those he's engulfed); Frenzy, who has bicycle wheels attached to his back, a top hat, and the power to move like a tornado; and the Quiz, a germ-phobic young woman who has every power you haven't thought of (and she loses each power once you think of it). They are a terrific cast of characters, and their colorful costumes, and even more colorful personalities, provide great conflict for the Doom Patrol when they steal the most powerful painting in the world.

In *Doom Patrol* #27, Mr. Nobody explains the plan: they will steal "The Painting that Ate Paris." It will provide a means to achieve his "dreams of global absurdity." The painting, depicted in isolation on the first page, before we (or the Brotherhood) even learn about its power, shows an infinitely recursive scene. In the center of the painting is the painting, and in the center of that smaller painting is the painting, etc. It never ends (although, the limits of comic book printing are such that it does end for us after a handful of recursions). Mr. Nobody's plan is to steal the painting from eccentric collector and scientist of the strange, Horst Eismann.

Meanwhile, the Doom Patrol is once again seen for only a few pages this issue. Morrison clearly doesn't feel the need to push the heroes to the forefront. They emerge as necessary, and he's willing to let them sit out as long as he's exploring his more interesting ideas. In this case, the heist of the painting is the main plot thread, and when the Doom Patrol does appear, it's to emphasize the theme of the story, which in this case is *recursion*. Rebis takes on the task this time, as it plays with a Russian nesting doll (a relic of its past life as a human female): "Push. Pop. Stack. Jargon of recursive sequence. Every doll an isomorphic mapping of every other doll." As I've pointed out many times in this book, Morrison is fascinated by the idea of patterns and layers. He's used chaos theory in every major work so far, and he uses the idea of the Mandelbrot set[137] once again in this scene. The smallest piece reflects the pattern of the whole. Basically, though, Morrison doesn't explore the idea in *Doom Patrol*, he just throws it into the mix. *Zenith* and *Animal Man* were far more contemplative looks at these ideas and themes. *Doom Patrol*, as Morrison himself has pointed out, is just Lee-and-Kirby-style[138] comic book fun. It's just that Morrison's frame of reference is much different, and his personal interests filter through and become part of the work.

So Morrison's interest in Dada leads the Brotherhood to steal the infinitely recursive painting and bring it to the base of the Eiffel Tower, where Mr. Nobody announces, "Dada is useless, like everything else in life... thus do we present this absurdist ritual for your entertainment..." They invoke the names of the great Dadaists (Duchamp, Tzara, Breton, and Cravan) to activate the painting. The police arrive to stop them, but Mr. Nobody throws a rubber chicken at their feet and continues, ultimately achieving success on the final page of the issue:

This final image mirrors the image on page one, with the obvious exception that the painting has now "eaten" Paris, though where Paris has gone within the painting and why the Brotherhood occupies the outer portion alone is never explained. It's Dada, remember? It's not supposed to make sense.

---

[137] The Mandelbrot set is a fractal pattern created by mathematician Benoit Mandelbrot – a pattern which is infinitely recursive. Mandelbrot, by the way, coined the word *fractal* in 1975.

[138] Stan Lee and Jack Kirby created, for Marvel Comics in the early 1960s, the model upon which most contemporary super-hero comics are based. Their work combined bombastic rhetoric with touching moments of humanity along with explosive action scenes. See *Fantastic Four*, *Avengers*, *The Incredible Hulk, X-Men* and everything since.

*Doom Patrol* #28 begins with Justice League members Booster Gold, Blue Beetle, and Animal Man[139] standing on the desolate wasteland, looking into the painting. As a self-referential joke, Animal Man says, "Don't talk to me about weird! I've been living my life in the 'Twilight Zone.'" (This issue of *Doom Patrol* was released in the same month as *Animal Man* #18, the issue in which Buddy Baker sees us watching him.) To subvert the heroic entrance of the Doom Patrol, Morrison has Booster Gold say, "Talking of nutcases... here comes the Doom Patrol." Morrison, at this stage in his career, is clearly uncomfortable with heroes. His protagonists are never shown respect, and whenever they are given a dramatic moment (like they would normally be in a story like this), he deflates their significance with a negative comment. The Doom Patrol, though, as ill-respected as they are, quickly solve the problem by transporting themselves into the painting (via Rebis's inherently contradictory persona – remember, it doesn't have to make sense, it's all dada).

Once inside, they find that every layer of the recursive painting represents a different art movement (and thus, has not only a different style, but different physical laws). Frenzy attacks, a whirling mass of speed, and launches them all into different layers in a twist on the super-hero tradition of splitting up and facing enemies. In this case, the divide-and-conquer strategy seems to work for the Brotherhood of Dada, since the Doom Patrol, as disoriented as they are, cannot fight effectively. This is the first time since Morrison took over that we actually see fight sequences between heroes and villains. They don't solve this problem with a riddle or with a surprise stab in the back – this is a good, old-fashioned battle of strength and super-powers. But it's Grant Morrison, so the fight takes place against an ever-changing backdrop of art history. One scene takes place in an impressionist setting, another in a world of futurism, yet another in a surrealist landscape. Ultimately though, the Doom Patrol seems overwhelmed by the situation,

---

[139] Animal Man you already know about, but Blue Beetle and Booster Gold were two relatively ineffectual members of Justice League International. Blue Beetle, a Silver Age hero, was like Batman (except Beetle-themed and much less serious), while Booster Gold was a Reagan-era creation who was mostly interested in benefiting himself. As unspectacular as these three heroes are, they still think they're better than the Doom Patrol.

From Doom Patrol #28 – Mr. Nobody and the Brotherhood of Dada defeat Cliff Steele inside an ever-changing painted landscape. Art by Richard Case and John Nyberg. Copyright © DC Comics.

and Cliff Steele faces defeat by the Brotherhood amidst an expressionist cityscape.

Morrison also gives us a traditional Doom Patrol trope here as well: Cliff's damaged body. Throughout Doom Patrol history, Cliff has been damaged, rebuilt, and repaired time and again, so this scene fits right into what has come before, although Morrison jazzes it up with a little expressionism and an ominous reference to the importance of Cliff's "nutrient tank." That's typical Morrison as well – throwing in something off the wall, like being inside a painting, right next to something practical but overlooked, like Cliff's need for a biological support system.

In his moment of triumph, Mr. Nobody declares that they will expand the power of the painting to envelope the entire world: "We could do anything we wanted! Paint faces on Superman's bare bottom! Use Batman as an ashtray! Yes! Let's make them all suffer!" He realizes that these self-important, humorless heroes would be tortured far more by humiliation than by any other means. Interrupting his moment of glory, Sleepwalk fearfully shouts, "The buried rider! The Fifth Horseman! It's coming!"

Morrison frames the story in *Doom Patrol* #29 with a narration by the self-proclaimed "kign uv the wurld [king of the world]," Frenzy, who looks out onto his domain as he writes a letter to his "momma." Such a technique recalls *Zenith*'s Phase Four, where the sole surviving human, Dr. Michael Peyne, tells the story of humanity's last stand. In both cases, Morrison gives us a single character, apparently alone atop a great tower, looking down on the world and providing an unreliable narration. (Peyne regressed to infancy as his story unfolded, so his writing became less and less coherent, while Frenzy has a child-like mentality, an inability to construct a sentence without errors, and an incomplete sense of story – we never learn why Frenzy considers himself king of anything.)

Frenzy's narration fills us in on what happened with the Fifth Horseman, who so frightened Sleepwalk at the end of the previous issue. He tells of how they saw signs of the creature before they ever saw it in person. First, Sleepwalk's warning, then they came across a giant hoof-print in the sand. Crazy Jane, who was able to overcome the Fog's attack, recalls "certain Gnostic Gospels"[140] which foretell of the Fifth Horseman, "'And his name

[140] The Gnostic Gospels, including the Gospel of Thomas and the Gospel of Mary

that sat on him was Extinction. And Oblivion.'" As the painting falls apart around them, the Brotherhood of Dada decides that it needs help from the Doom Patrol. This is, once again, another traditional super-hero trope: the teaming up of heroes and villains to stop an overpowering threat. The Brotherhood frees Rebis and repairs Cliff Steele, hoping that the heroes can stop Oblivion. Ultimately, though, it's Crazy Jane who realizes what needs to be done: she needs to control the Horseman; she needs to ride it from within the cage of its heart:

Jane isn't able to stop the Horseman, but she guides it through the levels of the painting until she reaches the Dadaist layer. As Mr. Nobody explains, "The rider requires ideas and meaning to give it power, but Dada is the anti-idea! Dada destroys meaning! Dada strips away all sense! All significance!"

Outside the painting, Superman, who has now joined other heroes assembled in what was once Paris, looks into the canvas and sees something coming out toward him. A wave of energy zooms out into the world, past Superman. Inside the painting, Mr. Nobody cheers. Booster Gold looks at what has come out of the painting, and asks, "That's it?" We don't see what he's looking at for several pages, but when it's revealed, we find out that the threat of Oblivion, the Fifth Horseman, has been turned into nothing more than a child's hobby horse. The Dadaist layer turned the Horseman into something absurd and ridiculous, stripping it of its power, and the joke here is that the word *dada*, in French, means "hobby horse."

Although the threat has been extinguished, the painting continues to melt around the Doom Patrol and the Brotherhood. Rebis transports the heroes out, as easily as they had arrived, but Frenzy and the other members of the Brotherhood (except for Mr. Nobody, perhaps) wish to stay. Frenzy touchingly says, "This man [Mr. Nobody] said, 'You don't have to belong in the gutter. We're all super-heroes man!'" Morrison, once again deflating the moment, has Mr. Nobody respond: "Lloyd, I was only joking when I said that."

The final page of the issue shows Horst Eismann, once again in possession of his painting (though now it is a blurred mess of abstract impressionism), locking it into his vault. Inside the painting, Frenzy finishes

Magdalene, are not accepted as canonical by mainstream Christians. None of the extant Gnostic Gospels mention a Fifth Horseman of the Apocalypse.

the letter to his mother, happy to be ruler of a world that doesn't really exist.

Crazy Jane was able to control the Horseman just enough to lead it to its own destruction (if being turned into a hobby horse qualifies as destruction) but at a great cost. When *Doom Patrol* #30, "Going Underground," begins, Jane is comatose and unresponsive. Cliff volunteers to try to enter her psyche by transferring his consciousness, through Rebis, into Jane's mind. Once inside, he finds himself underground, in an intricate subway system. Jane's multiple personalities each occupy their own station on the map, and one persona, Driver 8, drives the train from station to station, guiding Cliff through the tunnels.

After the Fifth Horseman incident, "no one down here wants to take control anymore, in case they get hurt," says Driver 8. She then refers to previously undisclosed personality K-5 as "the one who endured the first abuse." The name K-5 apparently refers to Kay Challis (Jane's real name) at age 5, when she was sexually abused by her father. Kay blocked these childhood memories for years, until, one day, it all came flooding back to her, and, as Driver 8 explains, "the woman could have killed herself or gone mad. Instead, she survived by creating other selves to bear her childhood trauma." Later, Driver 8 describes where the name Crazy Jane came from. It was not from the "Crazy Jane" poems by William Butler Yeats, rather it was from the "painting by Richard Dadd. Victorian artist. Schizophrenic. Killed his father." Clearly, Richard Case, artist of Doom Patrol based Jane's features on the work by Dadd.[141]

After delving deeper into Jane's psyche, Cliff understands more about Jane's past, but he still hasn't been able to rescue the Crazy Jane personae from wherever it has been hidden. Without Jane to take charge of the personalities, her body will remain comatose. As Cliff gets closer to uncovering Jane in the subway tunnels, her multiple personalities convene to bar his path. "Never trust a man!" says Jane's Black Annis persona, "I'll geld them all! With my own teeth! I'll do it!" Cliff replied, "I'm not a man. Not anymore."

Cliff's emasculation is exactly what allows him to pass through the

[141] Actually, Dadd's painting of Crazy Jane, which features a woman with a strong brow and strands of hair across her face, looks exactly like Richard Case's drawings of Doom Patrol member Crazy Jane. Case obviously referred to the painting on more than one occasion.

blockade. He strips off his clothes, revealing his sexless metal body to prove that he is no threat to the personalities, all of whom reflect a different way of dealing with the sexual trauma of the past. "Let me through," Cliff pleads, "I'm not a man." His wish is granted, and he recovers the Jane personality as she is on the brink of throwing herself into "the well," which presumably would destroy her. In the climax of the story, a huge, bloated, grotesque "Daddy" creature emerges from the well to devour Jane and anything in its path. Cliff opposes the creature, and Morrison once again uses the trope of the broken Cliff as the creature bites Cliff's metal body in half. Jane stops the monster by defying it, using her anger at the harm inflicted upon Cliff to summon enough courage to say, "I hate you, Daddy!" This act is immediately followed by Jane waking up from her coma, disoriented, but presumably in control.

The entirety of "Going Underground" follows the typical heroic quest pattern, as Cliff, the hero, descends into the depths to rescue someone in need and return her to the land of the living. His journey is blocked by archetypal beings like Threshold Guardians (in the form of her multiple personalities blocking his path) and Ultimate Evil (in the form of the horrifying "Daddy").[142] The difference is that Cliff does not rescue Jane, exactly. She brings herself back out of the pit, albeit with inspiration from her friend.

What's interesting to note is that after twelve issues under Grant Morrison, the Doom Patrol, as a team, has not faced one Earth-bound threat. Orqwith was extra-dimensional, as was Red Jack. The battle with the Brotherhood of Dada took place inside the universe of a painting, and now this most recent conflict occurred totally inside a character's mind. After Morrison's use of the multiverse in *Zenith* and his layers of reality and fiction in *Animal Man*, it's not exactly surprising, but it's still peculiar. Perhaps it was Morrison's way of keeping the Doom Patrol isolated, away from other DC heroes. After all, if there was a true threat to the planet, wouldn't the other, more powerful heroes be better suited for the job? The Doom Patrol handles the things no one even notices: the odd, mysterious happenings beneath the surface and between the cracks where things get really interesting, as Morrison reminds us again and again.

---

[142] These are all obstacles in the path of the hero of the monomyth, according to Joseph Campbell.

## Kipling, Stevenson, and Descartes

In my chapter on *Zenith*, I mentioned that the doubling motif was rampant throughout that series, and Morrison seemed particularly interested in exploring the relationship between the *mind* and the *body*. In *Doom Patrol* #31-34, Morrison returns to these ideas once again and adds some new complexity to the theme of *duality* by investigating the conflict between *being* and *nothingness*, between *reality* and *fiction*. But *Doom Patrol* is no philosophical treatise. Morrison explores these concepts in a manner that's uniquely his: part comic book pastiche, part action movie, part twisted fairy tale. Morrison, especially in *Doom Patrol*, is no quiet minimalist. He's a maximalist of the highest order, a creator who will throw one bizarre concept after another onto the page, creating a complexity that might threaten to overwhelm the narrative in the hands of a lesser writer.

Just look at the characters and concepts he introduces in one issue, *Doom Patrol* #31, "The Word Made Flesh":

(1) Willoughby Kipling: arcane investigator, former Knight of the Templar Order, part John Constantine parody,[143] part hard-boiled detective with bad grooming habits and a cowardly streak a mile long.

(2) Cliff Steele's new robot body: black, streamlined, with built-in weapons systems and sensory apparatus which allows him to literally *feel* for the first time since his accident.

(3) Fear the Sky: assassins in three-piece suits with heads like celestial objects who carry bladed weapons shaped like question marks.

(4) Baphomet: the pagan oracle, in the form of a disembodied horse head with a railroad spike embedded in its skull.

(5) The Dry Bachelors: oddities made from old love letters and dead skin cells, dressed in purple suits and fedoras, with hammers and exclamation point balloons as weapons.

(6) The Mystery Kites: scouts "made from specially selected murder victims stretched across bone frames."

(7) The Never, Never Boys: Wynken, Blynken, and Nod: demonic children wearing trench coats and gas masks as they ride their tricycles along

---

[143] John Constantine, created by Alan Moore, first appeared in *Swamp Thing* #37 (1985). Constantine is the prototypical occult investigator, with his trench coat, cigarettes, and sarcastic tone.

the walls and ceilings.

(8) The Cult of the Unwritten Book: the agency behind these terrifying and strange creatures who have been sent to capture...

(9) The Fifth Window: a young man covered in tattooed words who will be used to "summon the Unmaker [which will] mean the end of the universe."

All that, plus some plot and characterization, in just a single issue. It's certainly a stark contrast to the prolonged, slow-moving decompression that plagues current comic books.[144] Morrison's strategy for juggling all these new characters and ideas is to use Willoughby Kipling as a narrator. Kipling basically just shows up and tells the story, convincing the Doom Patrol to join him. Through his exposition, we find out who these strange creatures are and what they want – and what they want, apparently, is to destroy the world (of course), which the Doom Patrol certainly isn't going to allow to happen (which explains why the members instantly team up with Kipling – not that Morrison would have wasted any pages on debate or discussion when he had so many crazy new concepts to introduce).

The plot of "The Word Made Flesh" consists of Willoughby Kipling avoiding death by defeating or running from the agents of the Cult of the Unwritten Book. Meanwhile, the young man covered in tattoos, the so-called "Fifth Window," finds himself in a similar predicament. The difference is that the Cult wants to abduct the tattooed young man and they want to kill Kipling. The sequences involving the actual Doom Patrol are relatively brief and can be summarized in a single sentence: Cliff gets a new body before Willoughby Kipling shows up and leads them to the alley where the Fifth Window is hiding. That takes all of seven pages; the other seventeen pages feature the introductions of the abundantly strange agents of the Cult and the attempts to avoid them.

The *fiction / reality* dualism is explored in "The Word Made Flesh" (not surprising, considering the title), but on a different level than Morrison used

[144] The "grim-and-gritty" trend of the late 1980s and 1990s was replaced, in the first decade of the 2000s, with "decompressed storytelling," a technique which maximizes character moments but prolongs the length of the narrative. Each individual issue tells only a small part of a larger story. Nothing significant happens in any one chapter, and a reader has to buy six or ten issues (or wait for the trade paperback collection) to see how everything plays out. Morrison rejects that technique even today, and attempts to cram as much into each issue as possible.

in *Animal Man.* While *Animal Man* was full of metafictional moments, *Doom Patrol* maintains the integrity of its fictional world while demonstrating the power of words and language to invoke change. For example, to defeat Fear the Sky, the Cult's first wave of assassins, Kipling uses a 1903 edition of Robert Louis Stevenson's *A Child's Garden of Verses*. By reading aloud from the text, chanting Stevenson's poetry, the Fear the Sky agents are sucked into the book, "trapped forever," as Kipling narrates, "in one of Charles Robinson's illustrations." Later, Baphomet is described as being "in the guise of Falada from the Grimm Brothers' 'The Goose Girl.'"[145] Then, of course, the Never, Never Boys are called Wynken, Blynken, and Nod after the nursery rhyme of the same name (not identified in the issue, though) which begins: "Wynken, Blynken, and Nod one night / Sailed off in a wooden shoe – / Sailed on a river of crystal light, / Into a sea of dew." The fiction, all of it intended for children, is used in "The World Made Flesh" to control, inform, terrify, or destroy. Morrison explores the potency of fiction and expresses a deep knowledge of the horrific subtext of fairy tales and nursery rhymes.

The ultimate text in *Doom Patrol* #31, though, is the Fifth Window himself. He's covered with tattoos of words which will be used to summon the Unmaker and destroy, or negate, the universe. Kipling, at one point, calls him *the Book* of the Fifth Window, as if he were not a human at all (which he is to the Doom Patrol) but a mere text to be read (which he is to the Cult). Obviously, the Doom Patrol cannot afford to allow such a text to reach its intended readers.

In *Doom Patrol* #32, "Decreator," we see the steps the Doom Patrol takes to prevent the end of the world. We also see that Morrison doesn't plan on slowing things down, as he once again packs the issue with new characters and concepts such as:

(1) The Pale Police: assassins with "B.O. and absolutely no sense of humor" who draw the thumb print of their intended victim on their white helmets and only speak in anagrams.

(2) The Hiroshima Shadows: beings who "[flit] through the night and [moan] in Japanese" while attacking the Doom Patrol on behalf of the Cult of

---

[145] In "The Goose Girl," the title character talks to Falada each day, even though Falada's head has been cut off and mounted in the wall of an alley. Thus, Baphomet here appears as a mounted horse head who can speak.

the Unwritten Book.

(3) The Shroud of Stilts: "one of the minor grotesques," a mass of stitched-together burlap with a gaping maw hovering over long wooden legs.

(4) Holy Pop: 7-Up blessed by "a defrocked priest," a liquid used to erase all the names in the phone book except the name of the person bearing the Wound.

(5) The Wound: a laceration on the otherwise innocent Emilio Cuervo which acts as a portal between the headquarters of the Cult and the world of the Doom Patrol.

(6) Nürnheim: the ghost of a German town, "sometimes its hidden in an old photograph or in a drawing in a comic." It is the moving headquarters of the Cult of the Unwritten Book.

(7) The Plague of Bodiless Mouths: who argue and fly through the park.

(8) Whispering Jack: who "haunted the houses of unmarried women, suggesting indecent ingredients for unusual recipes."

(9) The Weeping Blades: headless muscle and bone figures with crowns of swords who spraypaint strange slogans on the walls.

(10) The Little Sisters of Our Lady of the Razor: deformed knife-wielding nuns in ragged habits with glowing eyes and faces wrapped in twine.

(11) The Decreator: a giant glowing bloodshot eye, peering down from the fragmented sky.

After an unbelievable amount of new creations in the previous issue, Morrison not only maintains the superabundance of new characters in *Doom Patrol* #32, but he adds even more, for a total of twenty new concepts in the first two issues of this storyline (with one more issue left to go in the story). Such a frantic creative pace perfectly matches the speed of the plot. The Doom Patrol members (and the readers) bounce from one new threat to the next so quickly that they become disoriented and uncertain how to proceed. Luckily, Willoughby Kipling is still around to explain everything and keep the heroes (and the readers) on course.

The plot continues from the previous issues, with the Doom Patrol trying to protect the Fifth Window from the Cult of the Unwritten Book because, as Kipling explains, the tattoos are "said to contain the secret name of the Antigod. The Cult wants to decipher the name, summon the Antigod, and bring about the end of the universe." To tie in with the *duality* theme, the

Antigod was created when God said "let there be light," thereby casting his own shadow. The shadow is "the Antigod, the Unmaker, the Decreator" according to Kipling.

*Doom Patrol* #32 is the second act of a three-part story, and one might expect that with all these agents and assassins confronting the heroes, a fisticuff or two might break out. Morrison gives us the obligatory fights, but not in any traditional way. When Cliff, Rebis, and Crazy Jane fight the Hiroshima Shadows, Morrison gives us a panel of the heroes running into battle, a splash page showing some action, and then a few shots in the background as Kipling talks to the Fifth Window in the foreground. In most comic book stories, the fight scenes are the foreground, and if there's a background, it might feature nameless victims and soon-to-be-damaged buildings. Here, we get two people talking in the foreground about the best place to hide from danger, while the barely visible fight scene happens in the distance (or off-panel). Later in the issue, Kipling is forced to confront an assassin from the Pale Police on his own, and instead of invoking some magical escape or using his ingenuity, he quivers and cries while he begs for his life: "Please... I'm not really involved with these people. They've led me astray. I... I have asthma." When Rebis shows up to rescue him, the fight lasts only one panel. Afterward, Kipling doesn't even try to excuse his cowardice. Such an inversion of the normal comic book action scenes is typical of Morrison. We saw it in the constant anticlimactic structure of *Zenith* and the ineptitude of Buddy Baker in *Animal Man*. Here, the Doom Patrol members are actually effective and efficient, but Morrison doesn't seem very interested in that side of the story – he'd rather focus on the odd and the strange.

One of the odd and strange occurrences in *Doom Patrol* #32 is that Cliff finds himself transported through the Wound into Nürnheim, the ever-moving headquarters of the Cult of the Unwritten Book. This time, Nürnheim isn't located in an old photograph, it's inside the very snow globe that's in Niles Caulder's lab located at Doom Patrol headquarters. Cliff has once again (just as he did inside Jane's mind) taken the typical path of the hero and gone inside the belly of the beast, only this time his descent has placed him inside something as ridiculous, and apparently innocent, as a snow globe.

The final odd and strange occurrence in the issue is the appearance of the

Antigod on the last page in the form of a gigantic glowing eye which hovers above the city.

As he did so powerfully in the previous issue, Kipling once again invokes a children's story, "Chicken Little" this time providing a note of humor upon which to end the issue. The giant eye of the Decreator recalls the startling moment when Buddy Baker, in *Animal Man* #19, looked out past the confines of the page and realized that he was being observed by people reading his adventures. The image above from the final page of *Doom Patrol* #32 puts us in the opposite place. This time, we are inside, along with the Doom Patrol, looking out at a higher power, embodied (if that's even an appropriate word in this instance) by a menacing, all-seeing eye.

The following issue, *Doom Patrol* #33, "The Puppet Theater," picks up the *vision* motif immediately, and Willoughby Kipling provides a bit of historical context. Describing the radiant eye of the Decreator, he says, "The Egyptians called it the eye of Horus, lord of force and fire. For thousands of years, the Hindus have known it as the annihilating eye of Shiva." Morrison used the Egyptian allusion before, if you recall, in *Zenith*'s Phase Four, when the former Cloud 9 members declared themselves to be rulers of the world and adopted the name (and eye logo) of Horus. Like the Decreator, the members of Horus in *Zenith* ultimately wanted to destroy the world. Buddy Baker, during that pivotal scene in *Animal Man* #19, had shouted, "I can see you!" which shows just how important *vision* is as a path to enlightenment (or terror). In *Doom Patrol* #33, the eye of the Decreator looms over the heroes like a judgmental voyeur.

Kipling goes on to explain how the Decreator will accomplish the negation of the world after Kipling angrily realizes that his cigarette has vanished:

> Have you ever seen a computer virus at work? When the virus gets into a program, the onscreen information begins to drop out of existence – letter by letter, figure by figure. That's what it's doing. The decreator is annihilating the universe, bit by bit. All the objects in the universe are dropping out of existence... And there isn't a single bloody thing we can do to stop it.

Meanwhile, Cliff Steele, still trapped inside the snow globe, finds himself confronted by two new agents of the Cult of the Unwritten Book: Hoodman Blind and Hoodman Shame. As Kipling's narration explains (and to be

clear, Kipling isn't present to witness this, but Morrison's conceit in this storyline is that Kipling is telling the tale after it's already been completed, and he has presumably heard all the details from Cliff), "[The Hoodmen] eat all the words that are on the tips of other people's tongues. They thrive on misplaced words, savoring the lost potential of each expression." Notice once again how Morrison connects language with power. To the Hoodmen, words are energy, both actual and potential, to be converted into electricity, which they use to disable Cliff.

As Cliff is dragged off to the center of Nürnheim, within the snow globe, and the ominous puppet theater that resides there, Rebis, Jane, and Kipling confront more agents from the Cult: the Starving Skins, fork-wielding humanoids held together by safety pins. Morrison still continues to throw new characters and concepts at the reader, even during the climax of the three-part story, but these agents are easily dispatched by the Doom Patrol. Cliff, unfortunately, was less effective, and his captors have brought him to their masters, the Archons[146] of Nurnheim, who are shown to be puppets. Their strings ascend up past the top of the panel.

The rulers of Nürnheim turn out, literally, to be puppets of a higher power. The Archons' strings rise up, out of the panel, and we never see who's ultimately in control. As revealed in *Animal Man*, Grant Morrison is the puppet master, but the characters in *Doom Patrol* never reach that level of awareness. The puppet rulers of Nürnheim don't even communicate with Cliff; they have their own smaller puppets doing all the talking, signifying the layers of power and reality Morrison explored so thoroughly when he confronted Buddy Baker in his final *Animal Man* issue. Here, the smaller puppets resemble the famous Punch and Judy[147] characters (another allusion to children's stories and their terrifying implications), and as Punch strikes Judy over the head with his club, he explains to Cliff what they hope to achieve by summoning the Decreator: "We achieve nothing. Literally nothing." Judy elaborates, her face and body covered in blood from Punch's

---

[146] *Archon* is an ancient Greek term for "ruler." It shares the same derivation as the word *monarch*. Morrison's perspective on government, as well as his metaphysical perspective, can be readily seen in the image of the Archons as literal puppets of some higher power.

[147] Punch and Judy shows have been performed for hundreds of years, but the basic story has always involved a hyper-violent Punch beating his way to victory by overcoming everything from the police, to the devil, to his own wife.

blows: "God, too, will come to nothing. All the strivings of humankind, all the pointless victories and triumphs of the human spirit. All for nothing...For ever and ever. Nothing." They are nihilists, and it's as simple as that. Cliff, in action hero mode, yells, "No Way!" and rushes up to the bell tower of the puppet theater to nosily alert the Doom Patrol that he's actually inside the snow globe.

On the outside, Crazy Jane, through the persona of Lucy Fugue, explains how they can stop the Decreator from fully forming: "The Decreator is a vibration, nothing more... We're going to set up a counter-vibration. An interference pattern." Her pseudo-science counters the Decreator, and both parallel events (Jane on the outside and Cliff on the inside) seem to be enough to disrupt the approaching Armageddon. When Joshua Clay, in Doom Patrol headquarters, hears the bells ringing within the snow globe, he throws it to the ground, shattering it. Cliff emerges unscathed, but Nürnheim itself seems to emerge as well, as it begins to expand into their world.

Then, nothing. It blinks out of existence, and the eye of the Decreator vanishes as well. Morrison once again provides an anticlimax, just as he's done a dozen times before. The threat, though, is not completely eliminated, as Kipling explains: "Objects and people will continue to vanish mysteriously, but it'll all happen so slowly that no one need ever know the old place is coming undone."[148] The Doom Patrol seems unsatisfied with that explanation, but Kipling disappears through a portal made from a smoke ring before they can stop him.

Ultimately, there's nothing more they can do, so Niles Caulder turns his attention to Cliff's new body: "I could have made a better body out of Campbell's soup cans," he says, in reference to the fact that Doc Magnus built this new shell for Cliff's brain, but the body was so easily defeated by the Hoodmen. Caulder seems annoyed by the prospect of having to fix someone else's mistakes, but he's going to have to do it himself if he wants it done right, he thinks. It's an early indication of his increasing (or increasingly transparent) *hubris*.

The Decreator storyline that runs through *Doom Patrol* #31-33 captures the essence of Morrison's writing. His prolific mind is evident here, with

---

[148] Before he departs, Kipling's pen disappears, proving that the Decreator is still at work, albeit slowly. It's a witty commentary by Morrison that explains all the missing socks and lost writing implements of the world.

dozens of new characters and concepts introduced in only three issues, and his fascination with the power of language to shape reality shines throughout the story. His favorite motifs and themes appear as well: *doubling / duality*, *eye / vision*, and *fiction / reality*. The battle once again puts the universe on the brink of destruction and ends with an anticlimax. It's Morrison through and through. The only dominant theme without much explication is the *mind / body* connection, but as you'll see, he addresses that thoroughly in the very next issue.

*Doom Patrol* #34, "The Soul of a New Machine," asks the essential question on the first page: "Does the body rule the mind or does the mind rule the body?" Beneath that question, we see a splash page of a brain in a nutrient tank, connected to dials, tubes, and gauges. It's Cliff's brain, and Niles Caulder complains egotistically as he rebuilds Cliff's body. Once he completes the repairs, but before he returns Cliff's brain back inside the body, Caulder leaves to procure some chocolate. "I refuse to perform a delicate operation without chocolate," he tells Joshua Clay. Moments after they leave, Cliff finds himself in a strange situation:

Cliff's body explains to his brain, "I've just developed consciousness. It's a little embarrassing and I'm not really sure how it happened. My guess is a faulty responsometer." He tells his brain that he wants to talk because he's worried what might happen if they put the brain back in to him. His body fears a loss of independence when the brain is re-inserted.

This entire issue takes the old philosophical question about whether the mind and body are independent or inextricably linked and turns it into a literal conflict. It's the "real life" demonstration of the basic concern addressed by 17th century Dutch philosopher, Rene Descartes, in his *Meditations of First Philosophy*:

> I have a clear and distinct idea of myself, in as far as I am only a thinking and unextended thing, and as, on the other hand, I possess a distinct idea of a body, in as far as it is only an extended and unthinking thing, it is certain that I, [that is, my mind, by which I am what I am], is entirely and truly distinct from my body and may exist without it.

Of course, Morrison inverts Descartes statement by showing a body that is an independent and thinking thing, a body that may exist without connection to a mind. Morrison's clearly having fun with the idea, and he takes it to ridiculous extremes, as I'll soon show, but within the context of the story,

Cliff is in real danger. His body, equipped with a diamond drill, cuts a hole in the nutrient tank in which Cliff's brain is housed. When Cliff's brain demands to know why his body is killing him, his body replies, "I call it a refutation of dualism. I guess I'm just a materialist at heart... When your brain dies, will your mind live on? You'll soon find out, Cliff." Cliff's body echoes one of the major concerns of Descartes's *Meditations of First Philosophy*, which attempts to determine whether there is such a thing as *mind* which is independent of biological functions. In other words, is the brain the same as the mind, or is the mind something transcendent? Descartes thinks it is, while Cliff's body claims that he "doesn't care one bit."

Morrison cuts away from that absurd conversation to show a parallel, and equally absurd, conversation occurring a few miles away between old Doom Patrol enemies Monsieur Mallah and the Brain. "Plato was the first to make the distinction." says sentient gorilla Monsieur Mallah, "He maintained that the body was simply a vehicle for the mind." The Brain, literally a disembodied brain in a skull-shaped metal housing is being pushed in a baby stroller by Mallah. The Brain says, in frustration, "I know all that! Are we almost there yet?"

The Brain's helplessness is hilariously signified by the baby stroller, and the poor evil genius is at the whim of a gorilla with bad manners.[149] As Mallah rationalizes on the following page, "perhaps, as Descartes argued, we beasts are mere automata... driven by instinct and mindless lust." The Brain quickly refutes that notion by saying, "Descartes was nothing but a miserable git who never had a good time in his entire life!" Later in the conversation, the Brain laments his state: "I long for a body." Their intent is to break into Doom Patrol headquarters and steal a robot body for use by the Brain. As they journey toward their destination, the discussion of Descartes continues,

---

[149] In the scene, Mallah looks for his gum, and finds that he has stuck it on the side of the Brain's head. The Brain, enraged, says, "Did I bring you up to be a slob? I think not." It's worth noting, by the way, that Morrison is presenting two classic *Doom Patrol* villains, the Brain and Monsieur Mallah, in a radically new context. The Brain was traditionally presented as a criminal genius in a skull-shaped tank, and Mallah was always shown as a hyper-intelligent ape, but they had never been shown in such a warped domestic manner as Morrison presents them in this issue. Their bickering only adds to the subtext and points to some strange partnership between the two characters which had remained unexplored prior to Morrison.

with Mallah, as before, taking the Dutch side, and the Brain taking the opposing view. The Brain rejoices in his past success with Mallah, saying, "You were an ape, a savage brute. And I made you a genius! I proved Descartes wrong!" Mallah happily agrees, but also describes he and the Brain as "a vivid and explicit expression of Cartesian dualism," meaning the independent body (i.e. Mallah), and the independent mind (i.e. the Brain). Ultimately, the Brain ends Mallah's later discussion of Descartes by simply saying, "Oh, shut up, Mallah."

Inside the headquarters, Cliff's body is expressing his newfound freedom: "I'm going to enjoy life instead of worrying," he says, indicating that thinking and worrying are the domain of the brain, and the body need not concern itself with such things. "I just act," he explains.

When Mallah and the Brain burst into the room, Morrison gives us a unique approach to the philosophical conundrum he's been investigating. Instead of mind vs. body, he gives us body vs. body (Cliff's body vs. Mallah) and mind vs. mind (Cliff's brain vs. *the* Brain) as Mallah literally throws his master toward the nutrient tank.

The Brain's wonderful line: "At last we are face-to-face in open combat!" and Cliff's brain's reply, "This is ridiculous," subvert any attempt to take these philosophical issues seriously. It's a farce, and Morrison knows it. It's a mockery of the attempt to "dignify some old costumed claptrap," as he once said in *Animal Man*. Morrison continues the absurdity of the farce after Mallah defeats Cliff's body. (Not surprisingly, the "battle" between the two brains was uneventful.) After a brief surgical procedure, the Brain finds himself in possession of a body, the body formerly known as Cliff. "It's a triumph, Mallah!" says the Brain. After an awkward moment, they agree to "stop pretending" and finally admit their mutual love for one another. "Kiss me, Mallah!" says the Brain, "but first... please... take that gum out of your mouth." When their lips touch, the robot body explodes. (Why? The reader isn't told. Perhaps a malfunction or a safety feature?)

All that remains of the two bizarre lovers is a flying beret which lands on the tank which holds Cliff's brain. The final page of the story mirrors the first page. It's the same image, with the same caption, but with three differences: (1) the stylish beret, (2) the wad of gum which Mallah inadvertently placed over the hole in the tank, thereby saving Cliff's brain, and (3) the answer to the essential question about whether the body rules the

From *Doom Patrol* #34 – With some help from Monsieur Mallah, the Brain's brain faces Cliff Steele's brain in "open combat." Art by Richard Case and John Nyberg. Copyright © DC Comics.

mind or the mind rules the body: "I don't know," says the caption.

The caption is not Cliff speaking, because throughout the issue, when his brain talks through the speaker box, the word balloons are shown with a pink background, and these captions are white. It's not Cliff's thoughts either, because when he had a brief hallucination on an earlier page, his thoughts were indicated by jagged oval captions, and these captions are rectangular. It turns out that it's not really a narration at all. The framing sequence which asks and answers the ponderous question simply quotes the lyrics of a Smiths' song.[150] By quoting those lyrics, Morrison shows that the issue of the mind and the body is as relevant in popular culture today as it was for philosophers hundreds of years ago.

## Transvestite Streets, Space Wars, and Alan Moore's Beard

Grant Morrison begins the multi-dimensional alien invasion epic, which runs through *Doom Patrol* #35-41, in an interesting way. In the first several pages, we meet a new character who will serve as an aide (and, in the future, a headquarters) to the Doom Patrol. It's Danny the Street, a sentient downtown block who can communicate through storefront signage, teleport from place to place, and dress in drag. (He's a *transvestite street* because even though his shops are the types of places frequented by men – hardware stores, gun shops, etc – they are decorated with bright, frilly patterns and pastel curtains.) Morrison apparently took inspiration for this creation from a famed 20th century British drag performer who called himself Danny La Rue (*la rue* being the French term for "the street"). Other than the name (and the penchant for cross-dressing), the concept of a sentient street who can move from place to place is a Morrison original, and it fits into the tone of *Doom*

[150] The song, "Still Ill," goes like this: "Does the body rule the mind / Or does the mind rule the body? / I don't know... / Ask me why, and I'll die. / Oh, ask me why and I'll die. / And if you must, go to work – tomorrow. / Well, if I were you, I really wouldn't bother, / For there are brighter sides to life. / And I should know, because I've seen them – / But not very often... / Under the iron bridge we kissed, / And although I ended up with sore lips, / It just wasn't like the old days anymore. / No, it wasn't like those days. / Am I still ill ? / Oh... / Oh, am I still ill ? / Oh..." The first few lines not only frame the story, but the rest of the lyrics demonstrate why Morrison was inclined to include a kiss between the villains.

*Patrol* which has become increasingly absurd since issue #19.

Danny appears at just the right time to help the Doom Patrol, because Niles Caulder has declared that they need to relocate their base of operations after the breach of security by the Brain and Monsieur Mallah in *Doom Patrol* #34. Caulder hasn't decided where they are moving to at the start of *Doom Patrol* #35, but he knows they must move somewhere, and we see Cliff Steele (in his classic orange robot body) moving boxes. When Cliff expresses disdain for the old metal shell he's forced to inhabit, Caulder tells him that he hasn't forgotten Cliff's "predicament" and offers apparent encouragement by quoting the Roman poet Juvenal, who said, "*orandum est ut sit mens sana in corpore sano*." The Latin actually translates as, "you should pray for a healthy mind in a healthy body," which is more of a criticism of Cliff's mental state than a helpful comment about his physical form, but Cliff's reaction, "Couldn't he have said it in English?" reveals that Cliff doesn't understand Caulder's allusion. It's a minor bit of dialogue, irrelevant to the plot, but it shows Caulder's sense of superiority over the other Doom Patrol members and establishes that the team doesn't really understand the level on which Caulder operates. It's relatively insignificant here, but as the series progresses towards its conclusion (or, at least, the conclusion of Morrison's tenure on the title), the teams' ignorance of Caulder's words and deeds will lead to catastrophic results. For now, though, they presume he has the best of intentions, even if they don't understand what those intentions may be.

*Doom Patrol* #35 also introduces some other new Morrison creations, including two new nefarious threats to the team (and the world at large), the surreal, but identical, villains called the Men from N.O.W.H.E.R.E. and their leader, the seemingly-banal-but-actually-psychotic Mr. Jones. Mr. Jones enters the issue in a sequence which parodies the American sitcoms of the 1950s. His first words as he enters his home are, "Hi, Honey! I'm home!" We can see his dutiful wife, in her pink dress and white apron, preparing the family meal in the kitchen as he enters with his words of greeting. But something's wrong: she has forgotten to push the "laugh track" button. So they repeat the scene again on the following page. After the successful entrance, and laughter from the crowd, Mr. Jones says, "Boy, I had a tough day at the office! Hey! That smells good! What is it?" His wife replies, "Why, it's your favorite. It's skinless stew." The laughter continues. Mr.

Jones turns angry, "my boss and his wife are coming over for dinner tonight and he's allergic to skinless stew!" "My promotion could depend on this," he continues. "I told you a million times, honey. Why don't you listen?!" With that he picks up a carving fork and thrusts it toward his wife's face. We see blood splatter in from off panel.

The scene, with its juxtaposition of sitcom clichés and atrociously violent action, recalls the Rodney Dangerfield sequence in Oliver Stone's *Natural Born Killers*. In that film, the oppressive reality of a dysfunctional family is undercut with a laugh track and sitcom conventions, even when acts of degradation or brutality are being committed. It's nearly identical in style and effect to this page. In this case, however, Morrison is not making a pop culture allusion. *Doom Patrol* #35 was released four years *before* Oliver Stone's critically acclaimed film. While it's possible that Stone was referencing Morrison, it's more likely that both creators were mining the same ground: the contrast between the profane horrors of society and the white-washed presentation of society as seen on television. The laugh track in both scenes is vicious because it's a hollow, mindless laughter, reflecting the emptiness of the audience, who laugh on cue, without feeling, because they are conditioned to do so. Yet we are the audience, and we have been complicit in the actions, even if we have never laughed out loud at a sitcom in our lives, because we too have been amused enough to bother watching, or lazy enough not to bother turning the channel.

Mr. Jones's last name represents the average, common man, and his first name, Darren, alludes to the typical sitcom husband who is so nondescript as to be interchangeable, as was the case on *Bewitched* when the husband, also called Darrin (but with a different spelling), was replaced by a completely different actor halfway through the series.[151] After he stabs his wife with the carving fork (she doesn't die – he merely poked out her eyes, indicating the *vision* motif once again – in this case, her blindness symbolizes her ignorance), he ventures into his wood-paneled den where he greets his team, the Men from N.O.W.H.E.R.E. This team, also clearly inspired, at least in name, by television archetypes (in this case, the 1960s television spy show called *The Man from U.N.C.L.E.*),[152] was formed by Mr. Jones, "to eradicate

[151] In 1969, Dick York was replaced by Dick Sargent at the beginning of the sixth season of *Bewitched*.

[152] U.N.C.L.E. stands for "United Network Command for Law and Enforcement."

eccentricities, anomalies, and peculiarities wherever we find them." This modus operandi will obviously put them at odds with the eccentric, anomalous, peculiar super-heroes like the Doom Patrol, but their first task is to confront an even greater threat, as Mr. Jones explains on page 18 of *Doom Patrol* #35:

> What we're talking about here is a sentient street. A street that can think for itself. Not only that, but it can also travel... Sometimes it's an alley in Peking, sometimes a back street in Toronto. And as if all that isn't peculiar enough, the whole street is lined with good macho stores, okay? Except that Danny has dressed them up in fairy lights and lace curtains. Gentlemen, this street is a shameless transvestite...we can't let this... this abomination threaten normalcy any longer... I mean, I'm as tolerant as the next guy, but what can I say, fellas? Destroy Danny the Street [laughter from audience].

The sitcom parody turns to a vicious satire of conservative "family values" in this sequence. Mr. Jones saves his true disgust for Danny's cross-dressing tendencies and tries to cover up his homophobia with by saying, "I'm as tolerant as the next guy," as if saying so makes it true. In word ("fairy," "shameless," "abomination") and deed (intending to destroy Danny), he reveals his intolerance. Even further, he and his team, the Men from N.O.W.H.E.R.E., are completely hypocritical because they are as abnormal as their victims: not only is Mr. Jones aberrant for his treatment of his wife, but his team members are dressed in boxy purple trench coats with striped socks and elfin shoes like the Wicked Witch of the East (another *Wizard of Oz* allusion), their shoulder pads are tiny smokestacks, their heads are blue eggs covered with scribbled words, their eyes dangle from small cranes planted on their heads, and they only speak in sentences which form the acronym N.O.W.H.E.R.E. Morrison exaggerates their peculiarities to accentuate the hypocrisy of prejudice and bigotry, but their absurd appearance fits the tone of the series perfectly. After the Brotherhood of Dada, the Cult of the Unwritten Book, and the love affair between an ape and a brain, "normal" villains would seem like a let down. Morrison must be aware of this, which is why he ironically gives Mr. Jones and his team the belief that, as insanely bizarre as they look and act, they are the only normal ones in the story.

Although my analysis of *Doom Patrol* #35 has primarily focused on the

---

*The Man from* U.N.C.L.E. debuted in 1964 and ran for 104 episodes. The show, a straight-laced espionage affair, is the opposite of the absurdist *Doom Patrol*.

newly introduced characters, Morrison does provide a few sequences involving the actual Doom Patrol members (besides the brief conversation between Cliff Steele and Niles Caulder I described above). One scene shows the team sitting in a circle engaged in group therapy with Caulder. (This scene, which immediately follows the introduction of Mr. Jones, his wife, and the Men from N.O.W.H.E.R.E., seems to be a counterpoint to that fake, sitcom-happy, suburban family – in the case of the Doom Patrol, its dysfunction is visible on the outside, yet they are a closer, more successful "family" than the Joneses.) The Doom Patrol members, in therapy, attempt to respond to Cliff's statements about his unhappiness, which, he says, is caused because he wants to "be a part of... well, life...," but his robot body won't let him. Various members discuss their ideas about life, each statement revealing insight into their characters.

Crazy Jane reveals her tortured multiple personalities when she says, "Life is hell. No. No. It's not," while the metaphysically-oriented Rebis states that "Life is information. It can be understood quite easily as bit strings with logical depths much greater than their lengths," and the timid Dorothy Spinner deflects the question entirely by saying, "Well... can I go to the bathroom, please?" It's yet another scene that is inessential to the plot, but it provides Morrison a chance to emphasize the fragile psyche of each member of the team and show how they are together not because they have a common mission, but because they are similar in their uncommonly damaged mental states. In case we have begun to think of them as super-heroes, Morrison reminds us that they still think of themselves as freaks (and not in a glamorous X-Men way, either – there are no exciting danger room simulations[153] here to prepare the team, just a lot of talking awkwardly while sitting in a circle).

By the end of the issue, the Doom Patrol isn't aware of Mr. Jones or Danny the Street, but when they arrive at the scene of a disturbance at the beginning of *Doom Patrol* #36, they find that the Men from N.O.W.H.E.R.E. have already begun their rampage against abnormality. Danny the Street is aflame, and its inhabitants (Danny has a tendency to pick up the lost and the

---

[153] As much as the X-Men characters play lip-service to their role as outcasts, they have cool, high tech equipment, like the "Danger Room," which lets them artificially simulate any combat environment. And while the X-Men reside in a luxurious mansion, the Doom Patrol members huddle together in a drafty warehouse.

lonely) are under attack. The Doom Patrol arrives in typically unheroic fashion: exiting a cab with slouched shoulders and no immediate sense of haste.

A police officer isn't sure what to make of them, as he says, "I hope you guys are super-heroes because we're out of our depth here!" Soon, the Men from N.O.W.H.E.R.E. engage the Doom Patrol in battle, and Mr. Jones (back at his house, apparently watching the action via a monitor – probably a television set) expresses concern that his team members "haven't been prepared for this," since they weren't planning on fighting the Doom Patrol until their *next* mission. The Men from N.O.W.H.E.R.E. are easily defeated by Cliff, Rebis, and Crazy Jane, who use their various abilities quite effectively. (Cliff's strength dispatches several of the villains, while Rebis destroys two with his energy being, and Crazy Jane's personality, called "the Sin Eater," devours one from within.) It turns out that Mr. Jones's team is not the true threat, but are, as Mr. Jones himself explains to his wife, "just bad, cheap copies of the real thing," although we don't learn what he's talking about in *Doom Patrol* #36. What we do realize, though, is that the events of *Doom Patrol* #36 (along with the previous issue) are merely setting the stage for something much larger. What seemed like a relatively straightforward storyline (weird villains whom the Doom Patrol has to stop) is just the prologue. The first ominous hint of the bigger picture appears on page 8, when Morrison directs our attention away from the final stages of the battle with the Men from N.O.W.H.E.R.E. to introduce something new (a space setting) with some strange beings (who look unlike anything we've seen before, and speak about events we don't yet understand). "The pupa is ready," one of the aliens aboard a strange ship covered with buildings and spires says, "but there is a suspicion that several geomancers of the Kaleidoscape have arrived ahead of us." At the end of the page, one of the aliens points to the Earth while the other says, "Hmm. Nice magnetic field."

These beings appear in only one more panel in the issue, but they are obviously creatures of immense power, and they are coming to Earth. Their words on this page are not totally incoherent either, since we've been reading carefully. Their reference to a "pupa" relates to butterflies which, in turn, recalls the second storyline from Morrison's run on *Doom Patrol*. If you remember, "The Butterfly Collector" narrative featured Red Jack's attempt to kidnap the comatose Rhea Jones for undisclosed reasons. The butterfly connection might be enough to lead us towards the realization that the comatose Rhea is in some type of "pupa" stage, and the mention by these alien beings of the Earth's "nice magnetic field" at the end of the page makes the realization even stronger, because if they're interested in the Earth's magnetism, they would certainly be interested in Rhea, a young woman with magnetic powers.

Besides that ominous interlude, *Doom Patrol* #36 introduces another character whose presence seems to indicate a much bigger story than we initially may have believed. This new character is Flex Mentallo,[154] the self-proclaimed "Man of Muscle Mystery." Mentallo first appears in the audience of a cabaret on Danny the Street during the attack by the Men from N.O.W.H.E.R.E. Mentallo is a thickly-bearded, shaggy-haired homeless man who seems to know something about these so-called agents of normalcy. During the battle, he warns Crazy Jane about their powers, and by the end of the issue, he reveals that the conflict on Danny the Street has triggered his memories: "They made me forget, but now I remember," he says. "Don't you remember me?" he asks the Doom Patrol. "Has everyone forgotten the Pentagon horror? Don't you know who I am? I'm Flex Mentallo." Mentallo flexes his biceps, but the Doom Patrol doesn't seem to know anything about him. His dramatic presence and his cryptic remarks contribute to the feeling that the story in these issues is part of a larger narrative, but Morrison is still setting things up – introducing the cast of characters who will play important roles in the larger epic.

Besides the introduction of the new characters, we also see more of Mr. Jones in *Doom Patrol* #36. He reveals that he created the "cheap copies" of the Men from N.O.W.H.E.R.E., and he prepares to defeat the Doom Patrol

---

[154] Flex Mentallo is featured prominently on the cover of *Doom Patrol* #36, as painted by Simon Bisley. Bisley's Mentallo looks *exactly* like Alan Moore. The similarity cannot be a coincidence. Was Bisley just having a little fun with the likeness, or was Morrison taking a jab at Alan Moore (or paying tribute in some way)? There's no real connection between Alan Moore and Flex Mentallo at all, other than their appearance, but as I've explained in previous chapters, Grant Morrison has had to emerge from the shadow of Alan Moore since he began writing for American publishers, and (as I haven't yet mentioned) Morrison has been notoriously hostile toward Alan Moore's writing in the press, slamming the critical attention paid to *Watchmen* and accusing Moore of plagiarism for his work on a two-part Superman story. It's clearly an angry Alan Moore face on the cover of *Doom Patrol* #36.

by himself with a homemade "delirium box" made from folded paper. His wife, now wearing ridiculous novelty glasses with eyes bouncing on the ends of springs to cover her blindness, expresses concern about their status in the neighborhood: "I heard the neighbors talking about us. I mean, you don't suppose we might be just a little bit quirky ourselves..." Her combination of conformity, common sense, and timidity are subverted by her actions as she says these lines. She blindly bumps into the coat rack and the guffaws from the laugh track coincide with her husband's dismissive response: "What a dumb thing to say!" Mr. Jones, in the role of the "normal, decent American" and husband, has the last word, as always, and in the next panel, Mrs. Jones smiles blankly behind him. Mr. Jones, though, is ultimately humiliated when his attempt to use the delirium box backfires, and he ends up being transported to the backstage area of a theater where he is given a makeover. When his wife turns on the light in the den, she finds Mr. Jones wearing fishnet stockings, women's underwear, a blonde wig, and plenty of makeup. Justice, in his case, is not in his physical defeat, but in his emotional suffering through embarrassment.

The issue ends with the butterfly (Rhea Jones) emerging from her cocoon (coma). Dorothy Spinner, on monitor duty at Doom Patrol headquarters, rushes to alert Niles Caulder and Joshua Clay. When they reach Rhea's room, they find a naked woman surrounded by (a) halos of energy, (b) floating metal objects, and (c) music. Her face is literally without features and on her chest, to once again tie into Morrison's fascination with the motif of *vision*, rests a large glowing eye. (Here, the giant eye seems to indicate her transcendence – she has risen above the bounds of the Earth and has attained both knowledge and power in her new state.)

*Doom Patrol* #37 begins with a one-page text summary of the series thus far.[155] Because it's supposed to be a jumping-on point, Morrison also provides a bit more exposition than normal at the beginning of the issue (even after a full-page of text). One of the interesting bits of dialogue between Cliff Steele and Niles Caulder, though, touches upon the essence of what makes the Doom Patrol special. Cliff says, "it might be nice to just stop a bank robbery or foil a criminal mastermind. You know, like the regular super-guys." Caulder responds by saying, "Nonsense, Cliff! It's essential

---

[155] DC was trying to attract new readers to the title, apparently, and they wanted the series to seem less impenetrable to newcomers.

From *Doom Patrol* #37 – Rhea Jones, after her metamorphosis, bears little resemblance to a typical teenage girl. Art by Richard Case and Mark McKenna. Copyright © DC Comics.

that we leave such feeble-minded pursuits to the musclebound cretins who enjoy them. Our work is far more important." It's a logical explanation of why the Doom Patrol has faced so many bizarre opponents, and it's a clever justification for Morrison to keep the plots from becoming routine and dull. To emphasize the non-routine, non-dull atmosphere of *Doom Patrol,* Morrison immediately follows up the conversation between Cliff and Caulder with a full reveal of Rhea's new look as the team members see what has become of her.

Rhea's physical appearance has changed drastically from the Paul Kupperberg issues. In those stories, she was a generically beautiful, athletic girl with long red hair and who went by the super-hero name of "Lodestone." Here, she has become an otherworldly, enigmatic being who floats above humanity and seems disinclined to return to the ground. Rhea explains that the Earth has a "nervous system" (lines of energy – magnetic energy – that run under the "skin of the world").[156] "I'm wired into it," she says, "so I can't hang around." Soon she flits away, speaking distractedly of the circus. Her newfound state has linked her directly into Earth's magnetic field, so we can understand why the magnetically sensitive alien creatures in the previous issue were so interested in her transformation.

To remind us of their interest, Morrison leaves the Doom Patrol behind on page 9 to show the aliens looking down at their target from their approaching space vessel. They speak cryptically this time as well, referring to the "Geomancers," "Huss," "the Cage," and the "Anathematicians" without providing any explanation about what exactly is going on. Morrison disorients us to make us feel uneasy about impending events. We don't know what's going to happen, but we sense it's going to be bad.

The Doom Patrol, meanwhile, tracks Rhea down at what Cliff refers to as "the spookiest circus [he's] ever seen." The details of the circus are unimportant to the main plot, but some of the performers we meet are typical Morrisonian creations: Cesarina, "the beautiful albino somnambulist"; the Girl of Glass who "fell from the moon one forgotten summer evening"; and

---

[156] Rhea seems to be referring to "Ley lines," as described in books like John B. Carlson's *Lodestone Compass: Chinese or Olmec Primacy?* The Ley line theory postulates that the great monuments on the Earth were aligned according to a geometric pattern. Carlson and others attempt to show that these lines coincide with areas of increased magnetic energy.

the Bountiful Baboushka, who "gives birth to a scaled-down perfect replica of herself" every nine months – a living Russian nesting doll, whom Rebis is fascinated by. Meanwhile, shadowy hooded beings observe the Doom Patrol on a monitor. These watchers are not the alien creatures we've seen before – they seem to be the opposition party, because they appear to work with someone or something named "Huss," whom the other alien creatures mentioned with disdain (or fear). These hooded observers mention that they "have the lodestone," an obvious reference to Rhea Jones, who seems to have disappeared from the circus mysteriously before the Doom Patrol can locate her, and the observers call Rebis "the Uroboros," and plan to abduct it as well. The Uroboros is the ancient image of the serpent devouring its own tail, which noted psychologist Carl Jung has described this way: "The uroboros is a dramatic symbol for the integration and assimilation of the opposite, i.e. of the shadow." This is a fitting description of Rebis, who is a combination of man and woman, as well as a combination of biology and energy (and has the power to release a negative being that looks like a glowing shadow). The hooded watchers also indicate that the circus was a false "tableau," which was a trap to catch Rhea (and Rebis, as a bonus), and they "collapse" their artificial circus remotely.

As the circus twists and disappears into a whiff of smoke, the first two aliens who have been monitoring Rhea from space finally arrive on Earth (in the final two pages of *Doom Patrol* #37) and realize that they are too late because one says, "The Geomancers have anticipated us!" Cliff Steele and Crazy Jane have been left behind in the wake of the departing circus, and they witness the arrival of these aliens. Cliff pithily replies, "Holy shit." Throughout the storyline, Cliff's matter-of-fact observations and unpretentious comments serve to undermine any sense of grandeur. Morrison uses Cliff to keep us grounded in reality and to provide more than a bit of humor.

The next issue, *Doom Patrol* #38, begins with an apparently extraneous prologue about a series of strange occurrences from the past. It's another example of Morrison setting the stage for events which will unfold several issues in the future. In this case, the ominous references to a character named "Wallace Sage" and his "sugar tongs" don't pay off until well after the current storyline ends in issue #41. I will point out a few other examples of foreshadowing as they appear, but I won't go into much detail about what all of these clues mean until we see their resolution.

The epic storyline between the Geomancers (the shadowy, hooded beings who abducted Rhea Jones and Rebis), who we finally see fully revealed in *Doom Patrol* #38 and the Emissaries of the Orthodoxy (the aliens who had been observing Rhea from space before she was taken), who we finally see named in the same issue, truly gets underway at this point and builds to a climax (and a resolution) in *Doom Patrol* #41. This narrative involves an inter-dimensional war, and the Doom Patrol members get swept up into it. It's a trope we've seen in comic books before, with the Avengers' involvement in the Kree-Skrull War[157] as the most prominent example. The battle in the *Doom Patrol* storyline, between the Geomancers and the Orthodoxy, involves, at its core, a civil war. As one of the Emissaries explains, an apostate by the name of Huss led the Geomancers in a rebellion against the rulers (a.k.a. the Orthodoxy) of the Insect Mesh[158] (their extra-dimensional realm). The Emissary explains that the war between the Geomancers and the Orthodoxy transformed over the years from a physical battle, to a telekinetic duel, to a war of plagues, to the most recent stage: "the war of nerves" wherein "each side would ignore the other in an attempt to irritate the enemy into submission."

The Emissary explains his presence on Earth as an attempt to stop the Geomancers from enacting their new plan which involves using Rhea Jones to "challenge the impartiality of the Judge Rock," a god-like being who is "the axle upon which time and space turns."[159] In other words, the Geomancers think that destruction of the Judge Rock will give them victory over the Orthodoxy. The Emissaries want to stop them. The Doom Patrol members are caught in the middle because they want to rescue their teammates, not necessarily because the Earth is endangered by the conflict.

---

[157] The Kree-Skrull war was was an intergalactic conflict between the technologically-advanced Kree and the shape-shifting Skrulls. The Avengers became players in the battle during an extended storyline which was published in *Avengers* #89-97 (1971).

[158] Insects as otherworldly beings. I've explained before how Morrison keeps returning to this motif. He explores it more fully in his later work like *The Invisibles*, but this *Doom Patrol* storyline is an early indication of his tendencies.

[159] The Judge Rock bears more than a passing resemblance to to the giant floating stone head in John Boorman's *Zardoz* (1974). The false god of that film, Zardoz, got its name from a fragment of a book: "The Wonderful Wi[ZARD] of [OZ]." Thus, the Insect Mesh storyline connects to the Wizard of Oz motif I've explained earlier.

(Morrison doesn't give us any evidence that the war affects anything but the Insect Mesh – by willingly risking their lives to join the fray, Cliff Steele and Crazy Jane show how much their makeshift family means to them.)

Morrison eschews clearly defined labels of good and evil for these two warring factions. While Cliff and Jane are listening to the Orthodoxy's side of the story, Rhea and Rebis, in no apparent danger, meet the leader of the Geomancers, Huss, and listen to his reasons for fighting the war. Morrison provides some complexity to the conflict that shows that both sides have legitimacy, although their true motivations are never clearly defined. Huss, who speaks in *dualities* (saying things like "venom stroke poison" [venom / poison] and "interest stroke curiosity" [interest / curiosity]), describes his plans to Rhea and Rebis:

> I desire to be remembered stroke admired as the one who made a change stroke difference. This war has been a war of faith. The orthodoxy believed stroke insisted theirs was the only possible route to salvation and the early Ultraquists challenged them. It is time a challenge of equal courage and foresight was made stroke accepted. Us must enter the zones.

The zones of which he speaks are powerful regions occupied by his forces (i.e. "The zone of dismay" and "The zone of transparent things"), and their ultimate goal is to destroy "the watchman of the powers. The last guardian angel. The Judge Rock" to reach the flower hidden at its center. This flower, "all that remains of the primal tree of knowledge stroke ignorance," will grant them victory in the war, according to Huss.

Meanwhile, Cliff and Jane, aboard the Orthodoxy vessel, travel though "webspace" (a type of hyper-reality) to reach the home of these strange creatures, a home filled with bone spires and red skies, a home called the Insect Mesh.

*Doom Patrol* #39 begins with another prologue, this time focusing on the middle-aged Delores Watson, who visits a fortune teller to find out about someone "very dear" to her: Flex Mentallo. This is more foreshadowing by Morrison, and he quickly returns to the Insect Mesh storyline by page 4 (although he does briefly return to a Flex Mentallo interlude for one additional page later in the issue, showing Dorothy giving Flex a clean shave and haircut). Inside the Insect Mesh, Cliff and Jane are taken to the Cage, which is the birthing center – the genesis of their world – and their only power source. The Cage is operated (or maintained) by the Anathematicians (notice how Morrison is finally revealing the details of these mysterious words we first saw several issues ago). Within the Cage, Cliff is attacked by a Smoke Dog, a creature sent to disrupt the Orthodoxy on behalf of the Geomancers. Before Cliff can react, he is dismantled (bitten in half – not for the first time in Morrison's run) by the beast. Jane transforms into her lethal Black Annis persona to eviscerate the Smoke Dog as Cliff's fluids drain out.

Rhea and Rebis, on a separate plane of reality (the Geomancers mostly operate from an ever-shifting dimension called the Kaleidoscape), listen to more relatively dull exposition from Huss regarding the war. Huss does say something interesting in this sequence, though. He refers to Rebis as being "in the early stroke preliminary stages of [its] transformation," and Rebis apparently agrees, because it says, "Yes. The Aenigma Regis is to come soon." This is another bit of foreshadowing that will not lead to anything for many issues. The rest of the issue concerns the build-up to the final battle. The Geomancers formulate their plan, while the members of the Orthodoxy perform a ritual which will help them unite to defend their world. Such commotion appears to be awakening the slumbering Judge Rock, but Morrison turns our attention to a more immediate concern: the terrifying sound of a giant spider which causes Jane to shrink in fear. As the creature turns the corner, we see what the Orthodoxy has done to repair Cliff's damaged body: they've given him six metal insect legs.

The next issue, *Doom Patrol* #40, again starts with a prologue, this time focusing on the Men in Green[160] who abduct Mr. Christmas, a man writing an exposé of "The Secret Government." Morrison doesn't attempt to tie this prologue into Flex Mentallo's story or the case of the sugar tongs, but by linking them all together in these successive prologues, he warns the reader that all of these situations must relate somehow. Once again, he spends only three pages on the prologue before throwing us back into the Insect Mesh storyline.

The assembled army of the Orthodoxy, with their insect armor, distinctly recalls the "Bug-Man" exoskeleton worn by the villains during the final storyline in *Animal Man*. Morrison seems to use the insect motif as a shorthand for cruelty and danger, and one look at Cliff's new body shows how effective such a motif can be. Cliff has never looked more lethal.

---

[160] A variation on the stereotypical government agents usually depicted as "Men in Black."

The two warring factions begin moving toward an ultimate confrontation by traversing various strange zones which each provide unique obstacles (walls that randomly shoot up from the ground, to give one example). As the Geomancers send Rhea Jones toward the Judge Rock and the army of the Orthodoxy marches onward, Cliff reveals some doubts about the whole situation to Jane: "This war doesn't make any real sense," he says. "There's something... I don't know... something disconnected and unreal about this." He doesn't go any further with his thoughts, but his expression of doubt provides a lifeline to the reader. This storyline has been fraught with exposition and falsely built drama. None of it has seemed as menacing (or entertaining) as Morrison's previous story arcs. Cliff, by providing a criticism of the war's unreality, allows us to recognize the flaws of the story without blaming Morrison. Because of Cliff's comment, the silliness of the entire epic is the fault of the characters at war, not the fault of a misguided writer. It's an interesting loophole in the plot, a way for Morrison to signal to the reader that there might be a reason why this conflict is more boring than previous issues.

Nevertheless, the war continues to escalate, with Cliff's hesitancy doubled by Rebis's criticism of Huss's motives for the battle. (Rebis accuses Huss of selfishly attempting to gain the flower to grant himself some sort of immortality instead of using it to help his people.) Also, the rigid "life" of the Orthodoxy seems less and less appealing the more we see of it. What seemed at first to be a case of both sides having equal legitimacy has, by *Doom Patrol* #40, denigrated into a story about both sides being wrong. As these internal quarrels occur, Rhea infiltrates the Judge Rock and retrieves the flower from its core. Although she's supposed to wait for Huss's signal before doing anything else, Rhea decides it's "Time to bring down the house," which leads to a pause in the action as the two factions are about to come face to face. Covered in shadow, they all stop and look up.

The looming shadow is the Judge Rock, and it's falling from the sky.

The ultimate chapter of the Insect Mesh epic, *Doom Patrol* #41, begins with what's labeled as "A Final Prologue." Dolores Watson, who had sought information about Flex Mentallo two issues earlier, visits a lost-and-found booth in a train station. The man in charge of the booth makes reference to a few of the mysterious occurrences that were described in the very first prologue before an inhuman hand reaches from behind a curtain an apparently kills Dolores Watson. "Is it real? Is it real? Is it real?" the lost-and-found man asks, not with a look of terror, but with a chilling smile on his face. The cumulative effect of these prologues is powerful. Morrison sets up a significant, mysterious threat that will surely challenge the Doom Patrol if they ever get a chance to return home. The prologues also ensure that we don't forget about Flex Mentallo, who will play a pivotal role in the narrative as soon as the Insect Mesh story is finished.

Meanwhile, the Judge Rock has landed upon the Doom Patrol, but Cliff is able to push a chunk of rock off himself to reveal that he has shielded Jane beneath his insect legs. Huss declares himself victorious for destroying the Judge Rock, but Rhea points out that it was she, not he, who caused the destruction. Instead of giving the flower to Huss, she throws it to Cliff and tells him to take it back to the Rock, saying, "You'll know what to do when you get in there." The leaders of the Orthodoxy refuse to accept defeat, and Huss, of course, continues to declare his victory.

Rebis, in an attempt to finally resolve the conflict, describes the American Indian tradition of the *potlatch*,[161] a competitive show of wealth whereby a tribe will destroy something of value to show that it doesn't need it. In return, the opposing tribe will destroy something of their own of even greater value to show their superior integrity, and so on, until one tribe finally admits defeat by refusing to sacrifice anything else. The Orthodoxy and the Geomancers enact this practice immediately, and, with their vast power, they quickly destroy everything of value in their world before realizing what they have done. Ultimately, though, it's Cliff's action of planting the flower within the Judge Rock that brings the war to a conclusion. The Judge Rock rises once again, but it now glows with knowledge from the flower. At this point, Rhea reveals the true origin of the Judge Rock:

> It was one of several angels sent to watch over man after the fall and one of its tasks was to transform from a physical reality into an abstract idea.[162] The thing is, Balzizras [the Judge Rock] thought God had made kind of a mess of the Earth and it decided to try its

---

[161] In a potlatch, the host gives away, or destroys, their possessions, thus displaying their wealth and power.

[162] Notice how this is the same goal as the members of Horus from Phase Four of *Zenith*. Morrison continually explores the relationship between the physical and the mental to show how the two are bound together inextricably.

> own experiment. It stole a cutting from the original tree of knowledge and then fled from Earth. Balzizras only wanted to create its own perfect world, but this planet was the result. The problem was it had no imagination. The only working dynamic it could think of was conflict... The power of real creativity was frozen in the flower. It's free now. Now you don't have to pray to a hollow head-in-the-clouds. The creator's come down among you, not as a judge, but as a sort of imaginative energy. Pretty neat, huh?

This is yet another example of Morrison's fascination with dystopias (as thoroughly explored in Phases Two and Four of *Zenith*) and his religious reverence of the power of the imagination. To Morrison, creation is a divine act, which is why his fiction often deals with the manipulation of reality. In his cosmology, imagination is the opposite of stagnation.

Rhea's revelation of the true nature of the Judge Rock leads to opposite reactions from the warring parties. Huss is despondent, saying, "My consciousness shall be extinguished stroke erased at death... I thought the flower would let me live forever! I didn't want this!" On the other side, one of the Geomancers proposes the building of a tower, with "Mesh and Kaleidoscape in collaboration. A beautiful tower with its roots in the foundations of the earth and its heights in the heavens."

The Geomancers agree to collaborate on the tower, which, as they build higher, will allow their "consciousness [to] ascend toward divinity." Their first creative act is to build what amounts to a Tower of Babel,[163] which we already know is destined for failure. But as Cliff says, in a typically subversive but humorous response, "I suppose it's better than watching TV."

In the brief aftermath of the war, Rhea, who has achieved some higher state of awareness (she does have that giant eye on her chest, remember), decides to journey into the stars rather than return to Earth with the Doom Patrol members, and Rebis turns his attention to the newly alive Balzizras and the concept of a transcendental tower. "The whole concept of the tower indicates a symbolic wish to transcend duality and achieve some kind of union with a fundamental state of pure consciousness."[164]

---

[163] In the book of Genesis, chapter 11, humans, all speaking a single language, build a tower intended to reach the heavens, but because of their hubris, God mixes up all the languages so they cannot communicate. Thus, they can't work together to finish the tower.

[164] Morrison once again directly tells the reader the theme of the story by putting it

Rebis's words about transcending duality (of mind and body, presumably) and achieving a union with pure consciousness sounds a lot like what Morrison explored in *Zenith*, *Arkham Asylum*, and *Animal Man*. In those stories, and in Rebis's dreams, true power is not mind over body but mind without the burden of body. But in all cases, real transcendence is ultimately impossible.

It's a theme that will resonate more fully in future issues, but really, Cliff's final line says it all, "Screw symbolism and let's go home."

## Secret Origins and Sugar Tongs

The secret origin story is one of the most common tropes in super-hero comic book history. Although some comic book series begin with a story illustrating how a character became empowered and / or adopted a costumed identity (*Fantastic Four* #1, for example, shows the four intrepid explorers as they are bombarded by cosmic rays, thereby gaining superhuman powers), many minor characters have their origins revealed years after they are introduced. In either case, the story is deemed a "secret" origin, presumably because the public at large does not know the full details of how the character gained his or her powers. DC Comics actually had a long-running series entitled *Secret Origins*,[165] an anthology series in which readers could find brief (8-to-12-page) stories describing how both popular and relatively obscure characters gained their super-heroic identities. Often, these origins provided streamlined, and slightly revised, takes on stories that had already been presented somewhere in the past. As such, the term "secret origin" implies not only a secret that's kept from the public, but a slight alteration on the previously accepted details of the character's genesis. (In other words, the writers of a secret origin pretend to reveal the "true" story as opposed to the exaggerated or over-simplified version that was previously published.)

Grant Morrison has used the idea of a secret origin throughout his work not just to provide background and character motivation, but to provide a narrative impetus as well. In *Zenith*, the title character sides with nearly anyone who has a clue about his parents' death, and the conspiracy that led to

---

into the words of a character.

[165] *Secret Origins* lasted for 50 issues from 1986-1990 and featured Grant Morrison stories in issues #39, #46, and #50.

his possession of super-powers is a main plot thread throughout all four phases of the series. Yet, Morrison never once gives us a clear-cut secret origin story for Zenith. The whole of the four-part series is, in essence, his secret origin. In *Arkham Asylum* and *Gothic*, Batman's origin, although never directly retold, is the traumatic event which binds the themes together. In *Animal Man*, Morrison uses multiple iterations of Buddy Baker's secret origin to reveal the reality manipulation of the yellow aliens and to play with the metafictional aspects of the series. In contrast to Zenith, Animal Man is given several secret origins, and, as is the status quo in the comic book world, the "true" origin is the one most recently published.

In *Doom Patrol* #42, Grant Morrison plays with this trope once again in a story entitled, "Musclebound: The Secret Origin of Flex Mentallo." (He will play with the Doom Patrol's own origin by the end of his run on the series, but that's a topic for later.) Flex Mentallo, a Grant Morrison creation, first appeared during the last storyline, and as I mentioned previously, a series of prologues over the course of several issues has emphasized that Flex Mentallo is a character we need to watch. *Doom Patrol* #42 is the beginning of the explanation of *why* we need to pay attention to him. The events of this story and the next take place while Cliff, Rebis, and Jane are off in outer space settling the feud between the Geomancers and the Orthodoxy. It is, therefore, at least in the beginning, a Doom Patrol story without any of the central Doom Patrol members in it. In issue #42, Flex narrates the story himself, showing an awareness of the trope in which he is participating when he says, at the beginning, "My origin story's fairly ordinary compared to some." Although Flex is telling his story in 1991, he explains that his origin goes back to 1954 (which would make him over 50 years old, assuming he was a teenager in the 1950s – he, like most super-heroes, looks to be in his mid-thirties at most, especially after his Alan Moore beard is shaved off and and hair is trimmed). In 1954, he was insulted by a bully at the beach. As Flex tells the story, the accompanying images mimic the famous Charles Atlas ads that used to appear in comic books. Those multi-panel ads, titled "The Insult that Made a Man out of 'Mac,'" promised muscular glory to anyone who purchased the Charles Atlas fitness books. What Morrison does in *Doom Patrol* #42 is to take those ads, which existed outside the continuity of the comic book stories in which they appeared, and make them part of the contextual history of Flex Mentallo.

Morrison is often accused of being a deconstructionist, and what he does here (and so often elsewhere) is take an established idea and bring it to its logical conclusion by treating the text literally (a common technique of literary deconstruction, but Morrison uses it creatively, not destructively). So, when the Charles Atlas ad shows a bullied kid who becomes ridiculously musclebound through the use of "secret techniques" from fitness manuals, Morrison sees that as a super-hero origin story. And when the artist of that Charles Atlas ad shows the musclebound bully-beater labeled with a "hero of the beach" sign over his head, Morrison takes that literally, and imagines that the character has gained some sort of image projecting power which allows the glowing words "Hero of the Beach" to form over his head when he flexes.

Morrison takes that kernel of an idea, directly stolen from the Charles Atlas ad (which explains DC's difficulty, years later, at getting this issue and the later *Flex Mentallo* mini-series reprinted) and expands upon it without contradicting anything shown in those famous ad panels. He contributes additional beats to the story. In the page from *Doom Patrol* #52, which provides Morrison's version of "The Insult that Made a Man out of 'Mac,'" panels 2, 4, and 6 mimic the first three panels of the Charles Atlas ad (with the exact dialogue as well), while panels 1, 3, and 5 show what was happening between panels. The original ad features a significant ellipsis between the day the scrawny boy orders the Charles Atlas book and the day he returns to the beach covered with muscles, so Morrison fills in those gaps in *Doom Patrol* #42. As Flex explains, "[The book – entitled 'Muscle Mystery for You'] contained... techniques that I can't even begin to hint at. Muscle power, developed to such a degree that it could be used to read minds, see into the future, into other dimensions, even." Not surprisingly, given his track record, Morrison gives Flex far more interesting powers than that of a typical strongman.

As Flex continues his narration, he describes an entire lost world that he was once a part of, but nobody seems to remember. Flex tells of fighting characters like Dr. Saucer and the Incendiary Baby. He says he joined a team of crimefighters along with the Zipper, the Atomic Pile, Mr. 45 (referring to the speed of a record, not a caliber of firearm), and the Fact.[166]

---

[166] None of these characters have ever existed in the DC universe. They are all

Flex also cryptically points out that all of his adventures "seemed to involve the color green," and when the Fact mysteriously vanished, all that ever turned up over the years were a series of "Fact cards" stained with green juice.

Flex describes how he met his beloved Dolores (while judging a "swimsuit parade") before his story takes a darker turn. He details his first meeting with a Kolchak-like[167] reporter named Norman Grindstone who told him about Harry Christmas and the government conspiracy. Flex says,

> I can't remember much of what he told me: something to do with sugar tongs and a U. S. Navy destroyer that was used in some kind of invisibility experiment that opened a hole in another dimension in 1943.[168] This guy Harry Christmas had found some connection between the missing sailors and a bunch of airmen who'd vanished back in '45. Disappearances. Mysteries. Crying telephones. The secret government.

Grindstone, Flex explains, was investigating these events but then disappeared right after telling Flex about the secret of the Pentagon horror. Flex, because of the gaps in his memory, cannot recall the exact details, but he knows that he tried for months to use his muscle mystery power to "turn the Pentagon into a circle." Such a nonsensical act elicits a surprised query from even Niles Caulder (who has certainly seen some strange things in his life): "What was the reasoning behind that?" To which Flex replies, "I don't know. Something to do with the geometry of anguish... I can't remember." As elliptical as Flex's answer is, Morrison does have a reason for Flex's attempt to transform the shape of the Pentagon, but until his memory is restored, Flex is as baffled as we are. All he can say about what he saw beneath the Pentagon is a few fragments of nonsense: "I saw it... gigantic... clock... barometer... ant farm... I can't explain what I saw. It's too terrible to fit into my head or into words." The mechanical words like *clock* and *barometer* denote a coldness to the monstrosity beneath the Pentagon, while the term *ant farm* denotes a creepy, mindless, inhuman presence. Note how

---

Morrison creations, and the reason for Flex's false memories will be explained later.

167 *Kolchak: The Night Stalker* (1974) featured Darren McGavin as investigative reporter who explored crimes with supernatural causes. The television series only lasted one season, but it famously inspired Chris Carter to create the *X-Files*.

168 *The Philadelphia Experiment* (1984) depicted similar events. The film is based on an urban legend regarding mysterious experiments conducted on behalf of the U. S. Navy.

From *Doom Patrol* #42 – Flex Mentallo narrates his secret origin and his encounter with Normal Grindstone. Art by Mike Dringenberg and Doug Hazlewood. Copyright © DC Comics.

Morrison once again uses insects to evoke a feeling of unease or even terror. Therefore, even if we cannot make sense out of Flex's words, his language creates meaning through its tonality. The unknown is more frightening than the easily explained.

Flex finishes his story by describing his flight from the Men from N.O.W.H.E.R.E. and his subsequent loss of memory and arrival at Danny the Street. Now that recent incidents have sparked his memory, Flex has regained his sense of purpose. He emphatically declares that he needs to save everyone from whatever lies beneath the Pentagon, and he refuses to wait until the Doom Patrol returns from space. Even though his amnesia has delayed his actions for 32 years (according to the dates given in the text), Flex cannot afford to hesitate, because, as he explains, "Three and two make five and that's their number. That's the number of death and the night of time."

The final page of *Doom Patrol* #42 reveals that his beloved Dolores is not dead as we had supposed in the previous issue. She is speaking still, but she has been turned into a literal puppet as we can clearly see a grotesque mechanical hand embedded into the base of her skull, seemingly controlling her words. Morrison has used this *puppet* motif before in *Animal Man* and *Doom Patrol* to show the absence of free will. Here, Dolores is not manipulated by a higher power, but is used as bait to trap Flex Mentallo.

Although *Doom Patrol* #42 provides a playfully postmodern reinvention of "The Insult that Made a Man out of 'Mac,'" it also sets up a storyline which will take many issues to resolve. (It's already taken four prologues plus this complete issue to introduce, so you can imagine how long the entire narrative might be.) Morrison, though, takes the conventional idea of a government conspiracy and expands it in a unique direction. While a traditional secrets-of-the-Pentagon story might involve murder and betrayal and cover-ups and a secret government agenda, how many stories include all that plus supernatural events, insect colonies, a muscle man with clairvoyance, and indescribably powerful sugar tongs? Morrison certainly doesn't hold back, and *Doom Patrol* #42 is just the very effective beginning.

*Doom Patrol* #43 leaves Flex Mentallo behind (for most of the issue) to give the reader some answers about the mysterious Pentagon threat. The issue begins with a motherly woman reading from an over-sized hardcover book entitled *Anyhow Stories*, which is, not coincidentally, also the name of this issue's story. Morrison isn't delving into metafictional territory here, however, but he is emphasizing the importance of that book of stories and the connection between fairy tales and horror. *Anyhow Stories*, or, more properly, *Anyhow Stories, Moral and Otherwise*, is the name of a real collection of children's' stories published in 1882 and written by Lucy Clifford. The excerpt being read in the beginning of *Doom Patrol* #43 is from the final paragraph of one of the stories, "The New Mother":

> And still the new mother stays in the little cottage, but the windows are closed and the doors are shut, and no one knows what the inside looks like. Now and then, when the darkness has fallen, Blue-Eyes and the Turkey creep up near the home in which they once were so happy, and with beating hearts they watch and listen; sometimes a blinding flash comes through the window, and they know it is the light from the new mother's glass eyes, or they hear a strange muffled noise, and they know it is the sound of her wooden tail as she drags it along the floor.

In the story, the children have been told that if they keep misbehaving, their nice kind mother will be taken away and replaced by this horrible new mother with the wooden tail. Morrison only gives us the final, horrifying fragment that I've quoted above, completely out of context, and yet it is enough to show the terror imparted by these stories, "Moral or Otherwise." In the final panel of the first page, we see that the motherly figure who has been reading this story is surrounded, in the darkness, by nude, skeletal figures who are silently listening to her tale. These figures are "husks," and we find out more about them from General Honey as he guides newcomer Sergeant Washington through the bowels of the Pentagon.

Morrison uses Sergeant Washington's tour of the sub-levels of the Pentagon to show us the true nature of the conspiracy that so frightened Flex Mentallo. Sergeant Washington acts as a reader surrogate, questioning what he sees and wondering about what it all means. He, like us, is baffled and concerned by what he finds. The first place he visits is the "Deja Vu Room," which features a giant green eye as its centerpiece. General Honey explains that the eye is part of "Ka-Bala" and says, "We never make any decisions down here without consulting Ka-Bala." As odd as it sounds, this is not another bizarre Morrison invention. "Ka-Bala" is a real board game manufactured in the late 1960s by Transogram Company Inc. It was a strange fortune-telling game which involved chanting, Tarot cards, and a glow-in-the-dark game board complete with glowing eyeball. In *Doom*

*Patrol* #43, Sergeant Washington asks it a question: "Will I ever pitch a winning game?" The ball, spinning around the game board, lands on "no."

Morrison fills the issue with the bizarre detritus of childhood (*Anyhow Stories*, "Ka-Bala," and later, "X-Ray Specs"). These are not items of nostalgia for most of us, though, because, though we may have heard of these strange things, we probably didn't actually own them. But if we had known about these things as children, we would have likely imagined them having great power, and that it is how Morrison uses them in this story. Just as he did with the origin of Flex Mentallo, he takes the claims of comic book advertisements literally, thereby granting a fortune-telling board game actual prophetic power and granting plastic glasses the ability to see the bones beneath the skin.

As Sergeant Washington's tour continues, General Honey explains the background of this whole program beneath the Pentagon. "It really started," he says, "on July Second, 1875, when Bell said, 'Watson, come here! I want you!' That was the summoning that gave it power." Sergeant Washington ominously refers to this thing called *it* and mentions how he had heard that the "ant farm was built to contain it." General Honey explains that the whole project ties into an attempt to "use the dead as soldiers," and he describes what happens when people die:

> Well, the higher self, the "I," ascends into the spirit plane and the lower self, which is to say the astral husk, descends into the "Abode of Shells." Got that? These astral worm-casts are all that remains of our human personalities and desires. Sometimes they hang around on the astral plane, picking up messages from the Nagual, the formative world. Those are what we call "ghosts," bugging sensitives and mediums with their crazy, meaningless talk...
>
> ...Anyway, the silver sugar tongs are what you might call an intrusion into the physical plane. In actual fact, they're only the tangible part of what we call the dead hand. We use the tongs to capture husks. One of our Men in Blue lost the tongs in '55. He was expelled, but he stole one of our 'surprise packages' and used it to make a Delirium Box. "Mr. Jones," He called himself.

Notice how Morrison connects the dots between the previously mentioned sugar tongs and Mr. Jones, explaining that it's all part of the governmental attempt to capture the "husks." General Honey goes on to explain on later pages that the mysterious occurrences on Flight 19 and the U.S.S. Eldridge (as mentioned in one of the many prologues in previous issues) had to do with misguided attempts to take the "husks" from the bodies of the living. He also tells how the *Anyhow Stories* are used to train the "husks" since they are "childlike, undisciplined." As General Honey says, "Those stories used to scare the shit out of me and I'm a hard bastard. Imagine what they do to the husks."

After further exposition we learn the following information: (1) The husks are given new bodies in turned into Men from N.O.W.H.E.R.E.; (2) Mr. Sage, a man imprisoned inside one of the walls beneath the Pentagon, dreams up all of the weapons used by the Ant Farm; (3) Mr. Sage made up his own comic book as a kid called *My Greenest Adventure*,[169] and according to General Honey, "That's what got us into all his trouble with Flex Mentallo." (The connection between Flex Mentallo, Mr. Sage, and the color green will be made clear in a future issue – but for now the relationship is merely implied.)

Morrison doesn't explain most of these ideas; he just has General Honey state these things as facts. In future issues, we find out more about the mysterious Mr. Sage and the Ant Farm, but for now they are bizarre concepts that provide a sense of unease and foreboding.

After spending the first half of the issue beneath the Pentagon, Morrison returns us to Danny the Street, where we see Joshua Clay talking to Dorothy Spinner about testing the nature of her powers. Cliff, Rebis, and Crazy Jane are still off in space as Dolores Watson arrives, asking for Flex Mentallo. We know from issue #42 that she is the puppet of something evil, but the Doom Patrol members, and Flex Mentallo, do not.

After Flex dons his old costume (leopard print undershorts, studded wrist bands, and wrestling boots) for Dolores, she begins to lose composure, apologizing about her betrayal as she turns to dust. Immediately, the real Men from N.O.W.H.E.R.E. arrive. They have shiny, metallic, bird-like heads and claws, and belts filled with gadgets. They present a far more imposing menace than their impostors.

The final few pages of the issue contain something rare for a Morrison comic book: a relatively standard fight sequence. In this case, though, the heroes are wildly overmatched, as these Men from N.O.W.H.E.R.E. are far more effective than the imitations employed by Mr. Jones. These Men from

---

169 An allusion to the comic book in which the Doom Patrol originally appeared, *My Greatest Adventure*.

N.O.W.H.E.R.E. also don't sound anything like the ones we saw many issues ago. The previous Men spoke in acronyms, while these speak in the language of comic book advertisements. The majority of their statements are ad copy: "So realistic he seems almost alive!" they say, and "more fun than a 'barrel of monkeys.'" It connects them thematically to Flex Mentallo, who was "born" from a comic book ad, and shows their relationship to the Ant Farm, which, as I've said, is filled with children's toys like the "Ka-Bala" game and the X-Ray Specs.

As defeat seems imminent, a voice from off-panel tells the Men from N.O.W.H.E.R.E. to "Get away from that man [Joshua Clay]!" and the final page reveals the return of Rebis, Crazy Jane, and Cliff Steele (with insect legs), accompanied by a Geomancer escort. "Really. I'm serious," says Cliff Steele.

In essence, these two issues, *Doom Patrol* #42-43, have merely set the stage for the confrontation between the Doom Patrol, Flex Mentallo, and whatever *it* is that lies beneath the Pentagon. Even when providing two back-to-back issues of mostly exposition, however, Morrison is able to inject his own unique perspective. He takes the traditional trope of the origin story and spins it in a strange direction, and he does something similarly bizarre with the trope of the governmental conspiracy. It's all in service of the story, and it fits perfectly into the tone he's established since the beginning of his run on this title. He's writing the about the members of the Doom Patrol, after all: muscle mystery and soul-catching sugar tongs are right up their alley.

## Reality, Illusion, Sex, and Violence

It's important to remember that *Zenith, Arkham Asylum, Animal Man, Gothic* and *Doom Patrol* were, for all intents and purposes, written during the same few years, early in Morrison's career. Because these works were contemporary with one another, Morrison's main concerns do not differ much from issue to issue or title to title. Some variation exists, obviously, as Morrison brings certain details to the fore depending on the situation, but through it all (at least at this stage in his career), he deals with the same re-occurring themes, expressed as dualities: *order / chaos*, *reality / illusion*, and *mind / body*. He explores these themes on many levels, using a variety of narrative techniques, but these themes are central to Morrison's work no matter what the plot seems to be about.

Take, for example, *Doom Patrol* #44. It is, ostensibly, the climax of the Flex Mentallo vs. the Pentagon storyline which has been building for several issues. And, on the surface, that's what it is, but the issue is really yet another chance for Morrison to explore the themes which fascinate him the most. First, and most prevalent, is the *reality / illusion* duality. As Flex Mentallo and Dorothy Spinner are escorted beneath the Pentagon (after being captured), General Honey explains that the Pentagon "was built on top of an older structure. Five-sided city of the white abyss. The Pentagon is a spirit trap, a lens to focus energy... from the fundamental reality." This "fundamental reality" and "white abyss" possibly allude to he reality outside the comic book panels – a reality fully explored in Morrison's run on *Animal Man*. In that series, the characters who literally broke through the sides of a panel could see nothing but whiteness, unless, of course, they were able to focus their gaze on the beings watching their every move, a.k.a. the readers. Or they could allude to the supernatural, Lovecraftian alternate reality explored in *Zenith*, a place where the dark gods ruled supreme. No matter what General Honey thinks about the "fundamental reality," it is an example of a character being aware of a totally different "reality" than the one accepted by the other characters. In any case, the other reality is more powerful than the commonly accepted "real" plane of existence, and because the other reality is termed "fundamental," reality as the characters know it is therefore an illusion – a flicker of shadows on the cave wall as Plato might put it.

The *order / chaos* theme is also heavily explored throughout this issue. General Honey explains exactly why they are harnessing the power from the "fundamental reality" to begin with. Their goal, he explains, is to "exterminate all eccentricity and irrationality in this crazy ol' world." After all, he says, "a world without quirks is a world without rebellion." By using Dorothy Spinner's illusion-casting / reality-warping power (and for Morrison, there seems to be little difference between the two powers – since reality is an illusion, a person who can create illusions can change reality itself), coupled with the mental powers of the mysterious Mr. Sage, General Honey plans to make his utopian ideal a reality. Notice once again how Morrison equated utopian idealism with fascism, as a new world order will be forcefully put into place whether the citizens like it or not. And, just as he showed in *Zenith*, the good guys are on the side of chaos.

Richard Case's illustration / collage on page 8, showing the Ant Farm – the central machinery beneath the Pentagon – reveals the oppressive order and the inhuman industrialization, he intends to inflict upon the world. The clocks emphasize the rigid timetable of efficiency, while the Piranesi-style[170] etching of a cold, lifeless factory offers a chilling vision of the type of future General Honey dreams about. Even the poor cropping[171] of the Men from N.O.W.H.E.R.E., operating the mechanism with sledgehammers, contributes to the effect of the image. They seem out of sync with their environment, and rightly so, since they are basically organic creatures (no matter what their origin), and they cannot mesh with the machine. It is not an attractive picture, nor should it be, since Morrison so clearly sides with the forces of chaos when faced with such an alternative.

Morrison elaborates on this even more on a later page, while simultaneously investigating the *reality / illusion* theme as well. On this page, Wallace Sage is revealed to have literally created Flex Mentallo and given him life because Sage believed in him. Sage's full revelation, that he drew "My Greenest Adventure" with a green pen on blank paper, and that Flex was just his comic book character who "came right off the page and... and into... real life,"[172] not only explains the preponderance of the color green in Flex's early career, but it shows that the wall between reality and illusion, between the concrete and the fantasy, are easily blurred. Sage also speaks the evocative lines, "They're going to exterminate imagination" and "They're building death camps for our dreams." By using words commonly employed to describe the Holocaust in such a context, Morrison emphatically denies the supremacy of order over chaos. To him, a rigid order is death to the imagination, death to dreams, death to life.

---

[170] In the 18th century, Giovanni Battista Piranesi produced a series of prints which showed horrific underground vaults filled with stairs and machinery. The Ant Farm looks like a Piranesi-inspired etching which Richard Case used as a foundation for the splash page. The rest of the character and images on the page look crudely superimposed.

[171] The Men from N.O.W.H.E.R.E. look like they've been cut out with scissors and glued onto the etching of the machinery.

[172] Sage seems to share a similar power with Dorothy Spinner, only with a longer-lasting effect. Like Dorothy, and like Dr. Destiny's Materioptikon, Sage can make dreams into reality.

The climax of the story features a nod to the *mind / body* theme as Flex regains his powers and, by flexing the muscles of his body, is able to mentally transform the Pentagon into a circle (thereby changing a rigid, orderly geometric shape into something more organic), which foils General Honey's plans and allows Dorothy Spinner the time to overcome her fears and defeat the Avatar. The Avatar, by the way, was the thing ominously referred to as *it* in the previous issue. It turned out to be a pretty standard monster with a telephone-inspired look. As Flex Mentallo explains, the Avatar is "the thing that's haunted the telephone system for fifty years and enslaved the dead." Ultimately, the Avatar isn't a very interesting threat, and Morrison has Dorothy dispatch him off-panel immediately before ending the issue with a joke. The monstrous telephone Avatar hangs from the ceiling, strangled by his own cord. Dorothy tells Flex, "he hung up."

The Avatar wasn't the real menace from Morrison's point of view, but he was the monster that served as a placeholder for the abstract threat of an imposed order. By defeating him, General Honey's plan was thwarted, and the forces of chaos won. Morrison reveals an awareness that such a victory may have come at no small cost, however, with the final panel after Dorothy's joke. It shows a candle which has burned out, and what it alludes to is the Candlemaker, a character who is not named until a future issue, but who appeared to Dorothy just before the final battle with the Avatar and frightens her (or gives her the confidence, perhaps) enough to unleash her powers on the creature. The Candlemaker is a chaotic force of a different type, and when he appears again, he will wreak some serious havoc. For now, though, Morrison just gives us a bit of foreshadowing and leaves that final image as a hint that the story is not over.

The very next issue, *Doom Patrol* #45, is a respite from the heavy themes, ponderous conspiracies, and metaphysical questions that have dominated the series. It seems like an aberration in Morrison's run at first, not because it lacks quality (it doesn't), but because it doesn't connect to anything significant in terms of plot or theme. It is a straight-up parody of the Marvel character known as the Punisher, and it's the first of three parodies Morrison attempts in the series – he parodies Lee and Kirby comic book storytelling in a future issue, and he wrote the *Doom Force* one-shot which ridicules the Rob Liefeld[173] school of bad comic book narrative. While *Zenith* and *Animal Man* featured some humor in the form of irony (and, occasionally, satire), *Doom Patrol* #45 is Morrison's attempt at just being funny for the sake of being funny. It works.

One of the reasons it works is that the parody is not totally restricted to the character or actions of the Punisher. It parodies the style of a certain type of comic book as well. Morrison mocks the hard-boiled first-person narration so prevalent in mainstream comic books, giving his protagonist, the ridiculously-named Beard Hunter, internal monologue in the form of caption lines like "I'm the best there is at what I do. What do I do? I hunt beards."[174] and "Can't let him see me crying." Morrison parodies the senseless violence of the urban vigilantes when he shows Beard Hunter kill a man who criticized his favorite comic book writer.[175] He pokes fun at the false bravado of the contemporary super-hero by having the Beard Hunter act tough and carry an arsenal of weapons even though he still lives at home with his mother, a woman who sarcastically comments on his love for bodybuilding magazines and refers to him as a "drama queen."

The plot is as ridiculously funny as the character. The Bearded Gentlemen's Club of Metropolis hires the Beard Hunter to kill Niles Caulder because he has "lost the use of his beard," according to the employer. The final battle of guns vs. brains takes place inside a supermarket where Niles Caulder innocently shops for his beloved chocolate. The Beard Hunter guns down an innocent clerk before confronting his intended target. "Niles Caulder," he says, "I've come for your beard." Then he narrates,

> When it comes to my top choice of automatic weapons, the stripped-down Uzi heads the list. Six hundred bucks of hot, sexy death. Smooth action. Thirty-six round clip. Makes me feel like a movie star. I let him think about that for a while. And then I move

---

[173] Rob Liefeld, creator of *X-Force* and *Youngblood*, is the supreme example of shallow depths to which super-hero comic book art had sunk in the early 1990s. I'll describe his work in more detail when I analyze the *Doom Force* parody later in this book.

[174] This is the catchphrase, such as it is, of Marvel Comics' Wolverine – except that Wolverine claims to be the best at much more lethal enterprises.

[175] Morrison also parodies comic book fan mentality in the story, by showing the Beard Hunter to be an avid fan who lives at home with his mom. Like many avid comic book fans, he will react violently when his favorite comic book creators are ridiculed.

in.

The Beard Hunter with his tight red and black costume, and his silly belt of trophy beards, eroticizes his Uzi in his narration, referring to it as "six hundred bucks of hot, sexy death." The belt may be absurd, but the narration, and the way it shows how we can glamorize implements of murder, satirizes America's obsession with violence as a substitute for sex. So even when Morrison is playing around with a goofy issue of *Doom Patrol*, he includes some biting observations about society (and the role comic books play in society today). As I've said in other sections of this book, Morrison has routinely condemned the grim-and-gritty approach to super-heroics and glorified the Silver Age approach to storytelling. For him, characters like the Punisher offer no sense of wonder, of imagination – they are lifeless and dull and offer nothing more than targets for ridicule.

The issue ends with Niles Caulder laying a trap for the Beard Hunter in a grocery isle, using aluminum foil and loose wiring to electrocute the silly vigilante. Perhaps it's another of Morrison's investigations into the *mind / body* duality, with Caulder representing almost pure *mind* (since he does not have the use of his legs) while the Beard Hunter represents pure *body* (since he barely has the use of his brain – or, more specifically, he uses his mind to think about his body more often than not). *Mind* wins, of course, but only by defeating the *body* through physical means. Perhaps it's the quintessential Morrison, showing that *mind* and *body* are inextricably linked. Or perhaps it's just an excuse to show how stupid the Punisher character really is.

A more thoughtful examination of the *mind / body* theme does occur, actually, in the next issue, *Doom Patrol* #46. First, though, the story begins with a bit more humor in a brief sequence that reveals the final fate of the characters in the Flex Mentallo vs. the Pentagon storyline. Most of the characters speak directly to the reader in this opening sequence, taking turns explaining where they ended up. Harry Christmas, the reporter who was planning to expose the Pentagon secrets but had his brain scrambled, for example, is now a critically acclaimed writer of "experimental fiction." Sergeant Washington, who was reluctantly appointed to his position in the Ant Farm, has given up his government job to become a cabaret dancer on Danny the Street. Major Honey[176] explains that he's "an anally-fixated

[176] He was General Honey in the previous storyline, so either he's been severely

oedipal paranoid with south-of-the-border schizophrenic delusions" and has found the ideal job: he's going "to run for President." (Apparently the Beard Hunter episode didn't purge Morrison of his need for jokey satire.) Finally, Flex Mentallo, as a pure Morrison creation (through Wallace Sage, that is), plans to reject the convention of the depressing modern super-hero and "put a smile on the face of the war against crime."

After that (relatively long) prologue (that's actually an epilogue), Morrison turns his attention to his pet themes: *mind / body* and *reality / illusion.* (The *order / chaos* dilemma has been put aside, at least for now – though Morrison gives us plenty of foreshadowing right away to imply that things are about to change in that regard.)

The bulk of *Doom Patrol* #46 deals with four parallel stories:

First, Cliff gets a new body, which combines the best of all previous versions because it's fully operational, and it allows him to feel again. Crazy Jane, with the teleportation help of Danny the Street, takes Cliff on a sensory journey where he can feel what it's like to be alive. In this plot thread, Morrison, through Cliff, shows a mind in turmoil trapped within an artificial body. It seems that, no matter how scientifically advanced the body, Cliff Steele will never be happy.

Second, Dorothy Spinner confronts her own image in the mirror and sees the Candlemaker staring back at her. In this sequence, her illusions are crossing over with reality.

Third, Niles Caulder ominously refers to his "private research," which has led him to isolate himself from the rest of the team. Later in the issue, Rebis confronts Caulder and says, "I know what you're planning, Professor Caulder. I have known for quite some time." Caulder replies, "Ah. And what do you intend to do? Stop me?" Rebis answers, "We'll see."

Fourth, Dr. Silence visits Mr. Girodias[177] inquiring about the Painting the Ate Paris (which is the place where the Brotherhood of Dada ended up).

All four storylines deal with the fragmentation of the team. Things are beginning to fall apart – the chaos is catching up to them. Yet Morrison focuses on the *mind / body* (with Cliff's inner turmoil and Caulder's confrontation with Rebis) and the *reality / illusion* (with Dorothy, the Candlemaker, and the Painting that Ate Paris) themes most prominently as

demoted by the military or this is a continuity error.

[177] These two characters appeared briefly in the first Brotherhood of Dada storyline.

things begin to unravel. Morrison doesn't explore much of anything in detail in this issue since he gives almost every character the spotlight for a few pages. He does, however, get to the gist of the problem in a sequence between Cliff and Jane, as Jane says, "We're not alone in this world. We don't have to be." Cliff tells her she's wrong to bring any hope into his life. "I'm never going to have flesh and blood again," he says, "It's got so that I don't even dream I've got a human body anymore... You can't help me, Jane. Really."

In essence, Morrison reminds us that we cannot ever really know another person, and we are all basically alone. It's a bit of existentialism that might help prepare us (and the characters) for what's to come when things go from bad to worse in the series.

To instigate a bit of chaos for the team, Morrison introduces a new character, the Shadowy Mr. Evans, in *Doom Patrol* #47. The Shadowy Mr. Evans is described in a lengthy text piece that opens the issue. "He can only be comprehended as the subject of a complex system of claim and counterclaim, rumor and denial," it says. Later, it explains more: "Lord of Meaningless Mottoes, Sworn Enemy of the Grand Old Dukes of Nothing in Particular, he dwells at length in his dreamy library of dust." He is a trickster character, an agent of chaos,[178] and he's compelled to disturb the mortal world (for undisclosed reasons), but he would prefer not to.

Mr. Evans, with his periscope head and palm-shaving boy-servant,[179] is an absurdist creation. He's perhaps a harbinger of Mr. Nobody's return, although that is never directly stated. What is shown, however, is that the Painting that Ate Paris, now owned by Mr. Silence, is developing a black stain that's slowly growing in size – it seems that the Brotherhood of Dada may be back sooner than we think.

Mr. Evans doesn't actually do much in *Doom Patrol* #47 – he saves his mischief for the next issue – but Morrison does throw some other plot threads

---

178 If you think it seems schizophrenic for Morrison to have the Doom Patrol defeat the forces of order in one storyline and then follow it up a few issues later with a villain who is the personification of chaos, you might be right, but consider this: the Doom Patrol exists somewhere between the two extremes, as do we all, and it must balance the scales not between good and evil but between order and chaos, because living in a world consumed by either force would be unbearable.

179 Clankie, Mr. Evans's servant, takes a safety razor and digs it into Mr. Evans's palm when Mr Evans says, "Shave!"

into the mix (besides the Painting). We see Willoughby Kipling, the supernatural investigator who has been absent since the Cult of the Unwritten Book storyline. Kipling speaks with a hooded character in a smoky bar and says things like, "I don't want to hear any more balls about the war between good and evil! You might as well say the war between up and down or left and right for all the sense it makes" (which verifies the idea that order and chaos are the true forces of opposition). Kipling also alludes to a coming apocalypse which will cause the Earth to cease to exist in 2012. This is a concept Morrison has returned to again and again, most openly in *The Invisibles* in which the final issue actually takes place in 2012. In *Doom Patrol*, though, the date is never mentioned again.

The remainder of *Doom Patrol* #47 deals with two other dominant threads. Both deal with the *mind / body* theme in different ways. The first shows Rebis learning of its mother's death (or at least Larry Trainor's mother's death) from Joshua Clay. Rebis shows no emotional reaction at all. Instead, Rebis says coldly, "She was an old woman. It was only a matter of time." Later, alone in a darkened room, Rebis removes its bandages to reveal a charred human form beneath. It's an attempt to reconnect with the physicality of being alive, and it's another step toward a metamorphosis of form that will culminate in the next issue.

The second thread shows Crazy Jane making a bold (and wildly inappropriate) public appearance as her persona called the Scarlet Harlot. In this incarnation, Jane say, "Daddy said I was a little slut and when I grew up, I'd do it for money. And you know what? He was right. Except I don't even want money. I just want to do it." Cliff drags her out of the restaurant before she gets into trouble.

Her horrifying comment about what her "daddy said" (her father, if you don't remember, raped her as a girl, causing the psychic trauma that led to her multiple personalities) and her flagrant promiscuity indicate that something is amiss in Doom Patrol land. On the final page, Cliff and Jane (as the Scarlet Harlot) see who's causing the problem: Mr. Evans appears, accompanied by a floating pyramid with multiple eyes, a baby attached to him by an umbilicus, and flying vegetables – the usual stuff.

Mr. Evans receives his comeuppance in *Doom Patrol* #48, with the "help" from the bizarre Sex Men. The Sex Men, who bear name tags like "Kiss" and "Cuddle" and have lipstick marks and blue pyramids on their heads, are not only off-putting in appearance, but they are ineffective as well. They do at least provide some helpful exposition (in the form of first-person Dragnet-style narration) about Mr. Evans, saying he has left a "total eroticization of everything" in his wake.

Mr. Evans himself agrees, but has a different perspective, of course, saying, "I am the life force, the sex ray, the thrill of living that accompanies the awareness of the presence of death. I am Satan!" In his cosmology, and perhaps Morrison's as well, Satan is not an evil force, but the force of unbridled life – in other words, chaos. But it's a specific type of chaos – it's the chaos that rejects conformity and sterility, as he goes on to explain in a sequence that provides a counterpoint to General Honey's rant about an ideal world "without quirks":

> People like you [the Doom Patrol and the Sex Men], by seeking to restrict the erotic urge, have aligned themselves with the negative forces of the unlife and undeath. Your kind are responsible for crippling the spirit of humanity... Look here! This sad tableau of 'ordinary life' [he indicates a suburban family with two kids, sitting around a television in a living room]. Innocent men, women, and children crushed by repression, unable to express their true desire. But mark my words, that frustrated energy finds its way out eventually in the twisted form of neurosis, heart disease, cancer! Mankind is sick, sick, sick!

For Mr. Evans, normal suburban culture (such as dreamed about by General Honey, and satirically mocked in the Mr. Jones sequence several months earlier) is the abnormal, degenerate behavior because it crushes life with its banality. Mr. Evans seems to think that the forces of order and conformity have already won, and the Sex Men represent the voice of the so-called "Moral Majority" who would suck the life out of anything in the name of protecting family values. It appears Morrison is condemning the puritanical views of sexuality in the Western world, yet the choices made by Scarlet Harlot and Mr. Evans are clearly not attractive lifestyles either. We would hardly wish for a fully sexualized world just as we wouldn't wish for a desexualized one.

It's important to note here that Morrison is raising this issue in a mainstream super-hero comic book. It's easy to forget how subversive this stuff is because he does it so often, but he's exploring the very nature of

From *Doom Patrol* #47 – Mr. Evans and the Sex Men depart, leaving Cliff Steele and Crazy Jane (in the form of the Scarlet Harlot) baffled. Art by Richard Case and Mark McKenna. Copyright © DC Comics.

metaphysical sexuality in a book that was drawn by Erik Larsen[180] only three years earlier.

Because it is a super-hero comic book, and because there are no easy answers from Morrison (at least on this topic), the story is resolved with a trope from Superman's conflict with Mr. Mxyzptlk.[181] To defeat Mxyzptlk, Superman must trick the imp into saying his name backwards. In *Doom Patrol* #48, Cliff tricks Mr. Evans into saying the word "kneecap," which leads to the image of Mr. Evans being sucked through a dimensional portal. The Sex Men teleport away as well, and once again, Cliff deflates any pretension, and echoes the thoughts of so many readers, with his final line: "Who were those lunatics?"

The story basically ends there, but there is a coda. When Cliff and Jane (now back to her "normal" self) return to base, they, and the rest of the Doom Patrol members, open Rebis's door to find that it has abandoned all physical form. In its place, a glowing green circle hovers above the ground. Rebis has become the Uroboros, the snake that swallows its own tail as foretold in the Insect Mesh storyline. It's the ultimate *mind / body* transcendence.

Speaking of that, let me go back to a point I glossed over rather quickly but is actually supremely important. Willoughby Kipling mentions that the apocalypse will arrive in 2012, and then the date is never mentioned again in *Doom Patrol*. 2012 is a date Morrison has personally mentioned many times in connection with a radical change in our reality. When questioned about what exactly will happen in 2012 in an interview on comixfan.com, Morrison gave this description:

> I think that if anything happens at all, it's most likely to come in the form of a mass consciousness change – possibly triggered by planetary electromagnetic field alterations predicted to occur around that time – so that basically everyone will start peaking on the acid trip that never ends. "Individuality" will dissolve and your minds will start to merge into one mass mind, which is likely to

---

[180] This is not meant as a criticism of Erik Larsen, only an observation about how radical the title became compared to the staid conventionality of the Kupperberg / Larsen issues.

[181] Mxyzptlk first appeared in *Superman* #30 (1944), and the imp from the fifth dimension embodies the absurdity Morrison strives for in his Doom Patrol issues. But whatever havoc Mxyzptlk causes in Metropolis is automatically reversed when he returns to his home dimension. In the Superman comics, there's no question that order trumps chaos.

> seem quite frightening and overwhelming, especially for the sheltered minds, and time will seem to disappear as we identify with the mitochondria in our cells, instead of identifying with the physical individual carrier 'bodies' we use to expedite the shuffling around of DNA.
>
> The world's current social structures should collapse quite rapidly when that happens and chances are, only people capable of handling the immense influx of new information will be those already familiar with heavily-altered states of consciousness. For everyone else, it will seem like the Second Coming, the arrival of the Space Brothers, the Rapture, Hell on Earth, the 32nd path of the Tree of Life or whatever they decide to see – everyone will get their own personal apocalyptic transfer into this new mode of being. Some poor souls will have to be guided out of hell, others will have to be coaxed down from sci-fi Ultraspheres but we'll all be living in a state of permanent psychedelic ecstasy and will have to restructure our entire existence to cope with the new consciousness. I have a feeling that psychedelic drugs provide a flashforward glimpse of this kind of consciousness and help prepare the human mind for when that mode of consciousness is permanent.
>
> If something like this occurs at the end of 2012, and it's also possible that nothing of note will happen – we should see a lot of people freaking out when we re-enter what some Australian aboriginals call Aljira (a word English is not up to the task of translating, so it comes out as "Dreamtime") and I call "the Supercontext." When we see in a new way and become new to ourselves, we'll also see lots of stuff that will probably scare people who didn't know it was there all along. People in delirium and on the brink of death see these crawling, replicating "wilkie-swilkie men" all over everything and soon, I think, everyone will start to see them. They are "the spaces between things, come to life..."
>
> As for me, I hope I'll be screaming "Yes!" like Molly Bloom as the universe rolls up into a silver paper ball for the quantum cats of Hell to play with.

Morrison's words here reveal how every theme I've identified in his comic book stories, from *mind / body* to *reality / illusion* to *order / chaos*, all tie into his philosophy of what will happen (if anything does happen) at the end of 2012. Kipling's apparently off-hand (and unexplored, in the context of the *Doom Patrol* series) comment about the apocalypse of 2012 is actually the key that ties all of Morrison's ideas together.

## Dada, Dandy, and the Legion of the Strange

These *Doom Patrol* issues are divided into three distinct storylines. The longest of the three, comprising issues #49-52, deals with the full-fledged return of Mr. Nobody and his new Brotherhood of Dada. The other two, in issues #53 and 54, deal with a Jack Kirby dream and a meditation on Rebis's alchemical nature, respectively. Morrison doesn't break any new ground in this batch of issues, but he does return to some of his favorite ideas and look at them with a fresh slant. The three storylines have very different voices, as if Morrison is channeling different sides of his personality each time.

In the Mr. Nobody storyline, Morrison's channeling his absurd, satirical self. His new Brotherhood exhibits many of the same traits as the last one, with its penchant for silly behavior and need for chaos, but now Mr. Nobody has a more specific goal – or a more specific mean by which to achieve his goal: he wants to become President of the United States. Morrison clearly satirizes the inherent absurdity of the democratic political process (as practiced in the U.S.) once Mr. Nobody kicks off his campaign, but first there's a narrative hurdle to overcome: Mr. Nobody is still trapped inside a painting.

As I mentioned in the previous section, the notorious Painting that Ate Paris has been purchased by Dr. Silence, and throughout the recent issues a large black spot has been growing larger and larger on the surface of the canvas. In *Doom Patrol* #49, the spot talks. "If I were you, Dr. Silence – I wouldn't," says the black shape in response to Dr. Silence's thoughts about destroying the painting. The blot, of course, is Mr. Nobody, and he needs some help to fully emerge from his imprisonment within the image. He gets this help from the newly assembled members of the new Brotherhood of Dada: The Love Glove, Alias the Blur, and Agent "!". Unlike the previous Brotherhood of Dada, which had a cast of strange but tragic characters, this incarnation is lighter, more bizarre, with less emotional weight. These new characters are odd and fun, but they merely serve a plot function – to rescue Mr. Nobody and fight on his behalf – and don't get a chance to be in the spotlight for any length of time.

The new Brotherhood visits Dr. Silence and the painting, retrieves Mr. Nobody through a nonsense poetry incantation, and helps Mr. Nobody achieve the first phase of his plan as they search through Dr. Silence's storehouse of relics. The object of Mr. Nobody's affection is revealed on the next page: the bicycle of Albert Hofmann. Hofmann, the Swiss scientist who accidentally invented LSD, conducted experiments on the mind-altering affects of the substance, most famously on April 19, 1943, when he rode his bicycle home after consuming a large quantity of the drug. Mr. Nobody narrates the story of Hofmann's ride home on the second page of *Doom Patrol* #50 over a series of hallucinogenic images:

> Riding a ghost train track down into the human subconscious, into a storm of signs and signals and unsuspected meanings. Legs pump on a treadmill, scenery painted by madmen rolls by on a thundering drum. Hoffman is Magellan, Columbus, venturing out through the door, beyond the blue horizon, over the rainbow, 'round the bend...

The bicycle itself, says Mr. Nobody, had "become a consciousness-altering device of outrageous potency, bought and sold by collectors of the arcane and the just plain daft." In the hands of the Brotherhood of Dada, the bicycle will lead to quite a trip, with all the meaning that word implies.[182]

Although Rebis was last seen in the disembodied shape of a glowing green ring, it reappears in corporeal form (attired in bandages as always) just in time to attend to this new threat to the social order. "I was having sex with myself," he explains matter-of-factly. Mr. Nobody's "consciousness-altering" plan hasn't reached the political level yet, so he spends most of the issue riding around town on his bike, shouting things like, "Monotony can damage your health!" and "Art for breakfast! Art for lunch! Art for Tea! Yahoo!" In his wake, the citizens become affected by the residual LSD trail. When confronted by Cliff Steele, Mr. Nobody defends his actions: "Society's to blame. We're crushed and molded and if it hurts they tell us not to cry out. I'm here to break the molds because someone must." After a series of fights and flights, Mr. Nobody takes a hostage and retreats in a flash of light, but not before saying to the Doom Patrol, "Next time we meet, we'll meet as allies!" The baffled (and ineffective) Doom Patrol just stand there. Jane says, "Oh, look! It's raining daisies." Cliff says, "You know what really worries me? What if he's right?"

Cliff's genuine confusion reveals a recognition of the futility of

---

[182] Regarding his own drug use at the time he was working on the series, Morrison says, in an interview at suicidegirls.com, "*Doom Patrol* shows the influence of shrooms from around the time of those Insect Mesh issues[,] but I was mostly doing it straight."

maintaining order in the face of chaos and shows an awareness that the "damage" caused by Mr. Nobody may result more from the flaws of an overly rigid society than from any malicious intent on the part of the Brotherhood of Dada.

In the epilogue, the Brotherhood begins to enact the second phase of its plan as it reconfigures an old school bus "with Hofmann's bike as its beating heart." Mr. Nobody plans to paint the bus in "cheerful and loony hues," turning it into a "luminous butterfly, a tool for mass-consciousness alteration." This vehicle is an overt allusion to the psychedelic school bus used by the Merry Pranksters[183] in the mid-1960s. The Brotherhood is very much a super-villain version of these real-life non-conformists. Mr. Nobody's bus, though, will not be used as mere conveyance. He plans to "run for President and win the race by fair means or foul." "We're going to invite the world to a party they'll never forget," he says, before finishing up with a grandiose final pose: "Utopia, here we come!" Mr. Nobody says as he stands on a hilltop, the American flag hanging from his back like a cape.

The issue's main story ends on this enthusiastically satirical note, but because it's a 50th issue, Morrison fills the story with extra treats for the reader. After all, as it says on the title page for the issue, it's "Celebrating One Hundred and Fifty Glorious Years of Doom Patrol Action!" This blurb mocks the hyperbole used in celebrating the so-called "Anniversary Issues" which were so common in the 1990s. (It was almost standard practice that, when a title reached issue 50, it would be labeled as a "50th Anniversary Issue" – a misleading and inaccurate claim which implied that the series had somehow been around for 50 years.)

In *Doom Patrol* #50, the extra pages are devoted to a series of fake recaps of various adventures that never happened, or as the unidentified narrator explains, are "impossible to tell." The pages are irrelevant to the larger scheme of the *Doom Patrol* narrative, but they are fun because (a) they each feature a guest artist, and (b) they tell of improbable battles with characters like "Doctor Chef," "Pinhead," "The Unbearably Tall Man Who Tried to Strike Out the Doom Patrol," "The Torso," and "The Sugar Tunnel." The issue ends with another falsity: an advertisement for Doom Patrol

---

[183] The Merry Pranksters, a group formed around novelist Ken Kesey, traveled around America in a multi-colored bus. They would hold "Acid Tests," distributing LSD to participants at various venues.

merchandise like "The Crazy Jane Cookbook," a "Robotman Radio and Bottle Opener," and a "Missing Piece Reality Puzzle." The ridiculousness of these items are amplified by the knowledge that super-hero merchandising isn't much different. After all, who hasn't owned Batman underpants at some point, right?

The following issue, *Doom Patrol* #51, features a unique cover. It depicts Professor John Dandy, archaeologist, transforming into Yankee Doodle, master of disguise. What's unique about it is that the artwork was done by original *Justice League of America* artist Mike Sekowsky, who had retired from comic books a decade before Morrison's *Doom Patrol* ever saw print. The art, as it turns out, was actually produced in 1964, and it was intended to be the cover for *Showcase* #50, a book which would have introduced the character of Yankee Doodle. That story, that character, and that cover never saw print in the 1960s, but Morrison used the cover to introduce his take on the Yankee Doodle concept. The story begins with the Brotherhood of Dada zooming across America in their magical school bus, sowing seeds of discontent in their wake. They are apparently gaining popularity with the masses. Meanwhile, Dorothy Spinner receives another brief (one-panel) visit from the ominous Candlemaker, who, as previously said, will have a major impact on the team in upcoming issues. For now, though, he's best set aside as we learn more about the government's response to this newly political Brotherhood of Dada. Once again, Morrison returns us to the lower-levels of the Pentagon, where we meet some new faces: Major Main and Ms. Roddick. They bounce across the floor of the Pentagon basement on children's hopping balls and speak of how they will "Fight fire with fire." They say they "want to use John Dandy."

As the U.S. military prepares for battle, Mr. Nobody and the Brotherhood seize control of a television station to broadcast their campaign message to America. "I can promise you that it will be Christmas every day!" says Mr. Nobody. Cliff Steele, back at Doom Patrol HQ watches in horror, but Crazy Jane has a much different response: "I think he's good. The whole thing's a dumb circus, anyway. At least he's admitting it. When's the last time we had a President who wasn't rotten to the core? Some of them just disguise it better, that's all."

When Cliff calls for action, Jane says "I'm not going to fight them." Rebis is also unresponsive, but for different, less human, reasons: "Time for the Aenigma Regis to unfold. And my life cycle must take precedence over the work of the Doom Patrol." Cliff, angered, is challenged by Jane as to why the Doom Patrol should do anything about the Brotherhood anyway. Cliff's response exemplifies the need to establish order in a chaotic world: "Because if we don't," says Cliff, "then the Brotherhood's right and there's no point... no point to anything. I can't live that way." Only Joshua Clay agrees to accompany Cliff on his mission to stop the Brotherhood, although Clay refuses to use his powers because he's "too old for that shit." Eleven issues away from the end of Morrison's run on the series, and already the Doom Patrol is fragmenting apart.

As the Brotherhood spreads its message, and the Doom Patrol battles from within, Major Main tells Ms. Roddick the story of Yankee Doodle:

> Using the code name Yankee Doodle, he went out there and kicked ass for Uncle Sam, no problem. Until some government big-wig freaked out and went down into the city under the Pentagon, taking a lot of sensitive documents with him. Somebody had to go down there after him... and Dandy volunteered... They sent him down into the abyss and waited... A year later, Dandy came back. Or at least something that claimed to be Dandy came back... He insisted he's swapped his original face for this new thing... and, well, then he did something to two of the soldiers...

Dandy has been transformed into an inhuman creature, crawling on the ceiling, with Scrabble pieces for eyes, a comb for a mouth, and disembodied screaming heads floating like a halo around him. *Doom Patrol* #52 begins with an omniscient narrator describing the innermost thoughts of Yankee Doodle as he prowls the rooftops on his mission: "One thought blazing, a magnesium flare in the center of his brain. 'Destroy the Brotherhood of Dada.'" Only an operative of the military could have such an uncomplicated, single-minded purpose, unlike the Doom Patrol members (Cliff Steele and Joshua Clay) who stand in the midst of an assembled audience, debating the first Amendment as Mr. Nobody prepares a stump speech.

Before he goes on stage, though, Mr. Nobody and the Brotherhood of Dada sit down for a last supper. In Richard Case's homage to Leonardo da Vinci, Agent "!" plays the role of John, the Love Glove is Philip, Alias the Blur is Thomas, and Mr. Nobody is Jesus Christ. Is Morrison signaling that Mr. Nobody is our savior? Possibly. Or perhaps it's just a literal sign telling us that this is, indeed, his last supper (at least with this group of guys), because soon after his speech, everything starts to fall apart.

The Love Glove considers betraying Mr. Nobody, but with a biblical flourish, he resists the "thirty pieces of silver."[184] Then, after Mr. Nobody proposes to the people of America that if they "wish hard enough, [they] can dissolve the boundary between the painting and this 'real' world," Yankee Doodle strikes. Yankee Doodle throws a flying blue head at Mr. Nobody, which causes him to turn back into "old Mr. Morden," Mr. Nobody's mortal, human identity. At that moment, Yankee Doodle drives a stake through his heart.

Yankee Doodle defeats the indescribable Mr. Nobody by *giving him a face*. Once he has a solid, identifiable target, Yankee Doodle is able to finish him off. The metaphor is obvious: an intangible concept cannot be destroyed, but a human being can. Give evil (or in this case, absurdity) a face, a presence, and then kill that person, thereby symbolically destroying the concept that being embodies. This has been the method of politicians since politics were invented, and we see it all too clearly in the present day. Morrison presents this fact of life with savage violence, and the reader, normally accustomed to rooting for the "good guys" and against the "bad guys," finds himself sympathetic to Mr. Nobody as he is eviscerated by the agent of the government. Cliff Steele is moved as well, and he tries to grant Mr. Nobody his last request: to be returned to the painting from whence he (most recently) came. But the painting is destroyed by a barrage of artillery as Mr. Nobody loses strength. He dissipates into smoke and ash as he says to Cliff, "One of these days, you'll miss me honey..."

The tragic death of Mr. Nobody is undercut by the arrival of the missing member of the Brotherhood of Dada: the Toy, whose simple question, "I'm not too late, am I?" and silly costume[185] diminish the dramatic impact of Mr. Nobody's demise. Would Mr. Nobody have had it any other way?

In the epilogue to *Doom Patrol* #52, Mr. Nobody's spirit lives on as a young girl finds a fragment of the painting. The captions throughout the page juxtapose the images with the words of David Rudkin's "Fire":

> Cherish the flame, till we can safely wake again. The flame is in your hands, we trust it to you our sacred demon of ungovernableness. Cherish the flame. We shall rest easy. Child

---

[184] Judas Iscariot betrayed Jesus for thirty pieces of silver, according to the *Bible*.

[185] The Toy has a tight yellow jumpsuit that reads "Play With Me," and toothbrushes over her ears.

> be strange, dark, true, impure and dissonant. Cherish our flame. Our dawn shall come.

In the final two panels, the little girl hurls a rock into the window of a car, smashing it. Thus, the saga of the Brotherhood is ended.

Morrison offers us a respite from the heavy political satire with *Doom Patrol* #53, a so-called "Journey into Wonderment" called "And Men Shall Call Him – Hero!" Like the Beard-Hunter issue, this is a comic book parody, but unlike that Punisher pastiche, this time Morrison seems much more affectionate about his intended target. In this story, which is framed as a dream sequence,[186] Morrison channels Stan Lee and Jack Kirby, and guest artist Ken Steacy does an amazing job of capturing the visual glory of those early Marvel comic books. On the opening pages, the normally somber, occult characters John Constantine and the Phantom Stranger are re-imagined as costumed members of "The Mighty Mystics." They speak in suitable bombastic dialogue: "When the gates of the infinite are briefly thrown wide, who dares say what might be waiting there to gain entrance?" asks the Phantom Stranger, who in this incarnation wears a cape and cowl and has a giant "PS" emblazoned on his chest.

We also meet Doctor Thirteen, the Multiple Man, (with the power to create and communicate telepathically with his thirteen bodies) and the "Ever-lovin'" Mr. E, the Malleable Medium, who can stretch his body while, presumably, contacting spirits from beyond the grave. Anyone who's ever read the somber adventures of DC's occult "Trenchcoat Brigade"[187] would surely thrill to read this over-the-top super-hero interpretation.

The Doom Patrol, re-imagined in this story as "The Legion of the Strange," are depicted as *Fantastic Four*-style adventurers, and we see Automaton (Cliff Steele) and Negative Man (Rebis) having a physical

---

[186] Danny the Street is having the dream. Only in Morrison comic books would a transvestite street dream of epic super-hero battles.

[187] "The Trenchcoat Brigade" was a term used by John Constantine to refer to the DC's occult heroes including himself, the Phantom Stranger, Doctor Occult, and Mister E. All of the characters wear ties and trenchcoats in most appearances. In this story, Morrison replaces Doctor Occult with Doctor Thirteen, a skeptic from the Phantom Stranger stories who would always try to find a rational explanation for supernatural events. In *Doom Patrol* #53, he re-imagines all of these characters as if they were costumed super-heroes with powers to match. Hence. Doctor Thirteen can create multiple selves and Mr. E becomes an occult version of Mr. Fantastic.

quarrel.[188]

The plot of the issue, as revealed by Automaton's thought balloons, closely parallels the famous story in *Fantastic Four* #51. In that classic tale, entitled "This Man... This Monster," an impostor has taken the place of Ben Grimm, the Thing, (after switching minds with him,) and plans on using the Thing's great strength for evil. When Reed Richards, Mr. Fantastic, faces death in the Negative Zone,[189] however, the impostor chooses to become a hero – he sacrifices his life to save Richards. In *Doom Patrol* #53, the mind of Cliff Steele has been replaced by jealous scientist Norman Caesar. Just as in the *Fantastic Four* story, this impostor undergoes a metamorphosis when faced with a moral dilemma: sacrifice himself by fighting Celestius the Man-God (a Galactus[190] proxy), or watch as an innocent blind child is devoured by the being.

Not only does Norman Caesar die a hero, but he stops the rampaging Man-God by using a portal into the infinite, and the battle somehow gives the little girl her sight back. His sacrifice was so great that it cured blindness.

Morrison's pastiche is spot-on, and although the issue has nothing to do with the "real" Doom Patrol (it is just a dream, after all), it highlights his love of Silver Age storytelling, when a sense of fun and wonder permeated the medium.

Following up the fun-loving Lee and Kirby spoof issue, *Doom Patrol* #54 is one of the most challenging comic book texts in Morrison's oeuvre. Morrison channels his metaphysical side here, and the entire story takes place as we follow Rebis, who has flown to the surface of the Moon to enact the final stage of its transformation to become the Aenigma Regis.

The key symbolic image in the issue is that of duality (both conflicted

---

188 Automaton was Cliff Steele's super-hero name in the first stories featuring the original Doom Patrol, and Negative Man was an original member as well. In this issue, they are modeled on the Fantastic Four, with Automaton chomping on a cigar like the Thing as Negative Man flies around and taunts him like the Human Torch. One of the recurring tropes of the *Fantastic Four* series is the constant quarreling between the Thing and the Human Torch. In early issues of the series, the Thing quits the team so he won't have to put up with the Torch's taunting.

189 The Negative Zone, an unexplored universe with great destructive potential, was discovered by Reed Richards in *Fantastic Four* #51, and it soon became an important part of the Marvel Universe.

190 Galactus, the Fantastic Four's most powerful threat, is a world-eater of nearly omnipotent power.

From *Doom Patrol* #53 – Norman Caesar, in the body of Automaton, confronts Celestius amidst Stan Lee-style bombast and Jack Kirby-style fisticuffs. Art by Ken Steacy. Copyright © DC Comics.

and unified). The entire story, in fact, seems to be a meditation on duality and the outcome of an alchemical union, which would result in a trinity (either physical, scientific, spiritual, or perhaps all three). Dualities leading to trinities explored or referenced in this issue include:

(1) Larry Trainor + Eleanor Poole = Rebis

(2) Sun, Earth, Moon (in linear succession on page 2)

(3) Past / Present / Future (images from all three times appear and disappear throughout the issue

(4) Barometer = Shine / Rain (physically embodied on page 12)

(5) Winged female (or hermaphrodite?) clutching two snakes (page 16)

(6) "Who is Mercurius?" (page 18) – Mercurius a.k.a. Hermes embodied duality. Mercury is a liquid and a metal, it is cold yet it burns.

And as Rebis explores more of the Moon, he finds remnants of the Apollo 11 lunar module. "If we really want to go into space," Rebis narrates, "we'll have to leave our bodies behind." "What did they see when the cameras went dead?" Rebis asks, and as he reaches the edge of a crater, he looks down to see two large trees bound together by a golden ring. A glowing golden sphere rests atop the branches.

These dual trees, joined by the golden ring and supporting the glowing orb, symbolize the union between Larry and Eleanor. As Rebis descends to the base of the trees, he finds a humanoid figure embedded in the roots. The figure has a drawer where its chest should be. Out of the drawer, Rebis pulls fragments of Eleanor's life: a photo, a book, bandages. "The dolls were a metaphor," says Rebis to itself, "the same doll giving birth to itself endlessly."[191] Morrison emphasizes the recursive nature of the universe as a way to explain the unity Rebis seeks in life. Ultimately, Rebis finds what it has been looking for all along, the final result of the foretold Aenigma Regis: a giant, radiant, green egg. Rebis has given birth – and the cycle continues.

Morrison's shifting authorial voice, moving from vicious satire to high camp to philosophical mysticism throughout this sequence of issues, shows his mastery of the medium and his mercurial spirit. He is not complacent, and as his run on *Doom Patrol* winds down, he will shake up the status quo even more.

---

[191] Infinite recursion. Morrison embeds the fractal principle into Rebis's self discovery.

## An Interlude with Liefeld

In the same month that *Doom Patrol* #57 was released, Morrison and company also put out a one-shot *Doom Force Special*. Because a discussion of that book would interrupt my analysis of Morrison's final issues on *Doom Patrol*, I'll take some time now to explain what the *Doom Force Special* was all about.

Much like *Doom Patrol* #53, which imagined the Doom Patrol as Stan Lee and Jack Kirby creations, the *Doom Force Special* also provides a parody of a famous comic book creator, only this time the parody is less kind and the creator less talented: Rob Liefeld.

Liefeld had gained immense popularity in the early '90s on titles like *The New Mutants* and *X-Force*. His art, characterized by figures with grotesquely balloonish muscles and gritted teeth, was the antithesis of the staid, angular, understated page designs of regular *Doom Patrol* artist Richard Case. And the heroes in his comics were aggressive and hyper-violent – exactly the opposite of the more cerebral and reactive Doom Patrol. Morrison obviously wanted to poke fun at the absurdity of Liefeld's over-the-top brand of super-heroics, and hence, the *Doom Force Special* was born.

The entire issue plays the Liefeld game with deadly seriousness. Even the text piece at the end, written by Editor Tom Peyer, explains the thoughtful process by which the issue was conceived:

> Grant breathlessly painted a vivid word-picture of a colorful band of super-outcasts who bravely battle the world's most powerful menaces on behalf of the very same human race that rejected them. Ironically, these youthful warriors have much more in common with their enemies than with those they fight to protect...
>
> "That's very good," I said, "but it needs something... An extra twist the readers won't expect..." He whispered three little words that would literally knock me out of my chair.
>
> "They're not mutants."

Peyer's hyperbolic promotion of the greatness of the issue continues as he says this of the artwork: "Our pencilers and inkers... seemed inspired to artistic heights they had never previously reached. If you doubt that, go back and look again at the sheer number of lines they put into each panel and onto every figure."

Such enthusiastic praise mimics the Marvel-style self-promotion as popularized in the "Stan's Soapbox" columns, and it also mocks the attitude of "more lines equals better art" which was the popular trend of the day with hot young artists like not only Liefeld, but Jim Lee and Todd McFarlane as well.[192]

The plot of the *Doom Force Special* is, of course, ridiculous. It's irrelevant, in fact, since the issue, in true Liefeld fashion, is designed to have as many action-packed panels as possible. In a typical example, characters like the Scratch, Flux, and the Crying Boy attempt to stop the evil machinations of Count Anton Zero and his sister, Una.[193] The climactic battle is filled with nearly naked women, musclebound "heroes," and lots of rendering lines.

By the end of the story, Liefeld is mocked, the overblown task-force mentality of current comics is ridiculed, and the Doom Force lives to fight another day. (In case you were wondering, it could potentially fit into Doom Patrol continuity since the story takes place in the future when Dorothy Spinner is a middle-aged woman and Doom Force member known only as "The Spinner.")

## Betrayal, Truth, Reality, and Life

When Grant Morrison took over the writing of the *Doom Patrol* series back in issue #19, he started with a storyline called "Crawling from the Wreckage." In *Doom Patrol* #55 he initiates a series of events that leads the team back toward destruction.

*Doom Patrol* #55 is structured around a theme: *the haunting effects of the past*. The major plot points that occur revolve around this theme, not just in this issue, but in most of the issues to come. Oddly, the events of this issue actually occur *before* the events in *Doom Patrol* #54, because we see Rebis leaving without emotion, and when it returns in a future story, it has given birth to the egg we saw last issue. But issue #55 isn't about Rebis, or even Willoughby Kipling (who makes a return appearance as he's informed that, contrary to what he'd assumed, the apocalypse is "set to break through

[192] All three of these artists, Liefeld, Lee, and McFarlane shared a similar style and were among the fan favorites who left Marvel Comics to form Image Comics in the early 1990s. Image Comics was known for promoting style over substance, and many of the early issues lack any kind of coherent story.

[193] All of these "characters" are original Morrison creations, used just for this special issue.

onto the physical plane today"). Issue #55 is about Crazy Jane and Dorothy Spinner.

Crazy Jane has gone missing from Doom Patrol headquarters, and Cliff finds a disturbing note in her room that seems to be written by the man who molested her as a child: "Baby lamb baby lamb," says the note, "I know where you are and I'm coming to get you Love Daddy XXX."

Meanwhile, Joshua Clay argues with Cliff about what to do about Jane and laments the problems of the team as Dorothy arrives to ask for help regarding her own problem. She says meekly, "Mr. Steele. Mr. Clay. I think I need help." Dorothy's problem is the Candlemaker, who we've been seeing for several issues (though the rest of the team has not), and who "wants [Dorothy] to make another wish so that it can get out and kill everyone else."

The Candlemaker, who first appeared to Dorothy when she was a child (and wished a school bully dead), is a relic of her past, just as Jane's father is a relic of Jane's past. The parallel nature of their stories is reinforced in this issue with a strong *candle* motif. As Dorothy explains the power of the Candlemaker to Joshua Clay, telling him that "You wish on a candle and the Devil comes," we see Jane in a cathedral, lighting a candle and remembering her days as Liza Radley, when she thought she was sane: "Every Easter we'd light a candle for... someone. Someone who'd died a long time ago and no one loved but us." That someone is Kay Challis, the little girl who "died" when she was molested by her father and was replaced by multiple personalities. Liza couldn't remember those things until she was raped in a confessional and her buried memories come rushing back. Jane reminisces about these horrible events of her past, surrounded by candles in the cathedral as a police officer asks if she's all right.

Dorothy, meanwhile, undergoes a seizure, trying desperately to hold the Candlemaker from coming out. Joshua Clay runs to Niles Caulder for help, but he finds Caulder's wheelchair overturned, just before being gunned down by a shadowy figure. The issue ends with an image that recalls the shocking scene witnessed by Buddy Baker in *Animal Man* when he returned home to find his family brutally murdered:

Joshua Clay lies dead of a gunshot wound on the tile floor. Blood pools beneath his lifeless body.

Just as in *Animal Man*, this scene indicates the beginning of the end for the characters, and the beginning of the end for Morrison's tenure on the title.

*Doom Patrol* #56 picks up the narrative with the aftermath of a deed committed by Jane. Between issues, she has unleashed the buried fury within her and killed the police officer who offered her help. The device of placing her murderous deed off-panel, between issues, may be an attempt by Morrison to keep Jane as a sympathetic character. Yet that seems unlikely, because she quickly lashes out at the police force that has her surrounded within the cathedral. She flies out of the doorway, blasting the officers (and their vehicles) with flames before walking calmly away. In the foreground we can see the dead bodies amidst flaming wreckage.

Showing the aftermath of her rampage is hardly an effort to keep her sympathetic.

Cliff, who apparently hasn't seen or heard about the events outside the cathedral (in Metropolis), seeks clues regarding Jane's whereabouts. He visits the hospital where he first met Jane back in *Doom Patrol* #19 and finds out from one of the doctors that Jane's father has actually been dead for ten years. The doctor says, "I should have thought the author of this note was obvious. This is Kay's own handwriting, Mr. Steele." Such a thought had never occurred to Cliff, but it doesn't make him fear for her safety any less.

The Dorothy plotline doesn't get much exposure in this issue, but Willoughby Kipling finds out more about his role in the upcoming catastrophe. He meets with the other Knights Templar,[194] and he's told: "The Doom Patrol has just become the focus for the first major assault in the final war of Armaguh-guh-geddon. And you've been chosen to help them, old man."

Jane, fleeing Metropolis without any further conflict, returns to her childhood home and literally descends down into the well. There, she recalls the torment of her father, but she also recalls his death in the hospital, where she saw him as a weak, helpless old man. Finally, she is able to get beyond her tormented past, and she opens an imaginary door at the bottom of the well to find a fairy tale landscape beyond the threshold. She has symbolically overcome the trauma of her childhood and reached a state of bliss.

---

[194] The Knights Templar, as depicted by Morrison, bear little resemblance to the soldiers who fought in the Crusades. Here, Morrison just presents them as a shadowy cabal who act almost like a secret occult police force.

In contrast to that, Cliff Steele, visiting Niles Caulder to ask for his advice about pursuing Jane, finds a snuffed out candle in the hallway. It's a meaningless item for him, but the reader knows what it implies: The Candlemaker is loose. Cliff, unaware of the threat, has more immediate concerns as he finds Joshua's dead body on the floor. Behind him, with a pistol, stands Niles Caulder.

The oblivious Cliff doesn't recognize the implication of the events, because, in *Doom Patrol* #57, Caulder talks to Cliff for eleven pages before Cliff even realizes who has killed Joshua Clay, and even then, Caulder has to spell it out for him: "Surely, it's obvious," says the man they called the Chief, "I killed Joshua. It was me." This is the second time in two issues that someone has pointed out the obvious to Cliff, establishing that his human brain is not his strongest muscle.

Dorothy's storyline progresses concurrently, as the wish she made to release The Candlemaker is revealed: she asked for Joshua to be brought back to life. The Candlemaker grants her wish, and then immediately snuffs out his life again, saying: "You thought I belonged to you, but you were just the door I walked through. When I'm ready, I'll kill you, too."

Caulder, meanwhile, has paralyzed Cliff using a fail-safe mechanism he'd installed in Cliff's new robot body. Having abandoned all pretense of heroic mentor, Caulder reveals the true nature of his plans, explaining that his scheme began when he was just a child: "Ever since I was young," he says, "I have been driven by one blazing ambition. To create life... I finally did it." Caulder reveals a humanoid figure, an artificial being with red eyes and no facial features save a mouth in the shape of an "O." This creature is part of Caulder's plan to investigate the nature of catastrophe. His experiments in that area actually began long ago, as he explains to the motionless Cliff:

> Catastrophe theory provides us with this topological model which represents the introduction of sudden, discontinuous change into a stable system. We cannot predict the effect of catastrophe, but we can use this model to help ascertain the conditions most favorable for its manifestations.
>
> Following my confrontation with Immortus,[195] I began to

---

[195] General Immortus first appeared in *My Greatest Adventure* #80, the first appearance of the original Doom Patrol team. Caulder once worked with Immortus before Immortus betrayed him.

> conceive my grand scheme. My world had been transformed by unexpected events, catastrophes. I became interested in creating similar effects in others. I spent some time looking for a perfect subject for these new experiments. And quite by chance, I found him. Cliff Steele. International adventurer. Daredevil... I wondered what would happen if I introduced a catastrophe curve into the life of such a man. I had to find out.

Caulder reveals that he not only caused the accident that destroyed Cliff Steele's body, but he also caused the accidents that created Negative Man and Elasti-Girl as well (among others – those three were the few who survived their catastrophes). "I contrived the means by which to bring us all together, as if by accident. And, as you know, we became the Doom Patrol." As Caulder explains, "catastrophe forces us to think in new ways," and as he grew bored with the original team, he conspired with General Immortus to destroy them, saving himself by means of a force field. His new plan, he tells Cliff, involves a catastrophe of much more significant impact: "Imagine a mass accident... a global catastrophe curve. What might happen then? ... I can remake the world and everyone in it." Caulder's catastrophe curve is very similar to the chaos theory that Morrison has explored so thoroughly in previous work. Caulder revealed his own fascination with chaos in an early Morrison issue of *Doom Patrol*, but Joshua Clay didn't realize the implications of Caulder's interest.

"I believe in catastrophe. I welcome it with open arms," says Caulder, after revealing his maniacal plan to Cliff. At that moment, in ironically catastrophic fashion, Caulder's artificial being attacks him and tears off his head. Panel by panel, as Caulder is torn apart, the artificial being begins to develop features and transform into the Candlemaker. This creature has taken this man-made body as his earthly shell, to be used to wreak havoc on the world. It's not the catastrophe Caulder had in mind, and he isn't going to be around to see how it turns out. Neither is Cliff, apparently, as the Candlemaker turns his attention on the paralyzed Robotman. We've seen Cliff torn asunder before – it has been one of the common tropes in the *Doom Patrol* series since its original inception, but even Cliff will have difficulty recovering from this as the Candlemaker tears out Cliff's brain and smashes it on the floor, shouting, "I'm King Candle. I'm the Candlemaker!"

Things look so bleak for the team that the "next issue box" at the bottom of the final page reads merely: "?"

*Doom Patrol* #58 opens with an obvious dream sequence: a fully human

Cliff Steele and a matronly Kay Challis living together in an idealized suburban home. Cracks immediately appear in the facade, however, as Kay removes her face to reveal a swarm of buzzing insects. Morrison once again uses the insect trope to signify destruction and chaos, just as he's done in the past with the "Bug-Man" armor in *Animal Man* and the Insect Mesh of earlier *Doom Patrol* issues.

For the bulk of the issue, Cliff's consciousness moves through a surreal landscape, looking for a way out, or an answer to the riddle of his imprisoned existence. "I see the others, my friends," Cliff says. "They've got no faces and they're kind of tending to this big computer or machine or something. I don't know what it is. And they're like bugs or bugs are behind it all."

Cliff's torment continues for pages until, in his human form, he attempts suicide by slicing his wrist open. But it's ineffective. Beneath the skin he finds only metal: gears and rods. He doesn't emerge from his nightmare until page 19, where he awakens to find Willoughby Kipling, Dorothy Spinner, and the decapitated head of Niles Caulder. Kipling explains how he saved Cliff even though Cliff's brain was destroyed by the Candlemaker: "Caulder downloaded your entire consciousness into his computer... I managed to get you out and onto a disc... There's a double-disc drive behind an armored plate in your chest." Cliff has difficulty accepting this existential dilemma: "I want my brain back," he says. "That was the only human part I had left." Kipling provides little comfort: "Look, can you just have your nervous breakdown after we've saved the world?"

Cliff doesn't get to spend too much time lamenting his fate because Danny transports them to New York City, but when they arrive, all they find are enormous piles of flaming rubble.

Such apocalyptic imagery is nothing new for Morrison. In *Zenith*'s Phase Four, he reduced the White House to a similar condition, although in that case it was the forces of order, the self-appointed dictators of the world, calling themselves Horus, razing the landscape. Here, it's a chaotic force bringing about Armageddon, in the form of the Candlemaker. The Doom Patrol are the ones who have to establish a sense of order to save the planet.

At the beginning of *Doom Patrol* #59, we learn that the destruction of New York hasn't reached a literal level yet. The image we saw at the end of last issue is, as Willoughby Kipling explains:

> the Manhattan of dreams and drug visions, the city beneath the

> skin of reality. It's always there, but most people are unaware of it... [The Candlemaker is] killing the dream self of Manhattan. Burning down the archetypal city. It's the end of the world, but nobody's going to know until it's too late and their spirits are dead.

This is yet another example of Morrison's use of alternate realities, only this time the destruction of the "dream" realm will inevitably destroy the "reality" as well.

Kipling admits that they can't really stop the end of the world, because as he and Morrison himself have pointed out before, that's going to happen in 2012. "What we can do, though," Kipling says, "is stop the end of the world from coming at the hands of this miserable bastard."

As if on cue, Crazy Jane arrives to rejoin the team. Except she's no longer Crazy Jane, just Kay, and she no longer has her multiple personalities or any of their powers since she has reconciled with her past: "We're a team," she says, regarding her formerly fragmented personalities, "and it's fantastic." Without her powers, though, she is useless against the Candlemaker. Morrison emphasizes the irony that the Doom Patrol is no good without its neurosis: a healed Doom Patrol is a team without strength.[196]

Even Rebis's dramatic entrance into the climactic battle reveals that truth. Although it strikes the Candlemaker with success, Rebis hesitates in battle and begins to tell Cliff about what has happened on the moon (as shown in issue #54). After that, Rebis can't get its negative form to work anymore, and the Candlemaker attacks, leaving nothing more to Rebis than a skeleton.

The conflict with the Candlemaker continues through *Doom Patrol* #60, and Willoughby Kipling provides a bit more context about the being's origin, saying that it's an:

> Eregore of some kind, generated by the unconscious tensions that surround historical crisis points. I'd say it's a personification of human fears about the bomb, World War III, that sort of thing... Dorothy's head's like a revolving door, see? Connecting the plane of existence with the astral, where the world of Armageddon is taking place.

Although in previous appearances, Kipling has been portrayed as a coward,

---

[196] Contrast this with *Arkham Asylum* which features a Batman who in ineffective until he unifies his sense of Self. Jane cured when she unifies her Self, but she is now powerless.

he stands his ground in this battle and pays a price: the flesh and muscle is completely burned off one of his arms.

As the climax escalates, Cliff is the only one left to defend the world against the Candlemaker, who chases after Cliff saying, "Nothing is real. Only me. I can do anything. Nothing is real." Cliff leads the Candlemaker away from the city toward the home of Doc Magnus, where Cliff hopes to find aid. As Cliff begins to explain his plan to Magnus, the Candlemaker blasts the front of the house, blowing off Cliff's legs in the process.

*Doom Patrol* #61 provides a resolution for the Candlemaker story. Cliff describes his plan once he and Magnus escape immediate harm (with the help of Danny the Street, who sacrifices his downtown storefronts in the aftermath). Cliff explains that they might be able to reprogram the nanomachines which compose the artificial body inhabited by the Candlemaker, telling the nanomachines to destroy the body from within. Since Caulder created the nanomachines at Doom Patrol headquarters, they use the computer there to enact the plan. Even with Doc Magnus working furiously, the Candlemaker continues to attack.

In a last-ditch effort, Willoughby Kipling wheels out Rebis's glowing green egg (as seen in issue #54) in a shopping cart.[197] The egg hatches into a new Rebis, complete with all of its old memories intact. This new Rebis, fully-powered, strikes at the Candlemaker as the nanomachines work from within to destroy its physical form.

It's only the final action of Dorothy Spinner, blowing out the last bit of flame, that extinguishes the threat of the Candlemaker forever, but it was Cliff's plan to use the nanomachines that led to their victory. His brainpower (such as it is) led to their victory.

Even though the battle has lasted for several issues, plenty long enough for a typical super-hero climax, Morrison's not done yet. Caulder's plan for a global catastrophe has already begun, as Magnus discovers while using the Doom Patrol computer. Caulder has created thousands of other nanomachines and programmed them to replicate themselves infinitely to generate a global disaster. The Candlemaker was a catastrophe he couldn't have expected, but this is the one he was describing to Cliff – the one that he had already gotten underway. As Magnus says in disbelief, "We have...

[197] This is yet another example of how Morrison undercuts the drama with humor. The shopping cart diminishes any sense of grandeur the story had until that point.

hours left before they swarm over the whole world."

Cliff can't believe it either. "How many times do we have to save the world in one day for Christ's sake?" shouts Cliff at the beginning of *Doom Patrol* #62. Once again, he's forced to save everyone. He volunteers to reload his consciousness back into the computer and try to override the nanomachines' programming from within the "think tank" (the name for the data matrix within Caulder's infinitely complex computer system).

This threat takes less time to defeat than the Candlemaker, as Cliff is able to overcome his fear of disembodiment, quickly bypass the security from within, and cause the program to terminate itself as the rest of the group waits impatiently. "This can't work," says Magnus, "it's insane." Rebis replies, "It will work, Doctor Magnus. I have left the realm of science and entered the arena of faith. It will work if we believe it." The screen soon reads, "Program Terminated." Cliff's consciousness has defeated the physical threat. Mind has trumped body this time.

Afterwards, Cliff returns to the hospital where we found him in *Doom Patrol* #19. He tells the doctor, "I don't even feel that... that rage and frustration anymore. There's just nothing and no way home. I feel dead, but I'm still walking around. Shit." He says he feels nothing, but he still feels a great sense of loss because Kay Challis has not been seen since the battle with the Candlemaker. "I just want to save her," says Cliff. "I want to save everybody."

Later, after Cliff returns home (which is depicted as a small black room with nothing in it except a table, a chair, a clock, and a large image of Jane hanging on the wall), Rebis visits him and tells him to come see something. Danny the Street has begun to expand. Cliff witnesses the event as Danny the Street becomes Danny the World, an alternate reality where "everything [is] marvelous or frightening or strange," a fairy tale world that exists outside of our own. Danny the Street will still be around to provide a portal between his new world and the old world, Rebis explains, but Rebis is going to stay in this new fantasy world forever. Cliff is left to decide whether or not he wants to stay as well or return to the real world.

Morrison ends his run on *Doom Patrol* with an issue that seems to initially call into question the reliability of the entire series. In *Doom Patrol* #63, we discover what's happened to Kay Challis. She's seen in a hospital where she's kept heavily sedated. She's referred to as "dangerous" by one of the doctors as she lies unconscious on her bed. The drab hospital scenes are cut together with hallucinogenic fantasies of a Cliff Steele in plate mail armor and a Rebis brandishing a sword. These are clearly delusions, and they call into question whether or not Kay Challis has perhaps been imagining these adventures we've been reading about for the past 45 issues.

Kay's therapy reveals more evidence that these adventures have all been imaginary, as her psychologist says, "The 'Doom Patrol' just keep turning up, don't they, Kay? What if I tell you I think they're disassociated parts of your own personality?" When Kay mentions the Candlemaker, the psychologist says, "I thought we agreed this 'Candlemaker' was nothing more than your father, Kay? All this fantasy stuff was just your way of dealing with those terrible abuses." Later, the psychologist offers a rational explanation for Kay's memory of the Doom Patrol episodes:

> Keysmiths, Scissormen, Men from N.O.W.H.E.R.E. – they all seem to represent faceless forces of authority, but it's an authority that's incomprehensible... The other characters she's spoken about – Red Jack, Shadowy Mr. Evans, the Candlemaker – are all nightmarish male oppressor figures. The omnipotent bad father.

In other words, the psychologist is trying to analyze and interpret the *Doom Patrol* issues, much like I've been doing. Morrison must be poking fun at such analysis, but he doesn't make the psychologist an unsympathetic character. Her analysis may be simplistic, but she does want to believe in something greater than surface reality. "People like Kay inhabit a world where everything is alive and significant. So we cure them," says the psychologist.

Another doctor decides to treat Kay in a more extreme manner and provides brutal electro-shock therapy[198] to "cure" her delusions. When the psychologist finds out about this plan, she rushes to save Kay, but it's too late, the damage has been done, Kay is "cured."

Eventually, Kay leaves the hospital, and with a blank stare, works at the checkout counter at a grocery store. "She didn't ever paint again," says the psychologist. "Just yesterday night," the psychologist narrates, "she walked out of her apartment and left a note: ['It's not real' says the note, affixed to a bedside lamp]... she went to the bridge and they still haven't found the

[198] This recalls Morrison's depiction of ECT in *Arkham Asylum*. In both cases, Morrison's depiction of psychiatric methods shows the violence and inhumanity which are called upon to supposedly cure those who are different from the norm.

From *Doom Patrol* #63 – Kay Challis is rescued, saved from the "cure" of sanity. Art by Richard Case. Copyright © DC Comics.

body."

As Jane leans over the edge of the bridge and rain pours down from above, we see a familiar shape, it's Cliff Steele. He's returned from Danny the World to pick up someone he's been missing.

The final page of Morrison's final issue of *Doom Patrol* shows a celebratory Danny the Street transporting Cliff and Kay away from the dreary bridge. The narration reads: "There is another world. There is a better world. Well... there must be."

Thus, Grant Morrison concludes what was, at the time, the longest work of his career. By ending his run on the series with such a touching moment, he brings the humanity of the characters to the forefront. He's given us plenty of absurd moments and crazy situations, and the essence of the *Doom Patrol* has been to reject conformity and embrace our uniqueness, but in the final issue, he reminds us that the heart of the story has been the relationship, the love, between Cliff Steele and Kay Challis. The mind and the body, the order and the chaos, all has pointed toward one idea: life, in all its complexity. And Cliff and Kay's humanity, in the face of tremendous physical and psychological damage, has prevailed.

And that's all Mr. Nobody ever wanted, really. Well, that and maybe a plague of flying fish.

# Conclusion

These five works, from *Zenith* to *Doom Patrol*, represent the early stages of what would become an amazingly prolific and influential career. Throughout it all, Grant Morrison has returned to the same themes and ideas: the relationship between the mind and the body, the nature of reality, the role of the hero, and the dichotomy between order and chaos. He keeps telling the same archetypal stories again and again, but always with a fresh, enthusiastic perspective that keeps readers coming back for more.

Morrison's stories, unlike most of his contemporaries' stories, have aged well. Their continued availability in trade paperback form show how important these stories are to audiences today. Even if he hadn't moved on to bigger venues, creating the mind-altering *Invisibles*, relaunching the Justice League in a magnificent *JLA* comic book, or putting his own subversive spin on Marvel's *X-Men*, his greatness would have been ensured by the stories covered in this book.

Luckily for us, he didn't stop with *Doom Patrol*, and we can read his recent work and look for the new patterns that emerge, and take pleasure in the fact that Grant Morrison is, indeed, a master of the medium.

# Grant Morrison Responds

*This interview was conducted via telephone and email in December of 2006.*

**Timothy Callahan (TC): *Zenith* deals with many themes and conflicts that seem to reappear in your work again and again. I'm going to name some of these ideas, and you can let me know how you think about these and how they play into your work.**

Grant Morrison (GM): Okay.

**TC: Youth vs. Age?**

GM: Utterly. Completely. 100%. I was a punk rocker in 1976. I was a teenager. I grew up in a world where we were told we were rebels and we kind of had to make our music and wear our own clothes and create our own bands. It was very much a DIY ethos, you know. It was very much anyone over 23 was old when I was young.

I was just brought up like that. I had kind of a harsh, Spartan code, you know. If you get over the teenage years, then you're past it. That's how we used to feel. I still feel a little bit like that, though. I don't want you to think that I didn't quite progress past that stage, because it was a difficult stage in my life, and I've been living it ever since to get it right.

**TC: Was *Zenith* basically a story of this kind of young punk in an adult world?**

GM: It's very clearly a response to a lot of stuff that was going on. You can see it was my answer to things like *Watchmen* or *Dark Knight*. While they were really technically great, they were really quite miserablist to me – as quite an optimistic person – and I wanted to present a character who was more like me, who was more cynical and brash and hanging out with girls and going to clubs, you know, because that was my life. I was in a band and I did these things. I was just expressing my own feelings, which made it seem a little different from the other guys who were doing comics who may not have had that kind of experience to draw on.

It was quite clearly... It was almost a manifesto, you know? It was something that had been brewing in my mind for years and years and years.

**TC: Relating to that idea of a manifesto, there seems to be, in *Zenith*, and your later work as well, a type of ideal transcendence but also the trap of the body – the idea that the mind cannot fully ascend from the body. What do you think about that aspect of your work?**

GM: Well, that's a theme I've pursued. I've always had a mystical tendency, and I've been interested in magic all my life. I'm a practicing magician, so these are things I've been dealing with every day, and transcendence is one of my themes, so yeah, it's present in *Zenith*, but I just think it's part of our lives. It's a type of perspective that people can grow up to have. It informs the work, but to me it's a natural progression of the way humans think and act, and the next stage is a transcendent stage, and beyond that there may be further stages.

**TC: Had your philosophy along those lines fully formed by the time you wrote *Zenith*, or has it continually evolved since then?**

GM: It's continually evolving. I mean, these are just ideas that you play with all through your life and try to define them and discover why they're so interesting to you. So magnetic to you. But they seem to be the themes that informed the way I've lived my life, the way things have worked out for me, so that's the trail through the labyrinth that I've followed.

**TC: A few moments ago, you referred to your youthful self as both optimistic and cynical? How do you reconcile those apparently opposite sides of your personality?**

GM: Like anyone else does. I see people – including myself – as essentially ridiculous, robotic, predictable, self-important, and dumb. They can also be heroic, funny, creative, gorgeous, and lovable at the same time. Although it can often seem otherwise, I maintain a belief so deep as to qualify as a religious conviction that everything is okay with the universe, and it's all going to work out just right in the end. In fact, it's already working out just right, but our lives are too short and fragile for us to get perspective on it.

**TC: Getting back to your work, there's another dominant theme: chaos vs. order. As I say in the book, you seem to be on the side of chaos, for the most part.**

GM: It's a punk rock thing, and as I've grown up, I've tried to get a bit more holistic about it. I don't really believe in these dualities anymore. I think chaos is just the other face of order, the reflection that order needs to see itself in and vice versa.

**TC: So it all fits together.**

GM: Yeah, well, the universe we live in is a kind of binary universe. It's all ones and zeros, so things have to fall into dualities so they can kind of proceed by dialectic. I'm interested in these things, but I have to think beyond them to the world. Where they're both united as one.

**TC: Do ideas like this come into play during the plotting stage? Do they evolve as you're writing? How do these ideas actually inform your work on a practical basis?**

GM: I think they're quite organic with something like *Zenith*. They were laced into the text. In the case of say *The Invisibles*, the story is actually about the ideas, almost. And about me as a creator trying to deal with these ideas. They were much more foregrounded and much more planned. Much more intended to fit into the text. *Zenith*'s kind of more organic because that's the way my mind works, the metaphors in there trying to describe these things – higher dimensional spaces, or whatever.

**TC: When you wrote *Zenith*, did you approach each phase separately? Or did you have an overall story in mind?**

GM: I knew where it was going to wind up but I didn't have all the moves worked out. As usual.

**TC: How about the connection, in your work, between fiction and reality and the blending between the two?**

GM: I think it gives me time to break down the barriers between categories, you know. Fiction and reality, what's the difference? When I was doing *The Invisibles*, they became no different because I so entwined myself into the text. I couldn't tell it apart anymore.

I see how the two things can be blended together. And you see it in our own world as well. When the World Trade Center towers came down, the first thing I though was, how many times have I already seen this happen in movies?

**TC: Yeah.**

GM: The whole thing was rehearsed in our imagination on the screen. The year the towers went up, King Kong was kicking the shit out of them in a movie. They've been knocked down by aliens, they've been knocked over by tidal waves.

**TC: What struck me about it was looking at the image of the falling towers and then looking at the traditional Tarot imagery of The Tower card and seeing this image that has been part of our lives and part of our culture for hundreds of years.**

GM: Completely. And even deeper symbolism on the subject we're actually discussing is that the two towers appear on the Tarot Moon card which is one of the main features of *Arkham Asylum*.

**TC: Absolutely.**

GM: The Tarots actually are the gateway between reality and illusion. On 9/11, they were knocked down. Magically, that was a day when reality and fiction started to collide.

**TC: Okay, I have a specific question about *Zenith*. In Phase Three of *Zenith*, you seem to be doing some sort of pastiche of *Crisis on Infinite Earths*, or at least a reaction to it. *Crisis* also informs your Animal Man work. How did you actually feel about *Crisis* as a reader back then, and what was your take on it?**

GM: I was enjoying *Crisis* when it came out. I really liked the story, but I think I was slightly old for it by that time. I was in my 20s and it was a DC book, you know? I was a lot more interested in other types of art by that point, so it was just kind of a DC book even though it was a good one. But, yeah, it worked its way into my head, and when I did *Zenith* [Phase] Three I wanted to do this kind of *Crisis* thing but have all these characters from different parallel universes not getting on at all. Unlike that kind of collaborative stuff that goes on in the DC books, have people just hate each other and fight all the time. Fuck up constantly. Leave guys behind on exploding planets. That was my take on all that. I just wanted to show the absolute chaos that would ensue if you had all these people from parallel Earths bumping into each other and planets being destroyed and people having breakdowns right, left, and center.

It was just my kind of cynical fun with it.

**TC: What other kinds of art were you interested in at the time that made you feel "slightly old" for *Crisis*?**

GM: In terms of comics, I was a lot more interested in the British scene at the time – both in the mainstream and on the alternative side. Stuff like *X-Men* or *Crisis* would have been exemplars of the types of comics we were trying to find a direction away from. Outside of comics, I was listening to a lot of indie records, going to clubs, making music, watching foreign movies and reading books about magic.

**TC: You have Lovecraftian gods in *Zenith*, and you contributed something to the Lovecraft tribute book. When were you first exposed to Lovecraft and how has his writing affected you?**

GM: I probably read my first Lovecraft book when I was about 15, which is when you're supposed to read Lovecraft. I heard about him via Conan comics, probably, and was swept up in that teenage way by his obsessive language and massive, dark conceptual canvas. He's the William Blake of Existentialism.

**TC: Getting back to Phase Three, did you worry at all about the copyright issues with the use of all those existing characters?**

GM: No. A lot of them were already owned by Fleetway, obviously. Things like Robot Archie, for example. But with the other ones, I kind of created analogues for most of the DC Thompson characters. Like Billy the Cat and Katie became Tiger Tom and Tammy. Desperate Dan became whatever his name was. Big Ben. All these kinds of characters were just turned into versions of themselves. And any other ones that we took were from completely defunct things in the 40s, so I don't think anybody cared anymore.

**TC: But aren't those the copyright issues that are keeping *Zenith* from being reprinted in America?**

GM: Not at all. The issue is basically that, back in the day, Fleetway, or whoever owned 2000 AD at the time, didn't really get rights from people. They said basically that by signing a check your were signing away your rights to things, which doesn't really hold up in a British court, but it's so difficult to fight in a court, we can't be bothered, which is why *Zenith* isn't coming out.

What I'm trying to say is that I own this thing, but I wasn't trying to say that I own it all. I suggested to them that we could put the books out and split, but they didn't want to do that. It just fell apart over the issue of who actually owned it.

**TC: At the end of Phase Three, Zenith seems to make this heroic sacrifice, but of course he doesn't. It was just Vertex all along. Throughout *Zenith*, and throughout a lot of your work from that period, your protagonists seemed quite ineffective. Why do you suppose that was? If these characters were in some way representative of you, were you saying something about yourself?**

GM: Yeah, definitely. They were obviously coming from a place where I had spent nine years on the dole, or on welfare or whatever you want to call it, before getting into doing comics completely, professionally – before I could make a living at it. So it was a long time being poor. And I kind of had a lot of self-esteem issues which found their way into the super-heroes.

I also think it gave them an interesting flavor, because to me it was: *What would 1980s man do in these situations?* So I saw Animal Man just kind of fucking up. I loved to see them fucking up and somehow still winning because it seemed to me to be more true to the human experience.

**TC: Yeah.**

GM: You can't really do that with every super-hero, obviously. You can't really do that with Superman, or maybe you could, but it would be less effective.

**TC: Right. Most of the DC icons are not as interesting when they're screwing up. They have to be confident. That's who they are.**

GM: Yeah, it's nice to see them portray that, but somebody like Buddy Baker can be a bit more complex, a bit more human.

**TC: On an aesthetic level, Phase Four of *Zenith* looks quite a bit different than the other three Phases because of the addition of full color. Did such a change affect the way you wrote the story in any way?**

GM: I can't remember giving it much thought.

**TC: Ultimately, does *Zenith* have a political message, or was the inclusion of Margaret Thatcher simply a logical choice, given the time period?**

GM: Everyone who'd grown up working class, and a few people who hadn't, I'm sure, was required by law to hate Thatcher in those days and she made it easy to do so. I think *Zenith* is informed by the aura of Thatcherism – the hero is the ultimate yuppie in many ways and is a cynical acknowledgment of the central contradiction of the times – that so many of we raging left wing opponents of the Iron Lady were actually making some money, buying nice clothes and generally doing rather well for the first time in our miserable lives under the yoke of the tyrant.

**TC: Moving on to *Arkham Asylum* – I have to wonder, what made you choose that particular Philip Larkin poem for the subtitle?**

GM: Larkin is one of my favorite poets, and I thought this particular phrase fit the mood. The poem itself doesn't really have any particular thematic resonance with the story of *Arkham Asylum* but this line ["a serious house on serious earth"] had a nice suggestive ring to it.

**TC: Your annotations and your original script reveal a lot of information about your intent for *Arkham Asylum.* In my analysis, I reference "The Waste Land" in relation to your work on the graphic novel. Was "The Waste Land" consciously in mind as you wrote that particular work?**

GM: I don't know if it was specifically in mind, but yeah, when you think about it, obviously it was part of the stuff that I'd grown up with and was familiar with, and it fits into the whole "dark night of the soul" scheme of the book – the idea of the Twentieth century moral wasteland, which is in the book as well. I didn't actually think about it, but now that you mention it, there's so many correspondences.

**TC: Yeah. The pearl imagery and the Tarot cards... it just seemed like *Arkham Asylum* was analogous to "The Waste Land" without specifically referring to it. It almost seemed that you were drawing from the same well.**

GM: It's good when things cross like that, and you can see connections because obviously we share these cultural touchstones, you know, and I'm quite sure that type of material was in my mind when I was working on something like *Arkham Asylum*, which was intended to be a kind of "arty" type of project.

**TC: In my analysis, I also take a stab at what Dr. Destiny might represent. In the annotations, you don't really write about him. You change his appearance radically, but you only have him in a couple panels. Why include characters like that? Did they each have a specific**

**symbolic weight?**

GM: In some cases. In other cases, you don't know why they're there. You have to start thinking about it. And Dr. Destiny's one of those. I seem to remember putting him in because I liked the idea of the visual: Batman kicking someone in a wheelchair [laughter]. I think it was purely for that visceral... kind of... Batman shouldn't be doing this. And Dr. Destiny seemed to be in the right position to have that done to him.

But then you have to ask yourself why it's the master of illusion that has to be the one to get kicked down the stairs by Batman. So who knows what was going on.

**TC: *Arkham Asylum* features a reference to David Bohm's "Implicate Order Theory," which reappears in *Animal Man*. When did you read Bohm's books, and how did you take inspiration from them?**

GM: I read them in my early 20s, I think, and just... poetically, I loved the ideas. I'm not really scientifically minded, but the poetry of those ideas – the idea of the unfolding order – seemed to me to explain things in a way that was quite appealing. It could provide a model which worked for me at the time. As you can see in *Animal Man*, it kind of tied to a lot of things in my head. Concentric circles in the rain and all that sort of stuff, when you're wool-gathering and walking along the canal to get story ideas. That's the way your mind runs.

**TC: My understanding of the Implicate Order Theory is that there is an order to the universe, but we just don't have the capacity to understand it.**

GM: Yeah.

**TC: To me, that relates to the ancient Greek plays, like the works of Sophocles – *Oedipus*, *Antigone* – which deal with that issue. The gods know things we don't, therefore our lives are tragic. Were you consciously aware of the classically tragic undertones of your work?**

GM: Definitely, but in terms of *Animal Man*, what intrigued me was that, as the god of his universe, I was actually trying to make something better. In *Animal Man*, they talk about the god that made their world, you know. Heaven was so rubbish, he had to make comic books to entertain himself. So I was more coming at it from that idea. The idea of the thoughtless creator who might make the world we live in. Then, by analogy, going down to the second dimension and making myself the creator of

Animal Man's world and seeing how the relationship might work between the creator and the created.

**TC: So you saw it as a parallel relationship? That there is a bigger being above us, doing the same things to us that you're doing to Buddy Baker?**

GM: That's completely how I felt based on the experiences I'd had. And the experiences I had during the writing of *The Invisibles* really made me feel that.

**TC: So it became even stronger since then?**

GM: Yeah. Things happened to me. Actual events happened in the '90s that seemed to be physical demonstrations of the type of reality that I've always been interested in, so I presume that somehow I've always known. To me, the underlying structure of the universe is quite visible everywhere. It's just that we're so familiar with it we've forgotten how magical it is. It's as simple as that. Art is one way to point again at how magical things are.

In terms of *Animal Man*, we are the implicate order from which his explicate order is unfolded. We're the kind of Platonic higher reality that he can only know if we decide to allow him to know. He's never going to get off the comic page on his own, but I can send in a little pressure suit into his world. A little drawing of myself to communicate with him. And I imagine that as being... that's like me sending my UFO, my landing craft into another dimension.

**TC: Or your angel, or whatever belief system you subscribe to, right?**

GM: Exactly.

**TC: Wrapping up *Arkham Asylum* – at the end of the book, Batman's psyche becomes integrated. Do you think he's healed at the end of the story? Does that ring true to you? Or were you compelled to include a happy ending?**

GM: I felt it had to happen. Basically, as I say in the [Anniversary Edition], the real last page of *Arkham Asylum* is that Bruce Wayne wakes up in his bed and says, "Oh my God, that was a weird dream, but I feel great. It's like something's been solved in my mind." I think there's a lot in *Arkham Asylum* that's kind of a psychoanalysis of who Batman was at the time, which was in a strange and dark place following Dark Knight and the lesser types of Batman stories that came after.

**TC: So was *Batman: Gothic* conceived after you'd written *Arkham Asylum*? Was *Gothic* a reaction to it in some way?**

GM: They asked me to do a five-part Batman story, and I thought, "God, I've no idea. What do I do now?" [laughs].

I was really fascinated by the Romantic poets, so working backwards from there I was reading a lot of stuff by the Gothic authors. I just decided, this is the way to do it. I'll go back to the source and do a Batman story that's completely based on the classic Gothic elements, you know. There's a corrupt monk, the devil pact, the evil scum of the underworld, all that stuff. So I worked a kind of literary exercise, to do a modern Gothic story with Batman in it.

**TC: You also seemed to purposely integrate as many conventional Batman elements as possible – you have the batarang, the bat-gyro, etc. Did you have sort of a checklist in mind of Batman traditions you wanted to cover?**

GM: Yeah, there was kind of that going on, and I also wanted to show people that I could just do a straight Batman story, as well. Because I think after *Arkham Asylum* a lot of people were quite bemused, you know? It did very well, and it got a lot of interest, but the traditional comic fans were quite surprised by it. So the Gothic story was just me showing that I could do it straight, and here was Batman in his early years, and here's his bat-gyro, and remember all this cool stuff? And that was it. It was more about me having fun.

**TC: What is it about Batman that compelled you to write stories which hinged on his origin? Is there something about Batman that makes his origin so dominant in his stories?**

GM: Not sure about that. If you're doing a "special" Batman story, as *Arkham Asylum* and the *Legends of the Dark Knight* stuff was intended to be, then it's natural to go to the most familiar elements of the character's world and play around with the preconceptions readers may have. The Batman work I'm doing now doesn't refer much to his origin, so I don't think it's a particular quirk of this character.

**TC: When I reread *Gothic*, it seemed to be the other side of the coin from *Arkham Asylum* – a chance for you to do all the things you couldn't, given the nature of that graphic novel.**

GM: You know, it's still not quite traditional, either.

**TC: Not at all [laughs]. It's your version of traditional.**

GM: I'm starting to do the stuff that's a bit more traditional. I'm starting to get it right.

**TC: Okay, let's jump over to *Animal Man*. In those first few issues, were you purposely doing an Alan Moore riff? Did you feel compelled to write in that style?**

GM: Basically, DC [came to England and] said, "what have you got for us?" And me and Neil Gaiman went up at the same day, and he pitched them *Black Orchid* or *Sandman* or something, and I'd come up with *Arkham Asylum* and *Animal Man*. I had no big ideas for *Animal Man*. I thought a bit on the train on the way to the meeting, because they'd asked me to pitch a couple of things, and all I had was *Arkham Asylum*, so by the time I got to London, I'd roughed up a kind of *Animal Man* pitch based on what I presumed they'd expect from a British comic book writer, because I really wanted the work.

So yeah, when you read it, you can see it was quite clearly influenced by what Alan Moore was doing in *Swamp Thing*. It was me sort of playing with all of his transitions and finding that they were clunky and kind of unpleasant [laughs]. I was losing interest in that by issue #5. I think it's interesting that you can actually see the thought process on the page in that book. It was originally intended as a four-issue miniseries, so I thought I'd give them a nice, tight little story with poetic captions and all that stuff, and then it would be over and done with, but they asked me to continue, and that forced me to think about what I wanted to do and who I wanted to be – which was not doing pastiches of other people just to get the job.

**TC: *Animal Man* really does break wide open in issue #5.**

GM: You can see it. That's just me planting a flag at that point, and saying from now on, everything's different.

**TC: Going back to the first four issues for a minute... You created Buddy Baker's family, right? He didn't really have much of a back story when...**

GM: No, they did exist before that. I think they get mentioned in a couple of panels or in the *Who's Who*.

**TC: They look like a typical Midwestern family, but the series is set on the West Coast. Was it your plan to capture a kind of generic, American, suburban family?**

GM: Yeah, I just wanted it to be America as seen by a Scottish person, you know? What it seemed like to me. The strange thing is that *Animal Man* was supposed to be set in Los Angeles but everyone who read it assumed it was supposed to be set in San Diego [laughs]. Obviously, I managed to blur the boundaries enough that no one knew where it was actually set. It was just a kind of an E.T. America, you know? The white picket fence.

**TC: What actually inspired "The Coyote Gospel" in issue #5? Was it the Chuck Jones cartoons? Was it the blending of fiction and reality? What made you say, this is the direction I want to take it in?**

GM: It was bunch of things. It was the fact that in the '80s, I was reading a lot of magic realist writers, like I was really into Borges and Italo Calvino and Thomasso Landolffi and people like that. And a lot of their stuff was about the relationship between the creator to the created. It was kind of the idea of the work being aware of itself – being able to question the author. And at the same time I was thinking of... I was looking for a new direction. I wanted to challenge what seemed a stale dead end: the realistic approach which, to me, was running its course.

So there was that, and then I looked back at the comics that really inspired me as a kid which were the Flash comics from the '60s, and they were just nuts, you know. Really psychedelic stuff where the Flash would get turned into a paving stone, or turn green – anything could happen. He'd be a puppet one month, then he'd be a living cloud. Those things had a big effect on me, and I thought that's the way I want to see comics. Instead of bringing their world down into our world and exposing the seams in Batman's tights and setting the super-heroes up as killers or losers or whatever.

**TC: The grim internal monologue era.**

GM: What I decided was to be an explorer who goes into their world. And I got started thinking, okay, what are the rules here? Where everything's primary colors and people can fly. This is their experience. This is the history of *Crisis on Infinite Earths*, you know? And they've got Superman living next door and all that kind of stuff. And suddenly that seemed to be a much more rich and interesting way of looking at the DC Universe.

**TC: Did you know when you wrote "The Coyote Gospel" that you'd eventually appear in *Animal Man* as a character yourself?**

GM: Yeah, the day I wrote that, the whole series just was mapped out.

The big influence on the series was basically the stories where the Flash actually vibrates on his cosmic treadmill through to what they called Earth-Prime which was this world where the stories were written. So it occurred to me that there was a bridge built between this classic, Silver Age, 1960s approach where the character could actually meet his editor and the work I was reading by the magic realist writers. I saw then that it was the way to move forward.

**TC: How did you come up with your unique approach to the two *Invasion* crossover issues of *Animal Man*? Both issues feature long monologues by villains who never appeared before or since. Did you receive any editorial pressure to feature your protagonists more prominently?**

GM: Not in those issues, no. There were two rejected issues from around this time – one was a bittersweet and farcical caper comedy called "Gorillas-A-Go-Go" which only had Animal Man on a few pages, and another really heavy, symbolic issue where Animal Man goes through a hallucinatory hell journey with images of flayed and tortured animals, intended to provoke a visceral response. I'm glad that one never came out, but the Gorilla story would have been good.

**TC: When you appear as a character at the end of your run on the *Animal Man* series, is that comic book version of Grant Morrison speaking from the heart, basically, about your attitude toward animal rights? Is he really you?**

GM: Yeah, completely. That was the way I was. I was really into animal rights, and I was a vegetarian at the time, so yeah, that was me. And *Animal Man* was kind of my way of putting those beliefs to the test, for me to create a way to challenge my own ideas. So in *Animal Man*, you can see the different sides of the coin. It seemed to me a quite black-and-white struggle, that humans were bad and animals were good, but the more I started to observe it, the more complex and gray it became. And I think you can see a little bit of that in *Animal Man*.

It's still quite sentimental, but it works in that way, and that's why I think it still appeals to people.

**TC: That's one of the ironies of your *Animal Man* work. You have the metafictional stuff, and you're breaking the fourth wall, and you're**

**pointing out that it is, in fact, a comic book story, but at the same time, you have these emotional issues with the animal rights stories and the death of Buddy Baker's family. How did you balance those two aspects of the series?**

GM: Well, that's the trick that you're trying to do. You're saying to people, "You're looking at a work of fiction, but the fiction is real. It's affecting, and it will tug at your heart, and you will care for these people." So they're actually real. And as I've said, Buddy Baker or Superman, or any of these characters, were created long before me and will still be around long after I'm dead, doing the same types of things [laughs]. As I always say, "who's more real in this equation?" I just come in to their strange, two-dimensional life for a while and keep it moving along. I put some energy from this world into it.

**TC: You had lost interest in "realism" in comics by the time you wrote the series, so why did you decide to spend a whole issue showing Buddy Baker's grief over the loss of his family in such "realistic" detail?**

GM: If I can clarify, when I talk about "realistic" comics, I'm talking specifically about the ones which posed the question, "What would super-heroes be like if they lived in the real world?" Although I'd tried a little of that with the first *Zenith* stories, I became more interested in the idea of imagining what it would be like to live in their world, where the laws of physics were different, where aliens and demons existed and where many, many human beings were endowed with special powers. I didn't want a "convincing," contemporary, "kitchen sink" backdrop, I wanted to work across the sprawling, colorful canvas of an actual fictional universe. Instead of dragging Batman into a facsimile of urban reality and watching his methods rub up against the laws of the world outside your window, I wanted to send myself into a world where anything could happen and generally did.

Even in a world where death can be revoked and identity and physicality can be completely fluid, I figured a man would go through a certain degree of emotional pain if his wife and family were killed, so while Animal Man was not physically like us, it was important for him to be emotionally like us. Also, at the time I wrote that, I was going through my own grief over the death of an animal I was very fond of. I'd never had anyone or anything I really cared about die on me, so it was something of a wake up call for my own emotions, and *Animal Man* provided an outlet for that and allowed me to analyze my own reactions at a distance and in the context of fiction.

**TC: When the comic book version of you talks to Buddy Baker at the end of your run on *Animal Man*, you express some disappointment with how everything turned out. Were you happy with what you accomplished with Animal Man?**

GM: Oh, yeah. I mean, I was really happy with it. Particularly the ending. The end was quite real. I was really trying to connect to the memories and things about animals as a child affected me – so yeah, it was all quite real, and I was really pleased with how it worked out. But by that time I'd begun work on *Doom Patrol*, which was the next stage beyond that. I was kind of getting more interested in that.

**TC: Did you feel, at the end of *Animal Man*, a little bit of, "how do I top this?"**

GM: It was just a case of following on to the next thing that interested me. I trusted the process that led me on to the next thing.

**TC: How did you get the *Doom Patrol* job?**

GM: They asked me to do it. Paul Kupperberg had been writing it, and it wasn't particularly successful by the time it reached issue #17 or 18. Then they asked me to come on board, and it was never something I'd been interested in at all. But I read the stories again, and I realized what they were trying to say. So how could I update that? And how could I tie it into all the stuff I was getting into at the time, like Situationism, and a lot of art history stuff, and surrealism, and Jan Svankmajer movies, and Cocteau, and Maya Deren? So there was a whole load of stuff I was getting into, and that all found its way into Doom Patrol.

**TC: How about the *Wizard of Oz* motif in *Doom Patrol*? Did you constantly think about the three main characters in those terms, or was that something that came up when you included Dorothy Spinner?**

GM: I didn't even think of it [laughs]. Although Dorothy Spinner was in it, I'd never considered the obvious. So, no, I hadn't actually thought that they were like the characters from Wizard of Oz, but of course they are, because these things always fall into the archetypes.

**TC: How about the insect motif? It appears in *Doom Patrol* and in most of your other work to some degree? Why do these insects keep appearing and what do they represent?**

GM: I suppose they represent the organized Other. It would be odd to write stories that didn't sometimes feature the dominant species on the planet.

**TC: What about the giant floating eye that appears in *Doom Patrol* and elsewhere? That image reappears again and again.**

GM: Since I was a little kid, I've always felt that I was being watched by someone, somewhere – one of the perks of being a Cold War surveillance baby who grew up watching *The Prisoner*, I suppose. This paranoid sense of constant surveillance, of dispassionate gaze somewhere, inspired me to dress up a little and turn my life into art during the '80s and '90s. I figured if someone was watching, I might as well put on a good show. Comics characters, of course, have every right to feel the same way. The eye is the gaze of the Spectator. Or the destroying eye of Shiva or Horus.

**TC: How did you come up with the Brotherhood of Dada? What inspired you to use them instead of the more traditional super-villains in *Doom Patrol*?**

GM: It was part of the thought process of *Doom Patrol*. If you had an original bunch of adversaries called the Brotherhood of Evil, then what would be the best way to update that to face the world's strangest super-heroes? And like I say, all the influences in my life at that point were brought to bear on the fact – like, I was really interested in Dada, and I was really interested in surrealism, and I was reading up on the history of it, and I was kind of applying it to my own life and my own practicing in the band, and trying to create this whole "life as art" thing. So, it was all part of that thing. It just fed into that.

**TC: Did you create a bunch of new characters and then pick out the best ones for the new Brotherhood? It always seems like you have a million ideas that you don't use.**

GM: Yeah, I mean there's just tons of these guys. Though, for this one, the whole team kind of came fully formed. Once the first idea came – to turn the Mr. Morden character into Mr. Nobody – and once I got that visual, which I sketched out myself, that Mr. Nobody visual, I thought it looked brilliant, it looked so not like anything else. And suddenly these things came together around him, and that kind of spirit of complete unreason and anarchy. It was very appealing.

**TC: When the Doom Patrol's fighting the Brotherhood of Dada – if it could be considered fighting – in "The Painting that Ate Paris," the**

**Justice League shows up and just kind of stands around. At that point in your career, do you think you were even capable – or interested – in writing a relatively traditional super-hero story?**

GM: Not at all. Basically, what happened after *Doom Patrol* is I stopped working, and I was enjoying the world for a long time, just traveling, and I kind of thought that would be the end of it for me, but I spent all my money [laughs]. So I came home, and I thought I'd better start taking my comic career a bit more seriously. I liked going around the world, but I needed to finance it.

So you can see me re-engaging with super-heroes in the *Flex Mentallo* series, and that's where I came back into it. That kind of allowed me... the last page of that is me preparing for the Justice League, I think.

**TC: *Flex Mentallo* was obviously quite brilliant. Is that series going to be reprinted sometime, you think? Or is it still a legal issue [with the Charles Atlas estate]?**

GM: They're sneaking him out in the *Doom Patrol* collections, and I have a feeling [the series] will eventually appear somewhere, even if they have to do it as kind of back-up in the *Doom Patrol*, or whatever. I do. I think they'll do it in the end.

**TC: A lot of people still haven't seen that series, and...**

GM: I'm just waiting for him to join the Justice Society [laughs].

**TC: How did you conceive of Flex Mentallo as a character, anyway? He and Danny the Street are two of your most interesting creations.**

GM: They were "found objects" – most of the characters in Doom Patrol are derived from dream diaries, conversations with friends (the characters Damn All and Darling Come Home from issue #25 were the actual imaginary friends of a friend) or fragments of songs I was listening to or movies I was watching at the time. (Red Jack was inspired by re-reading *The Ruling Class* – this play by Peter Barnes is another of the primal influences on my work and hints of it can be seen everywhere around this time, but especially here where the character even quotes from the play.)

Flex Mentallo was an off-the-cuff joke name given one afternoon to my friend, the comics retailer James Hamilton, by a member of his staff, who had wandered into the back shop while Jim was very intensely flexing a rocky bicep. The name Flex Mentallo, Man of Muscle Mystery, appeared from nowhere, and I was so taken by its absurdity, I asked if I could use it for a character and then created Flex, as we know him, using the Charles Atlas ad as the primal super-hero origin story.

With Danny the Street, I was signing in Dublin with Brendan McCarthy, whose work was a huge influence on me at the time. We were talking about the drag artiste Danny La Rue, whose name obviously translates as Danny the Street. This conjured the image of a transvestite street with tough macho stores all done up with fairy lights. I combined this idea with a street I believe I hallucinated in Paris and added the notion that Danny the Street could travel around the world and insert himself into any city anywhere. This element of his abilities was based on my misremembering Danny La Rue's signature tune, "On Mother Kelly's Doorstep," which I was sure began "On Mother Kelly's doorstep, I wandered the Earth..." It doesn't, of course, but from this complex of daft ideas sprang Danny the Street. The final touch was creating his origin story, where I decided he was the only material remnant of those fabulous otherworlds of our imaginations and dreams – like Wonderland, Slumberland, Never-Never Land, or Oz, or any of those places that hide in wardrobes and down holes.

**TC: How about the humor in *Doom Patrol*? You had whole issues that were parodies. How did you decide to add the humor? What was your thinking behind it?**

GM: That's my head. The way I look at the world is fundamentally stupid and absurd. I've got quite a cynical view and quite a very dark sense of humor, but generally it's funny. The whole bloody thing's funny to me [laughs]. And that sort of makes my work slightly different from some of the other British writers. I just see everything as fundamentally absurd.

**TC: That's one of the things that excites me about your work – even when some people misinterpret your work and think that it takes itself seriously. It's not really serious at all.**

GM: But at the same time, you should be able to make people cry and you should be able to make people feel emotions, but underneath it all, it's all bloody ridiculous.

**TC: Well, you spending time to write a 48-page Rob Liefeld parody is inherently absurd.**

GM: Yeah, Tom Peyer thought that would be really funny [laughs]. And it started as a list that Tom Peyer had made on his computer, you know. Remember when the Image comics started coming out? And the character names were all, "Brigade TM," everything "TM." Some lame concept they were claiming the copyright of. So Tom had started, one night, making this list up, which actually appears in the back of *Doom Force*, and it's like "Tree TM," [laughs] "Rimshot TM," and the whole thing kind of came out of that. It was just a stupid conversation one night in New York. And that's the way comics should get made up.

**TC: Another parody issue focuses on the Lee and Kirby era of Marvel Comics. I haven't seen you discuss that topic very often. How do you feel about Lee and Kirby's work from that period?**

GM: I can't say that I was a big fan of Marvel when I was a kid. They seemed a bit too scary for me. A bit creepy. But I remember the early *Fantastic Four*s and the kind of disturbing atmosphere.

**TC: Were these parody issues (besides the *Doom Force Special*, which was Tom Peyer's idea), something you came up with on your own?**

GM: Yeah, well in that case [the Lee and Kirby parody], I wanted a change of pace, you know, because there was a kind of big, heavy issue coming up next. So I started reading that early stuff and I was more interested in the way Stan Lee wrote comics, and how that kind of style was almost directly addressing the reader in the captions. That kind of bombastic approach that hadn't been used for a long time. And there were also connections between the early Doom Patrol, who were supposed to be called "The Legion of the Strange," and the Fantastic Four, you know? They were very similar. So I just kind of decided to combine them and do this kind of pastiche on "This Man, This Monster." Again, it was filtered through this *Doom Patrol* lens, so things are really amped up and kind of stupid [laughs].

**TC: They cure blindness at the end of the story!**

GM: Exactly. That's what happens when the cosmic gods disappear [laughs].

It was really, again, just having fun, but it also, I think... some door was opened there, because Alan Moore came out with *1963* not long after, and I think maybe everyone started to look at that stuff again through a different lens.

**TC: And all that stuff has since been reprinted in the Masterworks [line of hardcovers at Marvel] and the...**

GM: And now they're doing parodies an awful lot, but if you look back you'll find that *Doom Patrol* was one of the first things to ever parody Lee and Kirby. I tried to duplicate that style in a kind of postmodern, ironic way.

**TC: After that, in *Doom Patrol* #54, Rebis goes to the moon. I'm sure I'm missing a lot of the symbols in that issue, even though you have said that Doom Patrol doesn't have any symbolism in it.**

GM: Yeah. That one does. I mean, that one is really kind of Jungian. If you read the Jung stuff on Mercurius, everything's in there.

**TC: It's all Jungian?**

GM: Yeah, the whole image of the trees at the end – the golden band around the two trees. It's all alchemy, so... I was reading a lot of Jung stuff on alchemy, and I was interested in alchemy anyway. These kinds of ideas, of the union of opposites, I was interested in. So I was trying to express that through the character.

**TC: How early in your run on *Doom Patrol* did you know that Niles Caulder would be the evil mastermind behind everything? How did you arrive at that decision?**

GM: The moment I read Caulder's "origin" tale, it seemed clear to me that he had to be the twisted mastermind behind the whole thing. I based my insights into his personality on the way he treated his loyal robot X1 (or whatever his name was – I can't remember) in the 1960s story. I felt it was all already implicit in his character. [Note: Morrison refers to *Doom Patrol* vol. 1, issue #88, in which the origin of the Chief is revealed. In that issue's flashback, the loyal robot, RA-2 performs emergency surgery on Caulder to save his life, a deed which Caulder repays by blasting off the robot's head with a pistol. His explanation was that he had to destroy his robot assistant because it knew every detail of his work.]

**TC: Relating to the end of the series, one thing I point out in the book is that in one of the final issues of your run of *Doom Patrol*, you have a group therapy session, and you make it obvious that any attempt to heal these characters will remove their strength.**

GM: Completely, yeah.

**TC: Is that a comment on normality? What are you saying?**

GM: It all goes back to how I feel in the world. I sometimes feel that the world of imagination sometimes gets short shrift. And it's always been good to me [laughs]. So I kind of stand on the side of that, but again it goes back to Jung. There's a story that Jung tells of one of his patients, and she was a girl who believed that every night a demon lover came to visit her from the moon. And, basically, Jung cured her of the delusion, but in his book he writes about how bad he felt because he realized her life actually had more depth and more meaning when she did believe that she had a lover who came from the moon. So reading that story... you can see that as the backbone of almost everything in the *Doom Patrol*. It's me basically taking up arms on the side of the dreamers and the outcasts and the outsiders, because to me – and it's one of the themes of my work consistently, up until now – people can make their own stories to live in. And they have to seize control because other people will try to make a story for you, so a lot of what I do is about people seizing their own destiny. And it's usually poor people, or marginalized people, who suddenly become super-heroes, or they're suddenly given power that they didn't have before, and it's usually a power related to the fact that they believed in themselves, in what's possible in the universe.

**TC: Earlier we talked about how stories link together. *Animal Man* and *Doom Patrol*, the two longest works I cover in the book, feel unified. I know you had some general plans in mind, but you don't methodically plan out your work in advance. So where do you think that unity comes from?**

GM: It comes from me as a creator, I think. Again, it's the way I chose to work, which is slightly different from everyone else, because I kind of follow the logic of unreason, of the right brain. In a lot of cases, I'm not really writing stories, and it's a miracle I've gotten away with it for so long [laughs]. I'm actually trying to evoke feelings. In my head, and in the way I approach the work, it's a lot more like music. It's more of an evoking state, rather that being rational or linear, or whatever. So I think the thematic unity comes from the fact that you're actually watching someone working shit out in their head, you know, through a succession of projects. And you can follow the lines of thought, and hopefully that's what makes my work appealing to people, because it is a constant process of challenging what you used to believe or opening yourself to new information.

**TC: When you create the characters in these works who come from your subconscious, characters like Kay Challis, for example... Do you think about these characters after you leave them behind? How do you feel about them once you've moved on to other projects?**

GM: Always, yeah. I check out comics when people do them again. I tend not to read them [laughs], but I look at them just to see if they've got any of my guys in there. So, yeah, I feel for them, but I kind of feel that once I'm finished, that's it. It really doesn't matter what happens when someone else is in charge. They have to just get through that portion of their two-dimensional life. The stuff I do tends to be quite complete, in that the ending is there, and the end kind of sums up the feelings as I leave it. I tend to leave it so that other people can continue and write the stories, but at the same time there's a kind of finality to it.

**TC: While you're working, do you give much consideration to the artist? Do you think about how an artist will interpret your words? Does the act of collaboration change the meaning of your work at all?**

GM: I just write what I feel the need to write and expect my collaborators to be professional enough and creative enough to interpret my stuff to the best of their abilities.

On a couple of occasions, it hasn't worked out so well, and I might have had better results if I'd tailored my scripts more specifically to an artist's strengths, but I prefer to challenge them and see what they come up with. They all get the same kinds of scripts and some of them interpret the ideas more accurately than others, but that's the way of it. I'm not very precious about this kind of thing, even though I tend to get the blame for bad storytelling if the art isn't up to scratch, so I've usually moved on and lost interest by the time something comes out. The only artist I get a chance to talk to on a regular basis is Frank Quitely because he lives nearby and we've been friends for years.

One other thing I just thought of is that, reading your book – that whole Flex Mentallo shaving sequence which you thought was about Alan Moore was actually not [laughter]. It comes from Kirby and Lee. Remember the sequence – it's a classic sequence – where basically they discover the Sub-Mariner?

**TC: Yes. Sure.**

GM: And he's a bum, basically, and the Human Torch shaves off his beard. That's what it's from.

**TC: That Bisley cover looks...**

GM: Yeah, Bisley obviously drew Alan Moore there. Bisley used to do Alan Moore all the time in things. Even in the "Beard Hunter" issue of

Doom Patrol there's a picture of Alan Moore, and it says, "Our Founder." That was the artist who put that in there.

**TC: Everybody's referencing Alan Moore, but you were beyond that stage, right?**

GM: Pretty much. I loved *Miracleman* and I loved his *Captain Britain* stuff, but by the time *Watchmen* came out, he'd become competition [laughs]. And I was kind of all about critiquing that mode.

**TC: In retrospect, how do you feel about that period of his work? The *Watchmen* period?**

GM: When *Watchmen* came out, I must admit, I though the second issue was brilliant. The fourth issue, I thought, was brilliant. The issue where they spring Rorschach is brilliant. But I started to have problems with the whole idea of super-heroes in the real world, and I thought that the logic didn't hold out. I thought that it was, really, a traditional super-hero adventure story with a bit more rape and violence. And a bit more genius on the architectural side of the story construction.

But, ultimately, it ended up with tachyon particles and giant men, and really, to me, that story should have ended in just a welter of confusion and stupidity. That's how I would have done it, so I think it was actually really traditional, and that it wasn't actually advancing comics at all.

Some of the earlier stuff – *Miracleman*, that was the one, that was a big inspiration for me in the early days, you know, because it just seemed to break things open so well, and suggest so many possibilities. By *Watchmen*, I thought it was very mannered and it was no longer about punk rock. By that time, *Watchmen* seemed like Pink Floyd to me.

**TC: Do you think your work has influenced the direction of comics? Do you see repercussions from what you've done?**

GM: I've been working for thirty years, so I can see it – you can see the influence of *Zenith*, particularly, in a lot of – in Warren Ellis and Mark Millar, who were reading that stuff. So yeah, of course, I can see my influence everywhere, but it's [laughter] rarely acknowledged. Because I'm still in there working. You have to be gone before people really acknowledge you.

# Acknowledgements

I'd like to thank Mike Phillips and Julian Darius for giving me overwhelming support and encouragement throughout the completion of this project. They inspired me to undertake this project and helped make this book a reality.

I'd like to thank Grant Morrison for taking time out of his incredibly busy schedule to provide an interview. He was more patient and supportive than I could ever have imagined.

Primarily, though, I'd like to thank my family. Judy, Andrew, and Lauren Callahan all put up with a lot of neglect over the past year as I worked on this project, and I'd like to thank them for their patience and understanding. I hope those hundreds of hours during which I abandoned them in favor of writing about Grant Morrison in our basement did not cause any lasting injury. I'd also like to thank my parents, Richard and Linda Callahan, for allowing me to amass such an enormous comic book collection all of those decades ago and for supporting me in every way imaginable. I'd like to thank my aunt, Rae-Ann Winters, for filling the world with her kindness, and, most of all, I'd like to thank the late Raymond Winters, my grandfather, who not only drove my brother and me to the comic book shop every week but also provided the best role model anyone could ever hope for. I dedicate this book, and everything I ever accomplish in my life, to his memory.

# About the Author

'imothy Callahan has been a teaching writing and literature for over ten ears in the Berkshire hills of western Massachusetts. He holds a Bachelor f Arts in English from Hamilton College and a Master of Education from 'ambridge College. In addition to his scholarly work, he has written stories nd essays for literary magazines such as *As I Am* and *Upstreet*. He is narried to a beautiful and understanding woman, and he has a brilliant six-'ear-old son and a wonderfully inventive two-year-old daughter. Timothy nay be contacted via Sequart.com or through the Geniusboy Firemelon blog ıt http://geniusboyfiremelon.blogspot.com.

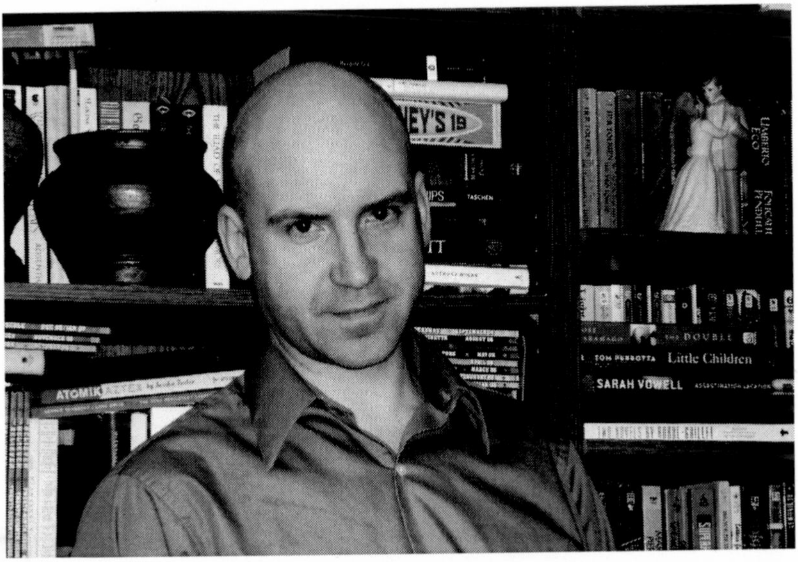

# New from Sequart.com Books

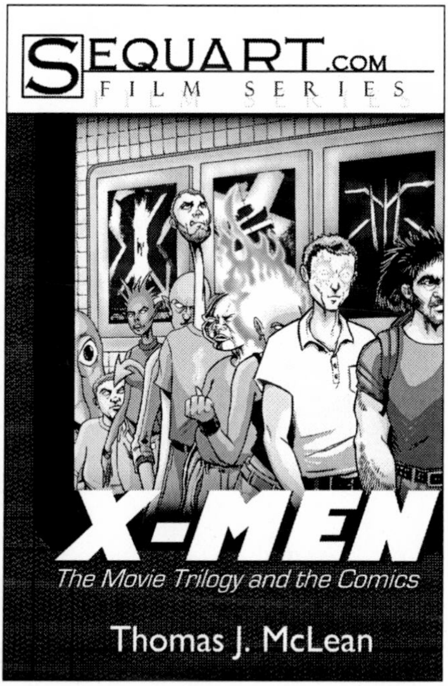


*X-Men: The Movie Trilogy and the Comics* by Thomas J. McLean offers the definitive study of the three X-Men films, directed by Bryan Singer and Brett Ratner.

This book contains scene-by-scene examinations of all three films, including notes on scenes cut from the films, paying particular attention to how they draw on their comic book source material. For all three films, the book also examines their sometimes controversial development process, their prequel comics (which featured exclusive content), their popular and critical reception, and their box office returns in historical context. A brief history of X-Men comics, a look at previous adaptations of the X-Men, speculation about the future of the franchise, and suggestions for future reading round out this seminal study of the popular and influential film trilogy.

312 pages / ISBN 978-0-6151-4086-5 / $19.95 MSRP

# About Sequart.com

Sequart.com features abundant resources relating to the study of comic books and graphic novels. Prominent among these resources are the Visual Shipping Lists, a list of comics shipping each week that includes covers, full solicitations, and links to more information such as previews; The Continuity Pages, a massive hyperlinked study of comic books by continuity, rather than simply by title; and a database of comic books and graphic novels with covers, other images, and links to other resources. This book is a publication of Sequart.com Books, the website's print division.

Sequart.com was founded in 1996 by Julian Darius, and has grown into an important part of the online comic book community. The site embraces the full diversity of the medium, from mainstream super-heroes to black-and-white independent comics, from Eurocomics to manga. It has no ideological bias, save that the medium should be considered an important and sophisticated art form worthy of study.

The term "sequart" itself refers to that medium and was created to avoid misleading, derivative, or derogatory alternatives. "Sequart" refers to the medium of comic books and graphic novels, of comic strips and manga – a medium that, like any other, can be employed to tell any sort of story. The term is specifically employed to refer to the medium itself, as opposed to specific formats or genre.

Run entirely by volunteers who love the medium, Sequart.com is a labor of love as well as a vast storehouse of information.